Power
and
Civil Society
in
Pakistan

Power
and
Civil Society
in
Pakistan

Edited by
Anita M. Weiss
and
S. Zulfiqar Gilani

OXFORD
UNIVERSITY PRESS

OXFORD
UNIVERSITY PRESS

Great Clarendon Street, Oxford OX2 6DP

Oxford University Press is a department of the University of Oxford.
It furthers the University's objective of excellence in research, scholarship,
and education by publishing worldwide in

Oxford New York

Athens Auckland Bangkok Bogotá Buenos Aires Cape Town
Chennai Dar es Salaam Delhi Florence Hong Kong Istanbul Karachi
Kolkata Kuala Lumpur Madrid Melbourne Mexico City Mumbai Nairobi
Paris São Paulo Shanghai Singapore Taipei Tokyo Toronto Warsaw

with associated companies in Berlin Ibadan

Oxford is a registered trade mark of Oxford University Press
in the UK and in certain other countries

ISBN 0 19 579414 1

Typeset in Times
Printed in Pakistan by
New Sketch Graphics, Karachi.
Published by
Ameena Saiyid, Oxford University Press
5-Bangalore Town, Sharae Faisal
PO Box 13033, Karachi-75350, Pakistan.

CONTENTS

page

PREFACE   vii
CONTRIBUTORS   xi

PART ONE: DISCOURSE AND CONTEXT OF POWER IN
          CIVIL SOCIETY IN PAKISTAN

1. Introduction   3
   ANITA. M. WEISS AND S. ZULFIQAR GILANI

2. Savage Capitalism and Civil Society in Pakistan   18
   MUSTAPHA KAMAL PASHA

PART TWO: SOCIAL FOUNDATIONS OF POWER IN PAKISTAN

3. Personal and Social Power in Pakistan   49
   S. ZULFIQAR GILANI

4. Gendered Power Relations: Perpetuation
   and Renegotiation   65
   ANITA M. WEISS

PART THREE: POLITICAL, ECONOMIC AND LEGAL
            POWER STRUCTURES

5. Business and Power in Pakistan   93
   IMRAN ANWAR ALI

6. Politics of Power and its Economic Imperatives:
   Pakistan, 1947-99   123
   SHAHID JAVED BURKI

7. An Uncivil Society: the Role of Shadow
   Privatization, Conflict and Ideology in the
   Governance of Pakistan   167
   OMAR NOMAN

8. The Military   186
   HASAN-ASKARI RIZVI

PART FOUR: NEW CONTENDERS AND ISSUES IN
          POWER NEGOTIATIONS

9. Power Configurations in Public and Private Arenas:
   The Women's Movement's Response   217
   FARZANA BARI AND SABA GUL KHATTAK

10. Microfinance in Pakistan: Perpetuation of Power or
    a Viable Avenue for Empowerment?   248
    LYNN RENKEN

11. Critical Engagements: NGOs and the State   275
    OMAR ASGHAR KHAN

    INDEX   301

PREFACE

We sat and listened, and listened, and listened. We were at a conference on Pakistan in the Lake District of England. Anita had journeyed with then three-month old Sulman from Eugene, Oregon, and Zulfiqar from Brighton, England. We had both come to the conference anticipating some kind of enlightenment, that gathered together with academic experts on Pakistan from throughout the world we would gain a greater understanding of the forces which were both ripping Pakistan apart while simultaneously rebuilding and restructuring it. It was the mid-1990s, still a time of some promise but by now sullied with over a generation of abject corruption and authoritarianism in Pakistan.

We had never met before. But as we listened to colleagues speaking of ancient art, Mughal kings and rural kinship structures, we found ourselves wondering why good, solid scholarship on contemporary Pakistani society is so limited. Anita was contemplating writing something like 'Leaving the Barn Door Open: The Disintegration of a Social Contract in Pakistan,' to grapple with why a country so rich in resources and cultural heritage was imploding. Zulfiqar had been struggling with the psycho-social bases of behaviour in Pakistan for some years. We both felt an overpowering need to understand, to interrogate, why this country with so much promise was on the brink of rupturing. Where is the solid class analysis that is so badly needed to understand structures of privilege in the country? Which text best analyses changes within the family in Pakistan today? Why are social linkages so ambiguous in the literature on Pakistan? We realized, then, that there was limited dialogue amongst and between scholars and social activists, and in order for us to understand the roots of these issues—the foundations of power itself in Pakistan today—we had to initiate a conversation with others.

We started talking to friends and colleagues. We set out to meld theory and praxis, to understand the myriad dimensions of conflict, contradiction, growth and transformation in today's Pakistan. Another friend shared his insights, that in Pakistan 'we are not a society, but just a crowd pushing and shoving each other to get by.' We refused to accept the laconic view that there was nothing there, in the first place, holding the people of Pakistan together.

We saw that for all the travails and negativity in the country, there were powerful triumphs as well. We could not shut our eyes to the fact that flowers continued to bloom in the graveyard of hopes and aspirations. People throughout Pakistan were demanding a voice—in the political arena, in economic circles, even within the family—and being listened to. Women were increasingly vocal, in print and in practice, in asserting their social place and practical power.

In conversing with others, over time the idea began to ferment: what were the foundations of power in Pakistan? Where did they lie, and how are they changing, particularly as NGOs and other groups constituting civil society were growing in importance and effectiveness? We decided to bring together US-based and Pakistan-based social scientists to forward the dialogue. We held a small conference consisting of contributors to this volume and a few others in November 1998 at Georgetown University. We are grateful to John Esposito, Director of the Center for Muslim–Christian Understanding, for assisting us in this effort and for inviting us to hold the conference on its premises—and for finally nailing us down to a date. We would like to thank the American Institute of Pakistan Studies for supporting one of the Pakistan-based contributors to attend the conference, and particularly Nadeem Akbar for all his logistical support. We would like to thank, too, the 'Pakistani friends' in the greater Washington, D.C. area who provided lunch for the hungry participants that day. Najia Ali Hyder and others in the International Studies Program at the University of Oregon did a great job in helping assemble the conference packets and Najia later came to our aid in assembling the index.

Aparna Devare and her colleagues from that American University did a terrific job helping out with various details, and we shall always appreciate their efforts.

A year went by as we each struggled with making sense of social issues that at times seemed to make no sense at all. We wrote, we revised, we were nearing completion of this volume when Pakistan again came under martial law on 12 October 1999. This time, however, power is not held by a Chief Martial Law Administrator (CMLA) à la Zia ul-Haq, who sought to legitimize military rule by adulterating religious beliefs, but by a Chief Executive Officer (CEO), Pervez Musharraf, who seems bent on making the country function again. After a dozen years of floundering democracy, a new breed of military rule seems to have emerged, hindered not by the politics of selfishness but by the sentiment of love of country and compatriots. It seems that the processes unleashed by Zia ul-Haq in July 1977 in reality continued until October 1999, despite the apparent 'democratic' interregnum. Can they turn the imbroglio around? The military government seems to be breaking new ground by assigning capable, qualified people to hold key positions in government, including one of our own contributors, Omar Asghar Khan, to serve as Minister of the Environment and Rural Development. We can but hope this trend continues. Perhaps the promise of a better future which prompted us to write this book will be realized sooner than even we had anticipated.

Nevertheless, we consider it necessary that we continue to remain mindful of the issues raised herein, and for others to expand upon them. This volume is but one step in a conversation of and reflection upon Pakistani society, and we hope that it will gather momentum.

Anita M. Weiss and S. Zulfiqar Gilani
December 1999

CONTRIBUTORS

IMRAN ANWAR ALI holds the Jamil Nishtar Chair of Agribusiness and is Professor of Economic History and Strategic Management at the Lahore University of Management Sciences (LUMS), where he has also been Director of the Centre for Management and Economic Research. At LUMS, he is also Associate Dean (Research) and Coordinator of Social Sciences. Professor Ali has an Honours degree from the University of Sussex, UK, and a doctorate from the Australian National University. He has taught in the Departments of Economic History at the University of New South Wales and the University of Melbourne, in Australia. He has also been an Honorary Research Fellow at the Institute of Commonwealth Studies, University of London, and a Visiting Scholar at the Harvard Business School. He has several publications on Pakistan and the Punjab including *The Punjab under Imperialism, 1885-1947* (Princeton University Press, 1988).

FARZANA BARI is Acting Director of the Women's Studies Centre at Quaid-i-Azam University, and editor of the *Journal of Women's Studies*. She received her Ph.D. in Sociology from the University of Sussex in 1991, and an MA in History from Quaid-i-Azam University. Dr Bari worked as a Social Development and Gender consultant in Pakistan 1991–3. She was a founding member of the Pattan Development Organization and the Islamabad chapter of the Women's Action Forum. Her publications include 'Gender, Disaster and Empowerment: A Case Study from Pakistan' (in *The Gendered Terrain of Disaster: Through Women's Eyes* edited by Elaine Enarson and Betty Hearn Morrow, Praeger, 1998), 'Road to Empowerment in Pakistan' (in *Women Claim their Rights in Local Politics* edited by Anne Seyfferth, Friedrich-Ebert-Stiftung, Bangkok,

1994), and her dissertation 'The Effects of Employment on the Status of Pakistani Women within the Family in Britain.'

SHAHID JAVED BURKI was recently Vice-President for Latin America and the Caribbean at the World Bank, and was formerly Vice-President for the China Country Program. He was a member of the interim government in Pakistan November 1996– February 1997 in change of the portfolios of finance, Economic Development and Planning. As an economist, he has published extensively on Pakistan, including *Pakistan: The first fifty years* (3rd ed., Westview Press, 1999), *Pakistan under Bhutto, 1971-1977* (2nd ed., Macmillan, 1988), and *Historical Dictionary of Pakistan (Scarecrow* Press, 1999). After taking retirement from the World Bank in August 1999, he has joined Emerging Markets Partnership—Financial Advisors, a Washington based firm, as its Chief Executive Officer.

SYED ZULFIQAR GILANI (co-editor) is currently a member of the National Reconstruction Bureau in Islamabad, and is Professor of Psychology at the University of Peshawar. He has been a Senior Visiting Research Fellow at the University of Sussex (1992–6). He received his Ph.D. in Cognitive Psychology in 1978 from Rutgers University. His current research concerns the psychoanalytic bases of leadership and politics, with special reference to Pakistan. Recent publications include 'Unveiling Bhutto' (*Economic and Political Weekly*, 1995) and 'Z.A. Bhutto's Leadership: a Psycho-Social View' (*Contemporary South Asia*, 1994).

OMAR ASGHAR KHAN is currently Federal Minister for Environment, Local Government and Rural Development, and Labour, Manpower and Overseas Pakistanis. He has long been an NGO activist and writer based in Abbotabad. He received his BA (Hons) in Economics from the University of Essex and his M. Phil. in Economics from Cambridge University. He had been a lecturer in Economics at Punjab University, Lahore, prior to being dismissed in 1983 by the military government for allegedly supporting the Movement for Democracy. He is a founder of the Pakistan Institute of Labour Education and Research and of the SUNGI Development Foundation, one of the leading national NGOs involved in policy advocacy and community development. He has served as a development consultant with a range of national and international organizations, co-authored the PDA White Paper on the rigging of the 1990 elections, and has written extensively on issues of development, NGOs, and political economy.

SABA GUL KHATTAK, Research Fellow and Deputy Director at the Sustainable Development Policy Institute (SDPI), received her Ph.D. in Political Science from the University of Hawaii. Her work includes feminist analyses of the Pakistani state, militarization and security discourses, women's issues, and refugee issues. Her writings based on this research have been published in *Alternatives* and in *Development,* as well as in several book chapters. Currently she is engaged in two research projects, one focused on women workers in the national and global economy and the second on women in conflict situations in the Afghan refugee and Karachi contexts. She is a member of the Women's Action Forum as well as the Legislative Watch Group in Islamabad.

OMAR NOMAN, an economist, is currently working with UNDP in New York and had played a key role in crafting Pakistan's momentous *National Conservation Strategy* in the early 1990s. Recent UNDP published reports include *Poverty in Transition?* (UNDP, New York, 1998) and *Central Asia 2010: Prospects for Human Development* (UNDP, New York, 1999). He has published extensively, including *Pride and Passion: an Exhilarating Half Century of Cricket in Pakistan* (Oxford University Press, 1999); *Economic and Social Progress in Asia: Why Pakistan did not become a Tiger* (Oxford University Press, 1998); *Economic Development and Environmental Policy* (Kegan Paul International, 1996); *The Child and the State in India and Pakistan: Child Labor and Education Policies in Comparative*

Perspective (with Myron Weiner) (Oxford University Press, 1995); *Pakistan: a Political and Economic History since 1947* (Kegan Paul International, 1990); and *The Political Economy of Pakistan 1947-85* (Kegan Paul International, 1988).

MUSTAPHA KAMAL PASHA is an Associate Professor of Comparative and Regional Studies in the School of International Service at American University, Washington, DC. Professor Pasha specializes in Third World political economy, international relations and South Asian studies. He was educated at the Forman Christian College (Lahore), Punjab University Law College, and received his doctorate from the Graduate School of International Studies, University of Denver. He is the author of *Colonial Political Economy: Recruitment and Underdevelopment in the Punjab* (Oxford University Press, 1998 and co-author (with James H. Mittelman) of *Out from Underdevelopment Revisited: Changing Global Structures and the Remaking of the Third World* (Macmillan Press, 1997). Professor Pasha serves on the editorial board of the *Bulletin of Concerned Asian Scholars* and was chair of the Global Development section of the International Studies Association (1998–9).

LYNN RENKEN is the Central Asia Program Officer for Mercy Corps International. She received her M.A. in International Studies from the University of Oregon in 1996 after completion of Fulbright research in Pakistan. Her M.A. thesis (with *distinction*) was entitled 'Micro Loans, Macro Returns?: Banking on Women in Pakistan.' She is currently working on Mercy Corps International's projects in Central Asia focused on microcredit, microenterprise, and other means through which the NGO can support the empowerment of local women.

HASAN-ASKARI RIZVI, Professor of Political Science at Punjab University, Lahore, was recently the Quaid-i-Azam Professor (1995–9) at Columbia University and Iqbal Fellow at Heidelberg University (1988–91). He holds a Ph.D. and MA in Political

Science and International Relations from the University of Pennsylvania. His books include *Military, State and Society in Pakistan* (London: Macmillan Press, 2000), *Pakistan and the Geostrategic Environment* (New York: St. Martin's Press, 1993), *The Military and Politics in Pakistan* (Lahore: Progressive Publishers, 1986), and *Internal Strife and External Intervention* (Lahore: Progressive Publishers, 1981). He has also published extensively in professional journals and edited volumes on the role of the military in Pakistan's political life.

ANITA M. WEISS (co-editor), Professor of International Studies at the University of Oregon, received her Ph.D. in Sociology from the University of California at Berkeley. She has held several research fellowships and consultancies in Pakistan, and has published extensively on social development and gender issues. Her most recent book, *Walls within Walls: Life Histories of Working Women in the Old City of Lahore* (Westview Press, 1992), was awarded the First Prize of the Allama Iqbal award by the Government of Punjab in 1994. She is also the author of *Culture, Class and Development in Pakistan: the Emergence of an Industrial Bourgeoisie in Punjab* (Westview Press, 1991), editor of *Islamic Reassertion in Pakistan: the Application of Islamic Laws in a Modern State* (Syracuse University Press, 1986), and numerous articles on culture, women, and development in Pakistan. Recent publications include 'Envisioning Women's Human Rights in Pakistan: Contexts, Debates and Challenges' (in Suad Joseph [ed.] *Women's Human Rights in the Muslim World,* in press); 'Much Ado about Counting: the Conflict over Holding a Census in Pakistan' *Asian Survey* (July/August 1999); 'Women, Civil Society and Politics in Pakistan' *Citizenship Studies* (3[1]1999, pp. 141–50); 'Pakistan: Some Progress, Sobering Challenges' (in Selig S. Harrison, Paul H. Kreisberg and Dennis Kux [eds.] *India & Pakistan: The First Fifty Years* Cambridge University Press, 1999, pp. 132–52); 'The Gendered Division of Space and Access in Working Class Areas of Lahore' (*Contemporary South Asia,* vol. 7, no. 1, 1998), and 'The Society and its Environment' (in

Peter R. Blood, editor, *Pakistan: A Country Study* Area
Handbook Series, Library of Congress, 1995). She is currently
writing *Interpreting Islam, Modernity and Women's Rights*,
addressing how Muslim states—specifically Pakistan, Malaysia
and Tunisia—are responding to having become States Parties to
CEDAW, so as to construct a practical understanding of the
convergences and divergences between international and Islamic
views on women's human rights. She is a member of the
executive committee of the Berkely Urdu Language Program in
Pakistan (BULPIP) and of the editorial committee of *Citizenship
Studies*.

PART ONE

Discourse and Context of Power in Civil Society in Pakistan

1

INTRODUCTION
Anita M. Weiss and *S. Zulfiqar Gilani*

Pakistan today is faced with a multiplicity of crises which are discernible in a variety of arenas. We have witnessed traditional centers of power and authority within the social fabric of society eroding, seemingly without any coherent alternatives. What results are social breakdowns and random acts of violence, coupled with institutional inefficiency and corruption. These are unanticipated everyday responses to this unparalleled institutional malaise. The loss of a 'social contract' between Pakistanis seems to have wreaked havoc not only in the economy but throughout the country's infrastructure: in the educational system, the government bureaucracy, the economy, and even in the arts.[1]

These crises are manifest in various profound ways. Between 1988–99, eight different governments have headed the country; the fifth was an interim government led by a non-Pakistani citizen (Moin Qureshi). In November 1996, the elected government of Benazir Bhutto was dismissed on the grounds of mismanagement and rampant corruption. However, despite the lack of a no-confidence motion, there was no popular protest against this action. Instead, the action was greeted with an initial sense of relief by many people, which was soon followed by heightened skepticism, cynicism and uncertainty regarding legitimate authority. Accountability—holding politicians and civil servants accountable to civil society for their actions— became the unprecedented consideration in the February 1997 elections which followed, resulting in Nawaz Sharif's re-election. In October 1999, the military resumed its political hegemony, this time charging Nawaz Sharif's government with corruption, mismanagement, embezzlement, and larceny.

Additional manifestations of these crises are apparent when we consider the fundamental cause of the devastating 1992 flood, which has in part been attributed to the prevalence of nepotism within the bureaucracy. This flagrant practice resulted in unqualified personnel ill-prepared to make timely, critical decisions of when to open the flood gates in the Punjab. In that same year, torture cells run by various political parties were uncovered in Karachi and the interior of Sindh. The administrative system of law and order has broken down to the point where few police are trusted by most people, and their ties to criminal and odious activities are abundant. For example, in September 1996, the then Prime Minister's brother was fatally shot in front of his own home by police in Karachi.

Substantive indicators of Pakistan's human development position further underscore these crises as they remain among the lowest in the world: adult literacy in 1997 was at a dismal 40.9 per cent (female adult literacy was even worse, at 25.4 per cent); Pakistan has one of the highest percentages of underweight children under age five in the world (38 per cent), far higher than that of Burkina Faso (30 per cent) or Sierra Leone (29 per cent), two of the world's poorest countries; nearly half (44 per cent) of the population does not have access to proper sanitation; and Pakistan's ranking in the United Nations' Human Development Index (HDI) places it among other countries with far lower GDP per capita rates.[2] The hyperinflation which hit Pakistan's economy in late 1996 contributed to lowering people's already weak purchasing power, and hence lowered morale further as the government was forced to introduce austerity measures to prevent the economy from going into default. Pakistan continues to be on the brink of economic crisis while most elites, individual as well as institutional, are living in ostentation.

What emerges from this current imbroglio is that at all levels of society there is an accelerating drift towards non-acceptance of formal authority in public domains. Indeed, real authority is notable by its very absence. The result is a dramatic increase in the perception and tendency that it is necessary and acceptable to attain power by any means. These trends have significantly contributed to a sense of uncertainty and social chaos, that society in Pakistan is adrift, in a state of anomie, and embroiled in conflicting power plays. Money, gained by any means (morally legitimate or otherwise), has become an important instrument and signifier of power. Consequently, there is a surface-level conformity amid growing cynicism and skepticism about the legitimacy of authority.

While there is widespread recognition of the crises of state and society, scholarly attempts at understanding these crises have been limited. We see a need to move beyond simply characterizing groups into constituent parties or classes. Instead, we seek to understand the extent to which certain segments of society hold power, over what aspects of social, political and economic life they hold this power, and the interconnections and contradictions between their objectives, those of the state, and those of others, particularly grassroots groups and non-governmental organizations (NGOs).

It may be useful to keep in mind that discussions of power fall roughly into two broad but inter-related arenas. There is power operative in politics. This has traditionally led to discussions of the state and its various organs being the instruments of power. The other is social power as manifested in sociological and psychological hierarchies and interactions which are more subtle and necessitate micro-analyses, which may explain why they have been addressed far less than the former. In this work we will be examining both kinds of power and attempt to provide linkages between the two.

The task of this book is two-fold. First, we seek to understand historic relations of power and authority in a range of social relationships in Pakistan as a means to create a baseline understanding of traditional conceptions of power. While these vary somewhat by region, class and gender, ample common features exist to form a foundation of what can be termed

'Pakistani society.' The second task of this project—and one far more onerous—is to grapple with understanding the causes behind the disintegration of a moral consensus within Pakistani civil society, with the ultimate objective of reconceptualizing development priorities.[3] We focus on shifting power relationships in various social domains as we examine how changing power dynamics are precipitating or responding to the erosion of existing local social contracts, and ways in which they are affecting the emergence of alternative contracts between the peoples of Pakistan. Our purpose is not to criticize but to contribute to the rebuilding of a diverse, confident and culturally rich society.

Historical Backdrop

Though the crises we mentioned above are current, they have a deep and organic link with the history of the evolution of society in Pakistan. In Pakistan today there are a number of cross-currents and contenders for power. At the most obvious level is the state. However, in this case it may be more useful to move away from the state-civil society distinction and utilize the more complicated concept of the *salariat*.[4] These are the state functionaries, big or small, who wield a great deal of power in actually getting things done. The salariat emerged as a dominant group through association with the colonial British civil bureaucracy, and continues to wield great power from within the state itself, though they are not perceived as 'the rulers.'

Pakistan's founders envisioned its civil society within a pluralistic framework despite that significant power remained in the hands of traditional landed and/or religious elites in the founding party, the Muslim League. There was an important contradiction in the positions which the Muslim League and Quaid-i-Azam Mohammed Ali Jinnah its leader, took through the period of the struggle for a separate state. For reasons of practical politics, Jinnah had to appeal to the traditional landed and religious elites. This was a continuation of the British policy of consolidating control by patronizing the religious leaders (the *pirs*) of Northern India. The British had skillfully strengthened the religious leaders through land grants in the Punjab and Sindh and in this manner created a powerful section of society which provided it support. When the struggle for Pakistan started gathering force, Jinnah realized the significance of those sections of society, especially in the rural areas. Thus on the one hand he appealed to the urban middle classes through messages of modernity and secularism, while on the other hand he accepted the support of the religious leaders in the rural areas of the Punjab, Sindh and NWFP.

Results of the 1937 provincial elections demonstrated the power of the local *pir* and the landlord in the Punjab. The Muslim League won only 1 of the 86 Muslim seats. The pro-British Unionist party, with the support of landlords, *pirs*, and local state functionaries, symbolized by the Deputy Commissioner, won 96 of the 175 seats, including the bulk of the Muslim seats. Thereupon Jinnah entered a pact with the Unionist Party, whereby the Unionists became part of the League while continuing to be members of their parent party. Jinnah thus opened the Muslim League to the traditional power-wielders, although the modernist and liberal sections of the party were unhappy with this decision. Jinnah managed to outflank the Unionist party politically and by 1945 the Muslim League emerged as the sole representative of the Indian Muslims (Saeed, 1980: 1–31). Thus in the Punjab the Muslim League won 79 of the 86 Muslim seats in the 1946 elections. The central thrust of the Muslim League campaign was the Islamic nature of the League and the promise that after its victory the government in harmony with the Qur'an will be established. The argument went something like this: the Muslim League is the only party which can ensure an Islamic government, and those who opposed it or the demand for Pakistan were therefore *kafirs* (nonbelievers). The top leadership of the Muslim League was modern and secular in its approach but to attain a mass base it had to appeal to traditional landed and religious elites. From the very outset the religious idiom was being used as a means to attaining power and the creation of Pakistan. Jinnah was sensitive to this and soon after independence tried to clarify that Pakistan was not to be a theocratic state. Because of his prestige and influence, Jinnah's view prevailed and the theologians had to lie low for a number of years after independence (Engineer, 1984: 1–12).

Jinnah had thrown his weight behind the modern-secularist view. Thus the religious elements lost significance and the state functionary, the 'salariat',[5] started emerging as the greatest wielder of power. Shortly after August 1947, the salariat started asserting their hegemony. Within the salariat, the civil bureaucracy was dominant. From 1947 to 1958, particularly after the assassination of Liaqat Ali Khan in 1951, one witnesses a number of civil bureaucrats becoming prime ministers and riding roughshod over representatives of civil society. Those who wielded power were more interested in making arrangements for the perpetuation of their power rather than moving on to the second stage of national liberation, i.e., the socio-economic empowerment of the people (Narain, 1984: 13–21). They continued with the British policy of patronizing the traditional feudal and religious elites and thus strengthened only select sections of civil society.

Different experiments were tried with the very definition of the state. For example, the issue of a unitary versus a federal state remained contentious. The constitutions of 1956 and 1962 gave different versions of how the state was to be defined. Running through all the debates was the problem of distribution of power; the one thing common to both; constitutions was that power remained concentrated in the feudal-religious-bureaucratic elites. Thus the notion of parity was developed and West Pakistan was cobbled into One Unit in 1955. This move effectively neutralized the numerical superiority of the Bengalis of East Pakistan, suppressed the Pakhtun movement of the NWFP and Baluchistan, and helped in perpetuating the dominance of the Punjab. The coup of October 1958 brought a military leader (General Ayub Khan) into the seat of power and all pretensions to political processes were suspended.

General Ayub crafted his own brand of 'Basic Democracy', representative at only its lowest levels. This takeover by the military was a harbinger of all future politics of power in the country. The usurpation slowly elbowed the civil bureaucracy and the feudal-religious elites into secondary roles.

There was resistance to these trends, especially in East Pakistan, Baluchistan and NWFP provinces. This resistance was expressed through oppositional politics. However, since the constitutional structure of the state did not provide space for such aspirations, and large sections of the population remained outside the political process, the resistance failed to have much impact on the power configuration of the larger society. Further, the timing was during the heyday of the cold war and Pakistan was squarely aligned with the United States. The Pakistani military state, supported by the U.S., maintained a firm grip on power.

This situation continued and the power elites prevailed by further entrenching themselves and their positions. The resentment nevertheless kept increasing as the nature of economic and social activities inevitably were undergoing changes and throwing up new actors into the scenario. On the surface conflicts of interests were not visible because the prevailing power elites were refusing to acknowledge the discontent. This situation started unraveling after the 1965 war with India but things did not start coming out into the open until late 1967.

The movement against General Ayub Khan was primarily urban based, and led by the left and sub-nationalist forces. The major cities had undergone significant economic and technological changes and people were no longer content with the prevailing power structures. In East Pakistan, the movement took an ethno-nationalist color and went on a trajectory which culminated in its secession and the emergence of Bangladesh. In West Pakistan, Zulfikar Ali Bhutto successfully managed to symbolize and articulate the discontent. He openly and defiantly questioned and challenged the prevailing power structures and thus struck a vital populist chord. His appeal was populist, targetting people's hearts and minds. The average person started questioning the basis of hierarchy and power in society, and many began demanding reforms.

The break-up of Pakistan was significant in many ways. The popular aspiration and movement for a change in the power configuration was derailed. In West Pakistan, Zulfiqar Ali Bhutto's popularity increased as he was seen as someone who could repair the damage to the very identity of the people and the existence of the state. While Bhutto's initial appeal was in the slogan of 'All power to the people', his subsequent actions and policies ran counter to it. The genie of peoples' power had been let out of the bottle but the those who wielded power at the level of the state clubbed together to try and put it back. Bhutto played a contradictory and ambivalent role. On the one hand he had unleashed the forces which were straining to overturn the power apparatus. On the other, after coming into power, he started making institutional changes to ensure that power was concentrated in his person. The old power elites thus saw him as the penultimate enemy seeking to alter traditional power configurations. In practice changed little.

The secession of East Pakistan in 1971 had reopened issues of national identity and the configuration of power dynamics in society. Animosity continued to grow between *muhajirs*[6] and Punjabis, the two most powerful economic ethnic groups in the country. The pluralistic perspective, shaken somewhat in the mid-1960s and early 1970s as divisions and distinctions between these and other ethnic and class groupings became more conspicuous, was definitively discarded in February 1979 when Zia ul-Haq's administration declared the right to legislate what was 'Islamic' and what was not.[7] Over time, as the formal state attempted to extend its reach into new social domains, civil society and its institutions became increasingly weakened.

The Zia ul-Haq era (July 1977–August 1988) generated a number of forces which furthered divisions and significantly eroded the moral consensus in society. The manner in which he came to power and the way he ruled intensified the perception that power configurations were a result of individual whims.

Zia successfully took some critical steps to undermine political parties and a participatory political process. His regime significantly furthered the weakening of civil society and dismemberment of the people. For example, the military intelligence agencies penetrated political groups and other sections of civil society with the purpose of dividing them. The logic was simple: a divided society is not a threat to the existing power structures. He also put forward his interpretation of an Islamic agenda as the basis of his regime's legitimacy. In doing so, he elevated and later empowered religious and sectarian groups by selective invocation of the genesis of Pakistan. He openly joined hands with the U.S. in Afghanistan; notwithstanding the merits or demerits of his Afghan policy, that involvement exacerbated the pervasiveness of violence in Pakistani society.

Bhutto initiated, and Zia perfected, the control over meanings—especially of words and symbols—in society. Control over meanings is a highly effective method for attaining and perpetuating power. Hamid Kizilbash had argued that the educations system, the most important socializing agent after the family, was restructured so as to perpetuate existing power relations between different sections of society.[9] The elite, in collusion with the state, ensured limited social mobility by allowing the quality of public education to decline while preparing their own children for positions of power through the parallel English-medium public school culture for the select few which developed during Zia's regime. The press was curtailed through selective use of incentives and sanctions. In the 1980s the army, through a systematic use of information, managed to create social trends which continue to plague Pakistani society. The electronic media—radio and television—was run by the state and played a considerable role in molding popular viewpoints over time. The common thread which connected the meanings assigned to words and symbols was a particular interpretation of Islam. This inevitably strengthened religious factionalism while also encouraged the rise of sectarian terrorism, problems which continue to haunt Pakistan today.

The traditional elites on which the Muslim League had relied upon during the struggle for Pakistan continued to solidify and entrench themselves throughout the 1980s. Nevertheless, there was a horizontal expansion amongst those who held power. Thus by 1988, the main power wielders were the army, the civil bureaucracy, the landed gentry, relatively new industrial groups, and new kinds of religious leaders who surrounded themselves with zealous, committed followers. We have not detailed the socio-economic dynamics of the rise to hegemony of these groups (such a study would be a separate volume itself). Importantly, however, the 'special relationship' between Pakistan and the U.S. played an important role in influencing the trajectory of power configurations in the country.

The death of Zia in August 1988 coincided with the start of a process of unravelling and the deepening of the crisis of society and power. It is this crisis which provides the starting point of this volume.

Organization of the Book

The book is organized in four broad sections: civil society, in general, in Pakistan; social foundations of power; political, economic and legal power structures; and new contenders and issues in power negotiations. The separate chapters address key themes in the discourse of power in Pakistani society, and how both groups—established and new—envision themselves as contenders and arbiters of power.

This first section addresses contending discourses addressing the very notion of civil society in Pakistan. Following this introduction, Mustapha Kamal Pasha offers his interpretation on the precarious existence of civil society in the country. Section II proceeds to locate foundations of power in Pakistani society and how they are perpetuated within essential socialization processes in Pakistan. Section III examines political, legal and economic structures, including ways in which local power dynamics affect the economy and the state's military organization. Section IV analyzes new power dynamics resulting from on-going renegotiations of power between social groups positioning themselves as stakeholders in Pakistan's emergent civil society. The prospects for these groups and the issues they bring with them—gaining a voice in a participatory political process, providing working capital to the poor, and constructing new institutions accountable to the people—is the focus of this section, which posits hope for the country in the hands of disparate groups negotiating, interacting and collaborating with one another as they reassemble a working social contract.

This introductory chapter frames the book's argument, situating the process of the formation of the state in Pakistan in the context of different groups vying for power, traditional class dynamics, and ensuing ideologies of the state. This introduction provides an historical 'signposting' of the major contenders for power in Pakistan: within the family and personal arenas; the place of Islam and religious action in public and private domains; and the tensions and contradictions between the state and civil society. It attempts to link these micro-processes (within the family, and generally in civil society) to macro-outcomes: political action and attitudes, economic achievement and the functioning of government. By underscoring the tensions and contradictions inherent between the state and civil society on a general level, this chapter locates, in particular, the different manifestations of authoritarianism at various levels of Pakistani society. The following chapter elaborates on the theoretical dimensions of civil society in Pakistan's postcolonial context. Mustapha Kamal Pasha argues that a modern civil society is beginning to emerge in Pakistan, albeit it is taking a 'savage' cast as it is linked to a particular form of capitalism, that which prevails in this 'economically poor, multi-ethnic, multi-lingual contexts engulfed by processes of lumpen development'(p. 41, chapter 2).

In Section II, Zulfiqar Gilani's chapter situates itself within the family, the most essential social institution in Pakistan and one which retains a dichotomous view of 'insiders' and 'outsiders,' which often results from first-cousin marriages.[8] Gilani addresses the ways in which child-rearing practices and childhood experiences affect social patterns of relating, which in turn affect social values and perceptions of power. He argues that this results in complex entanglements existing between the individual and the wielding of social power. In articulating the links between the societal and the socialized individual, Gilani provides us with insights into the psychological foundations of the crisis of power and authority in Pakistan today. Anita Weiss takes this scenario a step further by revealing the gendered dimensions to power relations and perceptions of power, and how access to power within the family culminates and is perpetuated today in accepted social roles. She argues that men and women have markedly different perceptions of how Pakistani society is changing as well as different expectations of each other's practical exercise of power. Indeed, these conflicting notions regarding the place and power of women forces a constant renegotiation of power relations between men and women, resulting in profound consequences for social cohesion.

The third section elaborates on the origins and manifestations of power in various institutiona! structures within Pakistan. Three economists—Imran Anwar Ali, Shahid Javed Burki and Omar Noman—analyse different dimensions of the role played by the economy in affecting power relations and civil society in Pakistan today. Imran Anwar Ali examines various kinds of connections between business groups and power concerns. Shahid Javed Burki assesses choices made by elites in efforts to manage the polity and the economy, and why Pakistan's economic standing remains problematic. Omar Noman offers that the direct impact of economic policy is negligible on Pakistan's economic situation; instead, he argues that 'the environment within which economic policy is embedded is disturbed by a dysfunctional social structure' (p. 167, chapter 7).

Hasan Askari Rizvi analyses a group which has often been 'the default' in actually wielding power in Pakistan, the military. In Chapter 8, he argues that the military has become an all-pervasive force with expanded professional and corporate interests encompassing the government, the economy and the society. The long years of direct and indirect rule have helped the military to spread out in the government, semi-government institutions and major sectors of the society. Its political clout and influence no longer depends on controlling the levers of power but is instead derived from its organizational strength and its significant presence in the economy and the society. Rizvi analyses the ethnic character and social composition of the Army as well as the place of Islam in military ideology while interrogating how the military has acquired such a pivotal position in the country.

The final section addresses ways in which power is being negotiated in contemporary Pakistan by new social institutions, or at least new manifestations of older ones. Farzana Bari and Saba Gul Khattak analyse the relationship between the increasingly robust women's movement and prevailing power configurations, and ways in which it responds to and has tried to affect them. Lynn Renken takes the discussion of women's financial empowerment, the role of NGOs and business efforts a step further by evaluating how power issues have shaped microlending institutions and their microcredit delivery systems in Pakistan. In her chapter, she investigates the perception Pakistani women have of their banking system and in what capacities they utilize it. Importantly, Renken focuses on the creation of new microcredit facilities, particularly their financial backing, loan selection criteria, target groups, actual beneficiaries of loans, and how effectively the institutions meet their organizational objectives and respond to client needs. Omar Asghar Khan considers the relatively new negotiation of space within civil society that is occurring between NGOs and the state, placing the current crisis of power and authority in Pakistan into the context of political stewardship and debate in the country. It is within this realm that civil society is having the greatest expansion.

Power in Pakistan is being negotiated between different groups in new, unique and innovative ways. This bartering for power has resulted in unprecedented and unanticipated contradictions, which in turn have unleashed a descending spiral of confrontations, uncertainty and social turmoil throughout the country. It is in the course of negotiating the ground rules of changing power dynamics that we can envision a new balance that can lead to developing new, viable paths to rebuild discourse and consensus within the country. We anticipate that this book will make a contribution to that effort.

NOTES

1. We are using the term 'social contract' in the sense argued by the eighteenth century philosopher, Jean Jacques Rousseau, that members of a society have unwritten expectations of each other, which is a foundation for social cohesion.

2. Data is based on United Nations Development Program *Human Development Report 1999* (New York: Oxford University Press, 1999), pp. 136, 140, 147, and 148. A country's ranking in the Human Development Index (HDI) is compiled through a composite scale consisting of its ranking on a life expectancy index, education index and GDP index. Pakistan's overall HDI ranking is 138 (out of 174 countries); on the GDP index, Pakistan is at 0.46. Burkina Faso's HDI ranking is 171 and its GDP index is at 0.39; Sierra Leone's HDI ranking is 174 and its GDP index is at 0.24. Pakistan ranks low on the HDI not because of low income levels but because its education index (0.41) is one of the lowest in the world.

3. There is some important scholarship that exists on civil society in Muslim areas, including Jillian Schwedler (ed.) *Toward Civil Society in the Middle East?: a Primer* Boulder, CO : Lynne Rienner, 1995; Augustus Norton *Civil Society in the Middle East* Leiden and New York: Brill, 1995; and Anders Jerichow and Jørgen Bæk Simonsen (eds.) *Islam in a Changing World: Europe and the Middle East* Richmond, Surrey: Curzon, 1997.

4. Hamza Alavi has developed this term in a number of writings; see for example Hamza Alavi 'Ethnicity, Muslim Society and the Pakistan Ideology' in *Islamic Reassertion in Pakistan: the Application of Islamic Laws in a Modern State* (edited by Anita M. Weiss, Syracuse University Press, 1986, pp. 21–46).

5. The *salariat* had emerged as a dominant group through association with the colonial English masters. Those who became members of this group also became part of the colonizers. Thus an indigenous group of colonizers emerged in the form of the *salariat*, and that is still largely true although the situation is now far more complicated.

6. *Muhajirs* are immigrants or descendants of immigrants at the time of Partition, who located mostly in and around Karachi. They have created a

political party, the MQM (Muhajir Qaumi Movement), which has often been an antagonist of the government in power.

7. The second constitution, in 1962, introduced a religious dimension to the state by adding 'Islamic' to the country's name. The 1971 secession of East Pakistan further contributed to the unease that all voices may not have a place to be heard in Pakistan. Zulfikar Ali Bhutto opened up a 'pandora's box' of sectarian conflict when he adopted the slogan of Islamic socialism. However, the Islamization program launched by Zia left no question that some interpretations of Islam were to wield unprecedented influence in the state.

8. Ernest Gellner, writing about Muslim society in North Africa, argues that the origins of first cousin marriage preference lies in the concept of 'republics of cousins,' for without them, where would one graze his sheep, and from where would one get a wife? For further explanation, refer to Ernest Gellner *Muslim Society* (Cambridge: Cambridge University Press, 1981), p. 33.

9. Hamid Kizilbash made this argument at the conference of contributors to this volume we held at Georgetown University in November 1998. Unfortunately, he was not able to contribute a chapter.

2

SAVAGE CAPITALISM AND CIVIL SOCIETY IN PAKISTAN

Mustapha Kamal Pasha

A. Introduction

In a remarkable reversal of fortune, after decades of neglect and historical amnesia, 'civil society' has recaptured contemporary political imagination in place of 'the state' as the new avatar of development, democracy and emancipation. Bordering on euphoria, the embrace of civil society is pervasive: in recent discussions of democratic movements around the globe; in grandiose claims about the 'end of history'; in triumphal announcements about the arrival of a universal stage in human evolution. The celebration of civil society harkens a worldwide democratic revolution, the decided victory of liberalism and the failure of alternative constructions of social order.[1] From a nearly universal acceptance of liberal democracy as an ideal state[2] to the legitimacy of non-state societal action propelled in part by the advent of economic liberalization and privatization, the coming of civil society underlines the evolutionary optimism of a liberal social order generative of a higher phase of civilization.

Spawned by the failure of the state to be the progenitor of either development or democracy, the focus of much of extant discussions now lies on civil society, a site of unprecedented promise for agents that presumably inhabit this purgatory. Both liberal and Marxian theorists have rediscovered the importance of what goes on *outside* the state. Particularly in the post-colony, a burgeoning civil society appears to suggest that after decades of ill-conceived statism, economic growth and democracy under the aegis of civil society are now within reach with an elective affinity to civility, rule of law, and order. For entirely different reasons, writers of contrasting political hues—conservative, liberal, radical—see civil society as the site of vitality, civility, and freedom. The implications for societal development are not too hard to find; the emergence of civil society in the non-Western world augurs well for social well-being; in a one-to-one correspondence, the expansion of civil society means social advance.[3] Civil society is clearly ascendant—a proper site for economic progress, humane social projects, the principal agent for environmental preservation, the chief arbiter of moral progress.

Underscoring the close nexus between ontology and thought, shifts in the political climate in favor of *civil society* enjoy curious sponsors. A new cottage industry of eager protagonists of civil society now sprawl across the academic and policy terrains, ranging from social activists, academics, leaders of non-governmental organizations (NGOS) to new converts within the establishment. Not to be overrun by the discourse on civil society, self-serving skeptics have also joined the conversation by repackaging their ill-gotten wares. The divide separating deception and true understanding could not have been more opaque; with the common coinage of civil society has come its erosion as an analytical construct. An all-purpose panacea for wishing away problems of historical and structural import, 'civil society' has all-but-lost its utility as a bounded category. But can 'civil society' be allowed to fall prey to conceit, misrepresentation or predatory drives?

Repudiating illicit trafficking in borrowed thought and speech, one will find the concept terribly illuminating. This assumes, of course, that norms of acceptable social inquiry be observed. Neither piracy nor pretension can be a substitute for a *bona fide* engagement with the concept; rescued from pretenders, civil society can afford analytical and practical relevance. A full disclosure of civil society's true lineage and authorship, recognition of its philosophically embedded nature, and historicity[4] will dispel mistaken notions of either its modularity,[5] or the erroneous idea of its inapplicability outside the West. The view that different 'empirical' terrains require different concepts obviously conflates theoretical and historical temporalities. Thus, between unreflective romanticization and deliberately misleading skepticism, 'civil society' offers a potentially useful framework for examining the pathology of our times, including an understanding of several unresolved paradoxes of post-colonial political economies.

This chapter extends my earlier work on civil society, which has focused on the distinctive resonance of its structure and practice in post-colonial societies,[6] especially Pakistan. Here, I am more interested in linking the specific character of civil society in Pakistan to 'savage capitalism.'[7] The epithet 'savage' connotes a social order unchecked and unregulated by public virtue. An historical structure, savage capitalism subordinates public tasks to private aggrandizement via primitive accumulation. Often, savage capitalism relies on the existing institutional framework to realize its logic of accumulation-without-obligation. Parasitic in appearance, savage capitalism is not a static system of social relations. Sometimes relying on formal accouterments of bourgeois expressions of constitutionalism, legality, rights, and formal citizenship,[8] but usually bypassing these 'impediments' toward the goal of aggrandizement, the organic agents of savage capitalism institute the conditions for their self-reproduction in the political process. This may explain the relatively flexible character of the landed propertied classes, who have systematically exploited the political system to sustain a social order to their own liking, but also the stark absence of checks on the excesses of state managers.

To anticipate the analysis, it is not as much the absence of civil society in Pakistan but rather its entanglement with 'savage capitalism', which gives it a distinctive character. Forms of wealth creation, distribution, and the state's (often) feeble efforts to harness economic development become quite intelligible once a determinate link between savage capitalism and postcolonial civil society can be established. The most glaring expression of a 'civil' society engendered under savage capitalism is the rigidity of class and social stratifications, reinforcing the state's predatory role. This chapter proceeds in four sections. This first section situates the contemporary discourse of civil society. Straddling between idealization and rejection lie three constellations of the concept: (a) as a market-driven social order, extending the framework of the classical political economists; (b) as associational life, originating in de Tocqueville's reading of democracy in America, but now covering an entire spectrum of social life *outside the state;* and (c) as civilized society, underscoring the Enlightenment's dualistic conception of humanity in the Occident and Beyond.[9] In the later sections of the paper, I will rely mainly on a classical reading of civil society to demarcate a determinate connection between capitalism and civil society. To be certain, a failure to fully explicate the centrality of capitalism to civil society lies at the source of much confusion about the concept. Misguided concentration on the *discursive strategies* of colonialism alone, without an understanding of savage capitalism, dismisses the centrality of accumulation as the site for structural reproduction.[10] It also downplays the *dynamic* character of institutions and the rise of new social forces in the postcolonial period.[11] It is within the structures of wealth creation, distribution, and consumption that one can best locate the factors inhibiting social and economic development.

Section B amplifies the relation between capitalism and inequality. Rather than treating inequality as an exogenous nuisance, a (classical) political economy perspective regards (economic and political) inequality as an inherent feature of civil society.

Section C offers an investigation of the emergence of civil society in Pakistan. The analysis here is both schematic and illustrative, necessarily requiring much elaboration. Recognizing the specific character of civil society in Pakistan will help dispel the urge towards its unreflective and hasty rejection in favor of some other smuggled category.

Section D provides by way of conclusion a plea for more determinate analysis of emergent civil societies in the postcolony. Needless celebrations nor condemnations of civil society yield precious little in the direction of reversing the despair which pervades our social and political landscape. By recognizing the distinctive character of civil society in Pakistan, perhaps, we can better appreciate the source of the distemper in the social, political, and cultural terrains.

B. Revisiting Civil Society

As noted, a flexible instrument for social diagnosis and prescription for all kinds of actors and agents on different sides of the political divide, civil society appears to please all–globalizers and resisters to globalization; international donor agencies and local recipients; rights activists and neoliberals. Thus, in one instance, civil society provisions ideological sustenance to economic globalization and corresponding assaults on the Third World state.[12] As the state retreats into the background, increasingly becoming a mere enforcer of 'global' rules locally, especially in the arena of economic policy, it increasingly assumes the role of a conveyer-belt for globalization.[13] On the other hand, civil society is seen as the bastion against top-down globalization and the fountainhead for preserving 'indigenous' cultures and peoples. Where else would one find social movements resisting globalization except in civil society?

Neither blind faith in civil society nor self-serving skepticism toward the concept, however, is desirable nor justifiable. While promising new channels of ' interest articulation' and personal freedoms, civil society also congeals a new form of *social power* which requires a stronger, not weaker, counteracting role of the state. The prospects of democracy or development are better or worse, depending upon the manner in which civil society is stabilized by the state. The simple appearance of civil society on the horizon is an insufficient guide to be better tomorrow. Self-serving repudiation of civil society in postcolonial contexts is equally facile. Some skeptics invoke alternative sites for closer scrutiny rather than a civil society fractured by an overdeveloped state.[14] Often collapsing intellectual genealogies, paradigms, and research agendas, protagonists of this (alternative?) view fail to separate out the different discourses of civil society, each with its own set of core metatheoretical assumptions. As Krishna Kumar rightly suggests in his evocative article, 'Civil Society: An Inquiry into the Usefulness of an Historical Term,' 'we are dealing with a concept rich in historical resonances; a concept where a good part of the appeal in the sense of many levels and layers of meaning, deposited by successive generations of thinkers.'[15] Perhaps it is useful to remind oneself of the intellectual history of the concept to assess how far we have come in our own thinking, from a theoretically embedded concept to a mere description of 'associational life'. Though defending a contestable thesis that our current (postcolonial?) problems 'relate not to the institutions of civil society but to the institutions of the state and the reconstitution of a functioning political society,'[16] Kumar's excellent summary of the 'career of the concept' is quite useful. Kumar links the modern concept of civil society to the Enlightenment, providing important detail on the shifting meanings of the term since the time of Cicero and Aristotle to Adam Ferguson to the classical political economists, notably Adam Smith and Marx, but also the current European discourse. As Kumar suggests:

> Up to the end of the eighteenth century, the term 'civil society' was synonymous with the state or 'political society'. Here it reflected precisely its classical origins. 'Civil society' was more or less a direct translation of Cicero's *societas civilis* and Aristotle's *koinonia politike*. Locke could speak of 'civil government' along with, and as an alternative term for 'civil or political society'. Kant sees *burgherliche Gesellschaft* as that constitutional state towards which political evolution tends. For Rousseau the *etat civil* is the state. In all these uses the contrast is with the 'uncivilized' condition of humanity—whether in a hypothesized state of nature or, more particularly, under an 'unnatural' system of government that rules by despotic decree rather than by laws. Civil society in this

conception expresses the growth of civilization to the point where society is 'civilized'. It is, as classically expressed in the Athenian polis or the Roman republic, a social order of citizenship, one where men (rarely women) regulate their relationships and settle their disputes according to a system of laws; where 'civility' reigns, and citizens take an active part in public life.[17]

In marked contradistinction to political and social theorists of the eighteenth and nineteenth centuries, current popular uses of the term treat civil society as any realm of non-state action, a social space contrasted with the state. Recent discussions of democratic transitions in both the Third World and in Eastern Europe have elected to equate civil society with 'associational life'.[18]

In its simplicity, the emergence of a civil society in theoretical terms is synonymous with the creation and consolidation of the modern world.[19] For classical political economy, civil society is synonymous with a market-driven capitalist order. Implicit in the Enlightenment view is also a determinate connection between wealth and civility or civilization; civil society is equated with the sphere of civility, a recognition of 'civilization'. Following Hegelian and Marxian formulations, I view civil society quite narrowly as that distinct sphere of self-seeking which straddles between the household (family or other institution) and the modern state, yet connected to both with a myriad of distinct social practices. On the one hand, it is a sphere that arises out of the expansion of the social division of labor, the evolution of market relations and interests embedded in those relations. But, on the other hand, it is also a sphere that connects the realm of self-seeking to political society.[20] Key to the notion of civil society is the rise of new forces in society and their aspiration to create a private sphere separate from, yet connected to, the state. This view is in marked contrast to de Tocqueville's notion of political society or its more recent reincarnations as associational life. Again, Kumar's discussion of de Tocqueville's idea of political society is pertinent here to establish a more direct contrast with a political economy perspective adopted in this paper. Kumar writes:

Political society draws upon the fullest development of what de Tocqueville calls the most important 'law' controlling human societies, 'the art of association'. In civilized societies there are political associations, such as local self-government, juries, parties and public opinion; and there are civil associations, such as churches, moral crusades, schools, literary and scientific societies, newspapers and publishers, professional and commercial organizations, organizations for leisure and recreation. The life of all these associations, the 'super-abundant force and energy' that they contribute to the body politics, constitutes political society. De Tocqueville notes that it is usually politics that spreads 'a general habit and taste for association', so that 'one may think of political associations as great free schools to which all citizens come to be taught the general theory of association.' ...Political society supplies 'the independent eye of society' that exercises surveillance over its public life. It is what educates us for politics, tempers our passions and curbs the unmitigated pursuit of private self-interest.[21]

Political economy locates civil society in the processes of social reproduction, assigning a structural dimension to the concept. By contrast, the idea of mere association as the centerpiece of civil society misconstrues the logic of a transitional or advanced capitalist society. Alternatively, the notion of 'civilized society' conflates normative preferences with structural imperatives. On a political economy perspective, the mere presence of a non-state or non-governmental action provides no understanding of the logic of social reproduction. The (classical) idea of civil society as a market-based capitalist order, instead, supplies a determinate notion. As I have noted elsewhere, civil society is coterminous with the arrival of a market-based political economy:

At a minimum, the rise of a civil society (in contrast either to political society, a realm of non-state action or as civilized society with a necessary normative superiority),[22] is contingent upon the development of a certain type of political economy with distinct social practices, including (and not limited to) the following: (1) a new social division of labor coextensive with an expanding exchange realm and a self-regulating market which differentiates society, especially the labor process; (2) the creation of a new sphere of social institutions and interests linked to the former (realm of exchange) and (3) a system of rights linked to the complex of apparatuses of coercive power, both serving as a check on the latter's global reach in society *and* providing an alternative channel for interest articulation. The essence of a system of rights is captured in the idea of *legality*, which provides protection to this new sphere both against the arbitrariness of the state and the caprice of private want satisfaction. To stabilize civil society, therefore, the state's role is crucial; a weak state, lacking legitimate authority is likely to devour civil society, or it merely becomes its extension.[23]

Often in societies where capitalism is not fully entrenched *as a social order*, one is likely to encounter hybrid forms, given the multiplicities of actors, including social practices of pre-capitalist society. Forms of social life under these conditions tend to betray symptoms which deny the very existence of capitalism. This is most apparent in the cultural domain, which is inhabited by a cacophony of disparate voices, passions, and interests. To innocent observers who consider their own societies as universally legitimate expression of reason and human volition, the process of social transition in the postcolony usually appears as the expression of cultural schizophrenia,[24] or simply the birth-pangs of modernization.

There are multiple sites to examine structural transition and the rise of a civil society in the postcolony. The process of transition often encompasses: (1) the rapid commercialization of its social life and the consolidation of a market rationality; (2) a rearrangement of the social structure with the emergence of new social forces; and (3) the appearance of a new public morality, individuation, and patterns of self-expression. Mutually reinforcing, these elements by no means exhaust the compass of civil society.[25]

Expansion of what Hegel calls 'the system of needs' and their material provisioning through a more complex social division of labor and the market, are among the principal bases for greater differentiation of society. Differentiation here, it must be stressed, is not simply technical or occupational, but class-based. Personal dependence is gradually superseded by a complex system of interdependence via the market. Rather than function as 'accessories of economic life,' to cite Polanyi, markets become determinative of nearly all aspects of social life.[26] The pursuit of money becomes the organizing principle for conferring social power. Other cultural values are subordinated to the working of this logic.

Differentiation largely rests on the accumulation process. Here I will mention two trajectories of change and transformation: (1) the growing power of capital; and (2) urbanization and the shift in the constellation of forces toward the cities. In the process of capitalist transition, the social structure in most Third World social formations has shown a recognizable pattern. In agriculture, industry, and the tertiary sector *more* structural spaces have become available to be occupied by new and old social agents. But differentiation in itself is insufficient as a surrogate for an emerging civil society. Relevant here is the production of new interests, sensitivities, identities, with claims on both the state and society. It is the emergence of these new social forces that necessitate the creation of a new sphere, independent from either the state or primordial institutions. To the extent that this sphere is coterminous with the expansion of the social division of labor and the market, realization of these 'needs' is possible primarily through exchange. This is one of the ways in which civil society and the market are connected. Yet the market's inability to realize all social needs and the state's own limitations necessitate the creation of an autonomous sphere, autonomous from the market and the state, though obviously linked to both. Associations linked to interests which cannot be actualized by either the market or the state are a key facet of civil society. To ensure this autonomy however, the state must itself be reconstituted; the state must stabilize the conditions for civil society to exist and function unfettered on its own terms, through rights. Absence of rights, therefore, can be a major fetter on the development of civil society; without rights, the realm of universal egotism works against the collective good.

The rearrangement of the social structure pertains to the interplay of greater differentiation and polarization of society on class, ethnic, sectarian, and cultural lines. Needless to say, these processes characterize most Third World social formations-in-transition in the era of post-coloniality and globalization. The chief dynamics of differentiation and polarization include: (1) the transformation of the economy, self-discovery and break with the colonial past; and (2) greater integration into the vortex of global political economy. These dynamics embody the contradictory nature of an emerging civil society. In sum, a (classical) political economy perspective allows us to identify the sources and stresses of social transformation, and also helps us recognize the structural antecedents of a civil society. This is not to privilege a political economy perspective, but simply to underscore its present relevance.

C. Capitalism and Civil Society

The subsumption of civil society to associational life is a substantial departure from the historical link between the idea of civil society and capitalism and the modern liberal state. To the extent that capitalism creates a separate sphere for private individual satisfaction outside the household, it is tied to civil society. Through relationships of exchange and the market, the private individual can both satisfy needs and establish common interests with others of various hues. This realm of free association and self-realization is marked by a system of rights, including rights to political association, free speech, rule of law, and above all, property rights.[27] Such a system of rights gives members of society the status of free interlocutors and civil society its special status as a sphere of a modern society. Without exchange and the market, therefore, a civil society, in its classical sense, is inconceivable.[28]

Indispensable also to the stabilization of civil society is the existence of a liberal state. Associational life that emanates via exchange and private activity necessitates a state. A minimum framework of rights reposed in democratic institutions ensures a civil society. Political society presupposes a system of rights, but draws upon civil society for initiative and direction. Crucial to this notion is the presence of clear boundaries; a private sphere without proper limits is a shaky construct. The boundaries of both civil society and state action are established by a system of rights whose enforcement is primarily the function of the state. Often, these boundaries collapse, affecting the character of the democratic process. But the ideal of maintaining these boundaries gives democracy its basic temper.

Despite the assumed harmony which a capitalist order via civil society celebrates, however, social inequality is at the root of this construction. Wealth and income discrepancies impinge upon the capacity of private individuals toward self-realization. Unbound, the empire of civil society can swallow public life or promote socially degenerative ends. Behind the edifice of exchange and procedural democracy often hide patterns of domination, oligarchy, and structural inequality. Yet democratization via civil society still offers to its protagonists a better ideal than a statist or authoritarian model of a social order.

With economic globalization, characterized by internationalization of production via flexible accumulation, the ascendancy of neoliberal social engineering, the tele-communications revolution, the hegemony of global finance, and the overall compression of time and space, new pressures confront the postcolony.[29] The most powerful impact of globalizing tendencies, however, is an assault on the state as the final arbiter of economic growth and political legitimacy. Civil society as the realm of social action outside the state has emerged as the alternative site and actor for transforming Third World societies in economic and political terms. The presumed failure of the state to simultaneously deliver accumulation and legitimate government in many parts of the Third World has seemingly given civil society initiatives added significance. Statist projects have exacted enormous economic and political costs. Against the insolence of planning, the market offers a Promethean frontier of opportunity. But what is the nature of civil society which is being proposed under conditions of globalization?

The neoliberal notion of civil society takes the unfettered market as the principal basis for reconstructing Third World economies, while also injecting democratic values into an otherwise illiberal social fabric. Intrinsic to neoliberal globalization is the increasing commodification of social life, the introduction of 'rational choice' in the societal calculus, and the dismantling of social institutions that do not measure up to the growing demands of the global political economy. In this context, the role of the state is one of realigning domestic forces to the requirements of global production and the logic of profitability.[30] The shock therapy afforded by the neoliberal project proposes to unlock the genie of self-interest as an organizing principle of social existence in societies in which communitarian values resist subordination to the same principle. Yet, the severity and pervasiveness of the neoliberal project leaves little room for advancing a liberal cause. Invariably, economic liberalization has yielded societal conflicts, intolerance, and a breakdown of the social compact. In the context of marginalization of large sections of the population that has ensued, given the unequal effect of either structural adjustment and the systematic dismantling of the state, the concept of the social whole is being replaced by the idea of the atomistic individual.

Globalizing tendencies have also contributed toward fragmenting the mediating structures and norms that have sustained civility in the Third World. Cooperation, mutual regard, and a civic attachment to community now appear as forms of social practice designed to cope with the effects of economic liberalization rather than to realize the idea of society distinct from an aggregate of separate individuals. But increasingly, civility cannot be sustained when the social whole is subordinated to the individual without cultivating a system of rights whose ultimate sanction lies with a democratizing state. Instead, a market-based civil society—the ideal of neoliberalism—can be neither 'civil' nor 'society' in the strict sense of taking civic virtue and the idea of societal good as its key determinants.

Inequality and civility are not mutually exclusive. Economic hierarchy produces incivility only when the social compact that sustains a social order is threatened. This may appear as a plea for maintaining the status quo, regardless of its inegalitarian content. Clearly, conservative apologists for declining civility in advanced capitalist democracies may use this argument to deny an acknowledgment of diversity, maintaining rigid class and gender barriers, and excluding access to new social actors into public life and the economy. If the (neoliberal) ideal put forth is the establishing of a liberal order in the Third World, the route of a disembedded market (i.e., a market separated from its cultural and social milieu) is more likely to undermine civility. Alternatively, societies that have the capacity to resist a purely market-based social order are more likely to sustain both civility and economic development. Adjusting to globalization simply via economic liberalization and the institution of procedural democracy has rarely produced favorable results. It is in this changing and changed context that the life and times of civil society in Pakistan become more visible.

D. Civil Society in Pakistan

I suggest quite explicitly that the transition to capitalism as a social system has already produced the kernel of a civil society in Pakistan, albeit a civil society marked by 'typical' postcolonial stresses and strains. To the extent that the development of a self-regulating market is frustrated by structural and institutional constraints, observers mistakenly conclude that civil society in the 'Western sense' is absent here. In the name of invoking special theoretical privileges for analyzing postcolonial contexts, they ironically rely on the same discarded 'modular' forms which help specify postcoloniality. In the context of Pakistan, the imperviousness of the landed aristocracy to imbibe market principles concerning rights in land, on the one hand, and its unwillingness to discard social relations of personal dependence may be the principal factors stunting accumulation. The proverbial vested interests of an overdeveloped military-bureaucratic complex undermining productive investment are too well-known to rehearse in the present discussion. Relevant here, especially, is the shadow of security which looms large on civil society.[31] An overly intrusive state may also explain why some of the vital sectors in the economy have continued to suffer. Curiously, there appears to be a major divergence between the state's intrusiveness and its poor extractive capacity. Finally, one cannot discount the peripheral status of crony capitalism *vis-à-vis* global capitalism, necessitating protectionism and a general anxiety regarding competition in world economy.

Most significantly, the historical monopoly of political power in the hands of the military-bureaucratic oligarchy has allowed neither a system of rights to be stabilized, nor political society to channel the democratic and liberal aspirations of society. In this sense, the state has only been an overdeveloped structure of coercion, not an expanded state (in a Gramscian sense) blending coercion and consent.[32] Or to be direct, it has been a distinctively postcolonial arrangement, where civil society has not been guaranteed by the state.[33]

In Pakistan, the substance of civil society is colored by postcoloniality and an active process of decolonization. This is revealed most vividly in *nativization* of society, i.e., the rise of indigenous, non-westernized social forces with a variety of claims on the social process, the redistribution of economic and intellectual resources corresponding to indigenization, and the *Pakistanization* of Pakistan. The last factor is best seen against the legacy of colonialism, particularly the cultural partition of society into westernizing and non-westernized spheres, clearly with a wide array of yet indeterminate combinations. Under colonialism, this partition elevated westernized and westernizing elites to pinnacles of political power and leadership and the subordination of the vast majority of the so-called 'vernacular' masses. British land and policies of social engineering once implanted, reproduced a pattern of privilege throughout the greater part of the postcolonial period in which the beneficiaries were the westernized or westernizing elites. The paraphernalia of the colonial state, designed to keep the colony in perpetual subordination to the metropolis was more accepting of westernizing junior partners inclined to function only as intermediaries rather than as autonomous agents. This pattern, I suggest, is now changing. The power structure, for instance, is now more open to demands of non-westernized social forces; westernized elites must share center-stage with agents of non-westernized sectors of society. Whereas the power structure may betray an older pattern, the balance of forces *within* that structure as well as its relation to society is qualitatively different today.

In conjunction with the westernized and anglicized elites, historically suspicious of vernacular expression, a new element in the power structure is a more nativized layer. For instance, the military high command is increasingly distinct from the metropolis in thinking, habits and tastes, compared to their pliant predecessors. The new military elite, for instance, is inclined to assume a *more* indigenous posture on issues of security or ideology. This is not to exaggerate the autonomy of the post-colonial state, i.e., autonomy from global political economy, but to suggest *discontinuity* in patterns of historical evolution. Central to a rupture in historical linearity is the emergence of an indigenous social element and its desire to assume new identities. In blood and color, in taste, in opinions, in morals and in intellect, Pakistani society appears to be more comfortable in the role as its own interlocutor.

The process of nativization, one may add, is wider in scope than the mere arrival of a new social element. At the core lies a constellation of more robust and self-reproducing demographic, economic, social, political and cultural factors. It is also qualified by spatial and temporal unevenness; not all sectors of society are being nativized. In fact, a sizeable fraction of the upper crust of the middle class is being westernized through a variety of links: through service to growing multinational activity in the country; consumption of western (material and cultural) products; access to western education; and insertion into a global information industry. Westernization, in its obvious forms, still remains an insignia of privilege in a society known for parading self-significance and influence drawn from an historically received access to an anglicized power structure. Westernization, in turn, must be contextualized in a wider setting, one in which privilege and plenty are no longer the preserve of a westernized elite. An abundance of cash, both accounted and unaccounted, has become fairly disruptive of the old nexus between status and wealth, the former now being conditioned by the latter. New social hierarchies based on *new* wealth have emerged.

Unlike the prognosis of modernization theorists, social mobility has not necessarily produced an orientation toward westernization. Rather, it may have either strengthened the 'indigenous' component or promoted the emergence of newer vernacular forms. Often, the spatial and mental breakdown of the relative isolation of rural areas has shattered the mystique surrounding westernization. Access to the cosmetic or real trappings of modernity may only be vehicles for articulating an alternative lifestyle or outlook; it provides no guarantee for a linear march toward a westernizing ethos. Hence, labour recruitment to the Gulf states may afford greater means to improve one's material existence,[34] but does not immediately serve as a bridge to accept western ways of being. In the towns and the cities, the growth and expansion of agencies of ideological production, such as state-owned radio and television or the private print media, may facilitate channeling of non-Western, nativist sensibilities. Notably, the cassette revolution, contrary to popular wisdom, not only contributed toward Pakistan's integration into the 'global cultural economy',[35] but also the development of a nativist cultural industry geared toward local consumers. Together, these factors are contributing toward the crystallization of a nativized personality of an emerging civil society in Pakistan.

Generally, political and economic power remains entrenched in elites more comprador than nativist in their make-up and orientation, but the so-called vernacular groups are not so powerless either. In conjunction with the landed aristocracy—the class which continues to wield maximal power disproportionate to its economic standing in Pakistan, a new, more indigenized middle class is beginning to make its presence felt.

The rise of non-western social forces does not signal the ascendancy of anti-modernism, but of a more indigenous, proto-nationalist class, a rude reminder of the intrinsic difference between modernization and westernization. The new middle class perceives itself to be quite skilled in positioning itself to modernity *on its own terms*, entertaining instrumental rationality, without inviting a cultural intrusion into the domain of all social relations. Hence, in sexual matters, it seeks privacy. Yet it shows no reluctance in promoting itself materially. The near-impossible task of reconciling a received ethos with a changing objective reality unsympathetic to its ambivalent stance toward modernity often casts this class in mutually contradictory roles. The political expression of this class is often the strengthening of politics of sectarianism—religious or otherwise—though such politics is by no means confined to that compass and appeal. Zia's greatest legacy to Pakistan, in a sense, is the *institutionalization* of vernacular political interests in the state.

With the differentiation in the social division of labour, the expansion of the sphere of the market, and the growing commercialization of social life, the elements of the new order are already in place. What impact do these factors have on the state? Specifically, how is the state adjusting to the 'great transformation' or the emergence of civil society?

Alavi's ground-breaking thesis on the state in post-colonial societies has the considerable merit of capturing the specificities of the distribution of power and the dominant role of the military-bureaucratic apparatus in the 'over-developed' state bequeathed to Third World social formations by colonialism.[36]

But Alavi's state is primarily an administrative apparatus of coercion and policy-making; it lacks a rationalizing and legitimizing function. Perceiving the state only as an instrument of 'interests' allows Alavi to over-emphasize its effectiveness in the post-colony. An alternative formulation of the state, which recognizes the importance of hegemony (in a Gramscian sense) to the efficacy of the state, furnishes a very different picture of the post-colonial state. Lacking in moral leadership, the state is under-developed, not over-developed.[37] This is, perhaps, the summation of Pakistan's political history: a one-dimensional process of state-building in which coercion, rather than consent; repression rather than legitimacy; administration rather than rule have been the order of things. In a way, the state has not been 'over-developed' à la Alavi, but 'underdeveloped'; the coercive aspects have, indeed, been overdeveloped. Aspects which generate consent and raise the state above society—key to the notion of a modern state—have been poorly developed.

This basic disarticulation *in* the state largely explains authoritarianism. The framework of civil and political rights, rules of political conduct (especially those pertaining to succession), citizenship and the specification of mutual obligations, as well as networks that bind the governed to the state have been absent.[38] The state has been primarily an administrative apparatus, lacking in a substantive notion of rights. The 'over-developed' aspect is basically the 'underdeveloped' aspect of legitimation.

Within the coercive state, politics have been constrained. The number of alternatives has been restricted, but certain historical developments also ensured that these limits would not be transcended. Notably, as many observers have suggested, the legacy of a non-sovereign parliament subordinates the nation's will as reflected in that representative body to the whim of a non-elected individual, the Governor-General or the President. Mohammad Waseem's analysis of this problem is quite useful, including his identification of other components of Pakistan's slide into authoritarianism, particularly the concentration of power in the center and the denial of provincial autonomy, bureaucratic caprice, election fraud and the degeneration of political parties given the long tenure of unrepresented government. These factors, however, should be seen against the backdrop of a poorly developed system of rights, and a weak civil society given certain historical and structural reasons. Similarly, the role of political parties should be seen within the context of the general development or underdevelopment of society.

An important factor inhibiting the growth of a normal state is the absence of hegemony or the inability of the dominant social groups in the state to exercise leadership over society. Torn by internal dissension, state agents have presented mutually conflicting and incoherent models of social organization and development to the people. Nowhere is this evidenced more vividly than in the controversy surrounding Islamization in Pakistan. Hybrid in cultural and political orientation, the state has failed to reconcile *popular* with *official* Islam, the genuine desire in society for moral leadership to the state's narrow interpretation of Islamic ideology. In essence, the state has been unable to rise above societal tensions, merely struggling to maintain a precarious balance between itself and society's contradictory impulses. This is as true for the political function of the state as for its economic role.

The expanding realm of universal egotism has not been regulated by a legitimation process. Consequently, arbitrary behavior has been the norm rather than the exception; in due course, social Darwinism has become the abiding principle of Pakistani society. In society's relation to the state, the latter has been seen as an *external* agency, not a place of ethical life connected to self-satisfaction. A glaring example of society's disregard for the state is with regard to tax collection. But the general attitude is more pervasive, applicable to virtually all sectors of society, especially those with privilege and connections. The ability to circumvent taxes is only a small weapon in the armour of the *priviligentsia*; the entire legal, judicial, and executive system has been porous. A behavioural notion of corruption in these circumstances cannot fully expose the structural nature of the problem. Citizenship and education have not kept pace with the unleashing of impersonal social relations congealed in the market. On the contrary, the breakdown of the old social covenant has been typified by an absence of a new charter. Recourse to personal networks to overcome the wickedness of the invisible hand or reliance on the more dependable cash nexus, therefore, are not hard to locate.

To ensure the development of civil society, the state must represent some higher goal and furnish a mechanism for its realization. That has not happened in Pakistan. The state itself has been an arena of universal egotism: self-seeking has been an integral part of society and the state. But why is this so? To advance moralism or a blanket condemnation of human nature— options that are vigorously exercised—is not enough. Instead, one must look beyond the perceivable crisis of morality to more structural tendencies. A key symptom of these tendencies is the persistence of illegitimate government in Pakistan's recent and past history. Lacking in popular consent, rule has been unjust and rulers have been motivated by a quest for *bonum propium* rather than *bonum commune*. In the nation's political imagination, it is not surprising, therefore, to find the ideal of citizenship held in such low esteem. This has usually translated for the *priviligentsia* as unrestrained opportunism; for the unprivileged, on the other hand, an acceptance of secondary loyalties have been felt as an additional burden to the already crippling demands of necessity.

Paradoxically, the over-developed nature of the coercive apparatus of the state can in part be explained by the under-nourishment of civil society, both in colonial and post-colonial times. This may seem tautological, but the inverse relation between the state and civil society is not so straightforward. Alavi's argument of the primacy of metropolitan interests in defining the character of the state in colonial societies tells part of the story. The other part is the impact of the colonial state on processes that stifled or promoted the development of a civil society in the colony. Despite the *capitalist* nature of the colonial impact, expansion of the social division of labour and the market and the system of accumulation under colonialism fell considerably short of the prerequisites for the emergence of civil society. In fact, the colonial economy remained largely embedded in society, though the corrosive and anomie–generating influences were unleashed through primitive accumulation. Society's response to these influences were, however, mostly defensive. Social and political movements originating in this context were conspicuous for their stress on preserving the tradition, not displacing it.

The story, and this is the heart of the matter, is quite different in post-colonial times. With basic demographic, social, and political changes, the economy has begun to acquire an autonomy from society as a separate realm. The post-colonial state, furthermore, can no longer justify itself with coercion alone. Pressures from below necessitate a reconstitution of the state to expand its function. Even Zia had to learn this lesson after a long spell of arbitrary rule, sanctioned by force or the threat of its use. The dyarchical arrangement reflects the transitional nature of the legitimation process. Yet there are no guarantees that this is a linear trajectory. The possibility of severe reversals in the framework of discord amongst the political elites is always there. With this qualification, one must insist, that legitimation is no longer *external* to the state. Rulers must establish an 'inner justification' or be prepared for applying larger dosages of repression. Hence the greater the expansion of the state as a locus of universal (i.e., society-wide) consent, the greater is the possibility for the development of civil society and, perhaps, democracy. The qualification here is important. The rise of civil society on the scene is fraught with contradictions. On the one hand, it heralds the articulation of new interests; on the other hand, these interests can both enhance older social hierarchies or spawn more pernicious structures of inequality. A redistributive state, rising above these particular interests is, therefore, quite indispensable for helping attain societal good.

Hence, savage capitalism in Pakistan is characterized by the rise of a civil society without a commensurate reconstitution of the state.[39] In short, the so-called 'crisis of governability' is another name for the disarticulation between an emerging civil society and a developing modern state. No single social class, least of all the new bourgeoisie, has been able to capture the state and to exercise moral leadership over the rest of society. The state itself remains an arena for struggle among fractious elites, reflecting their own hybrid social origins.

To a bystander, political society in Pakistan is conspicuous by a de facto absence of rules of political communication, especially at the apex of political power. The political stalemate in Pakistan reflects a general paralysis of governance. In the past this paralysis has seemingly rationalized government by presidential decree.[40] The lingering dyarchical arrangement between the civilian and the political elites[41] virtually truncated authority; the tug-of-war in political society makes effective government only a pious hope.

E. Conclusion

As in other historical contexts, the development of capitalism as a social system in Pakistan has released contradictory tendencies. I have proposed in this paper that a civil society—a sphere relatively autonomous from the state, but depending on it—is indeed emerging in the country. Clearly, it is a civil society linked to a particular form of capitalism, whose principal feature is not simply uneven development (which is true of capitalism generally), but the absence of a system of rights, public obligation (even in the Smithian sense) and a durable framework of autonomous civic action stabilized by the state. In a word, *savage capitalism*. Too often, an exaggerated focus on the state, without corresponding analyses of the relationship between the state and society, including the practices of civil society has blinded our understanding of a changing social world.[42]

The view that primordial ties and relations of personal dependence define the social milieu of Pakistan is not without foundation. However, the postcolonial period also reveals the slow consolidation of a market-based logic permeating all aspects of society, including the family and *biradari*. To the extent that the state has cast its long shadow on civil society,[43] an autonomous realm of association and individuation has not fully emerged. But this is not unique to Pakistan. It is not an issue of the *absence* of civil society in the postcolony but the nature of civil society in economically poor, multi-ethnic, multi-lingual contexts engulfed by processes of lumpen development. To be quite explicit, a modern civil society is beginning to emerge; the preconditions for the expansion of the sphere of both self-interest and rights are gradually coming into being. However, the rude presence of massive inequality severely constricts the development of civil society. With increasing pressures to 'globalize,' the tensions of this nascent civil society are most likely to exacerbate.[44] This makes the task of building a better *society* in Pakistan, as well as in the rest of the postcolonial world, more complicated.

NOTES

1. The literature on this line of thinking is quite extensive. I have explored this theme in David L. Blaney and Mustapha Kamal Pasha, 'Civil Society and Democracy in the Third World: Ambiguities and Historical Possibilities,' *Studies in Comparative International Development* 28 (Spring 1993): 3–24.
2. Francis Fukuyama (1989) 'The End of History' *The National Interest* 16: 3–18.
3. *See*, Blaney and Pasha, 'Civil Society and Democracy in the Third World' op. cit.
4. Krishna Kumar, 'Civil Society: An Inquiry Into the Usefulness of an Historical Term,' *British Journal of Sociology* 44, 3 (September 1993).
5. Ernest Gellner, 'The Importance of Being Modular' *Civil Society: Theory, History, Comparison*, John A. Hall, ed. Cambridge: Polity Press, 1995, pp. 32–55.
6. I have explored the theme of civil society in the context of Pakistan in numerous papers and panel discussions, including the following: 'Democracy by Decree? Civil Society and Pakistani Politics', paper presented at the 19th Annual Conference on South Asia, Madison, November 1990; 'Social Forces, the State and Politics in Post-Zia

Pakistan' at the 20th Annual Conference on South Asia, Madison, November 1991; 'Social Forces, the State and the State: Dilemmas for Democracy in South Asia' at the 33rd Annual Convention of the International Studies Association, Atlanta, April 1992; 'Civil Society, Authoritarianism and Development in South Asia' at the Annual Meeting of the International Studies Association-South, Tampa, October 1992; 'Privatization, Civil Society and the State: the South Asian Experience' at the 34th Annual Convention of the International Studies Association, Acapulco, March 1993; 'Is Democracy Winning' at the 22nd Annual Conference on South Asia, Madison, November 1993; 'Transnationalization, Civil Society and Social Transformation in Pakistan,' at the Annual Conference on Pakistan, Southern Asia Institute, Columbia University, New York, March 1994; 'Rethinking Democratic Development in Pakistan' at the 23rd Annual Conference on South Asia, Madison, November 1994; 'Politics, Discourse, and Powerlessness in Pakistan' at the 24th Annual Conference on South Asia, Madison, October 1995; 'Civil Society, Economic Reform and Politics in Pakistan' at the 29th Annual Meeting of the Middle East Studies Association, Washington, D.C., December 1995; 'Fifty Years of Pakistan; Critical Reflections,' at the 26th Annual Conference on South Asia, Madison, October 1997; 'Liberalization, Globalization and Inequality in South Asia' at the 1998 Annual Meeting of the Association for Asian Studies, Washington, D.C., March 1998; 'In the Shadow of Globalization: State and Civil Society in South Asia,' at the 27th Annual Conference on South Asia, Madison, 16–19 October 1998. I especially draw attention to the following published articles: 'The Hyper-Extended State: Civil Society and Democracy' in *State, Society, and Democratic Development in Pakistan,* Rasul B. Rais, ed. (Oxford University Press, 1997); Security as Hegemony' *Alternatives* 21, 3 (July–September 1996): 283–302; and Blaney and Pasha, 'Civil Society and Democracy', op. cit.

7. The term 'savage capitalism' was used by Samir Amin to describe the nature of capitalism under conditions of globalization at a Roundtable Discussion at the 32nd Annual Convention of the International Studies Association, Vancouver, British Columbia, Canada, March 1991.

8. *See*, my article on 'The Hyper-Extended State,' op. cit.

9. *See*, my article on 'Security as Hegemony', op. cit.

10. Much of the recent and often fashionable literature on postcoloniality suffers from this defect, notably an inability to link discourse with historical structures.

11. I have examined this topic in greater detail on the curious conjunction and disjuncture between colonial and postcolonial settings in *Colonial Political Economy: Recruitment and Underdevelopment in the Punjab* (Oxford University Press, 1998).

12. Neoliberalism could not have embraced a more reliable ally in emptying out the state of its societal role. On this related theme, *see*, Mustapha Kamal Pasha, 'Globalisation and Poverty in South Asia', *Millennium: Journal of International Studies* 25, 3 (1996): 635–656.

13. *See*, Robert W. Cox, *Production, Power, and World Order: Social Forces in the Making of History* (New York: Columbia University Press, 1987).

14. On this point, *see*, 'Security as Hegemony' op. cit.

15. Kumar, 'Civil Society' op. cit., p. 376. The literature on civil society is quite extensive. For representative views, *see especially*, Andrew Arato, 'Civil Society Against the State: Poland 1980-81,' *Telos* 47 (1981): 23–47; Michael Bratton, 'Beyond the State: Civil Society and Associational Life in Africa,' *World Politics* 41: 3 (April 1989): 407–430; John Keane, ed. *Civil Society and the State: New European Perspectives*, (London and New York: Verso, 1988); and Jean Cohen and Andrew Arato, *Civil Society and Political Theory*, (Cambridge, Mass.: MIT Press, 1992). For a discussion of Gramscian and Foucauldian understandings of civil society, *see*, Neera Chandhoke's excellent book, *State and Civil Society: Explorations in Political Theory* (Thousand Oaks: Sage Publications, 1995).

16. Ibid., p. 391.

17. Ibid., pp. 376-77.

18. We have criticized this view in greater detail in Blaney and Pasha, 'Civil Society and Democracy in the Third World', op. cit.

19. Samir Amin expresses this idea quite explicitly: 'The autonomy of civil society is the first characteristic of the modern world. The autonomy is founded on the separation of political authority and economic life, made opaque by the generalization of market relationships. It constitutes the qualitative difference between the new capitalist mode and all precapitalist formations. The concept of autonomous political life and thus of modern democracy and the concept of social science result from the autonomy of civil society, for the first time to be governed by laws outside of human or royal will. The evidence for this is most immediately apparent at the level of economic relationships.' *See*, *Eurocentrism* (New York: Monthly Review Press, 1989), pp. 81–82.

20. *See*, 'The Hyper-Extended State', op. cit. *Also see*, Antonio Gramsci, *Selections from Prison Notebooks*, edited by Quintin Hoare and Geoffrey Nowell-Smith (New York: International Publishers, 1971).

21. Kumar, 'Civil Society' op. cit., p. 381.

22. For the idea of civil society as 'civilized society', *see*, Ashis Nandy, 'The Political Culture of the Indian State,' *Daedalus* 118 (1989): 1–26.

23. 'The Hyper-Extended State', op. cit., pp. 186–187.

24. *See*, for instance, Christina Lamb, *Waiting for Allah: Pakistan's Struggle for Democracy* (New Delhi: Viking, 1991), op. cit.

25. This section relies on 'The Hyper-Extended State', op. cit.

26. Karl Polanyi, *The Great Transformation: The Political and Economic Origins of Our Times* (Boston: Beacon Press, 1957) (Originally published in 1944).

27. Cohen and Arato, *Civil Society and Political Theory,* op. cit.

28. Blaney and Pasha, 'Civil Society and Democracy in the Third World' op. cit.

29. Mustapha Pasha, 'Globalisation and Poverty in South Asia', op. cit.

30. Cox, *Production, Power, and World Order*, op cit.

31. For details, *see*, 'Security as Hegemony', op. cit.

32. Christine Buci-Glucksmann, *Gramsci and the State* (London: Lawrence and Wishart, 1980), 57.

33. This argument is more fully developed in David L. Blaney and Mustapha Kamal Pasha, 'The Emergence of World Culture? Democracy, Civil Society, and the State in the Third World.' (Paper delivered at the 32nd Annual Convention of the International Studies Association, Vancouver, British Columbia, March 1991).

34. Jonathan S. Addleton, *Undermining the Center: The Gulf Migration and Pakistan*. (Karachi: Oxford University Press, 1992).

35. Arjun Appadurai, 'Disjuncture and Difference in the Global Cultural Economy,' *Theory, Culture and Society* 7 (1990): 295–310.

36. Hamza Alavi, 'The State in Post-Colonial Societies: Pakistan and Bangladesh,' *New Left Review* 74 (July–August 1971): 59–81.

37. Gramsci recognizes the importance of moral leadership for the dominant classes to legitimize their control over the economy. For a useful discussion of this theme, *see*, Dwayne Woods, 'Civil Society in Europe and Africa: Limiting State Power Through a Public Sphere,' *African Studies Review* 35 (1992): 77–100.

38. On Pakistan, *see*, Mohammad Waseem, 'An Underdeveloped Citizenry,' *Dawn* (Karachi), 19 August 1991. For a similar analysis on these lines in another context, *see*, John A.A. Ayoade, 'State Without Citizens: An Emerging African Phenomenon,' in *The Precarious Balance: State and Society in Africa*, eds. Donald Rothchild and Naomi Chazan (Boulder and London: Westview Press, 1988).

39. For a good analysis of political trends in Pakistan, *see*, Paula Newberg, 'Dateline Pakistan: Bhutto's Back,' *Foreign Policy* 95 (Summer 1994): 161–174.

40. I have explored this theme in more detail in 'Social Forces, Civil Society, and the State: Dilemmas for Democracy in South Asia,' paper delivered at the 33rd Annual Convention of the International Studies Association, Atlanta, April 1992.

41. Waseem's remarks here are quite instructive: 'The dyarchical arrangement for sharing power between the parliamentary and nonparliamentary forces has created a situation characterized by limited policy choices and an inherently unstable relationship between the permanent state apparatuses on the one hand, and political leaders and parties who participate in

electoral politics on the other. *See*, Mohammad Waseem, 'Pakistan's Lingering Crisis of Dyarchy,' *Asian Survey* 32 (July 1992), p. 634. *Also see*, Salamat Ali, 'Three's a Crowd: Strains Within the Ruling Trinity Begin to Tell,' *Far Eastern Economic Review*, 6 June 1991, p. 20.

42. For an historical account of this political legacy, *see*, Ayesha Jalal, *The State of Martial Rule: The Origins of Pakistan's Political Economy of Defence*. (Cambridge University Press, 1991). An alternative analysis is offered by Hamza Alavi, 'Nationhood and Communal Violence in Pakistan,' *Journal of Contemporary Asia* 21, 2 (1991): 152–178.

43. *See*, my article, 'Security as Hegemony', op. cit.

44. *See*, my article, 'Globalisation and Poverty in South Asia', op. cit.

PART TWO

Social Foundations of
Power in Pakistan

3

PERSONAL AND SOCIAL POWER IN PAKISTAN

S. Zulfiqar Gilani

It is a truism that power is inevitably operative in every social group. Various institutional arrangements evolve or are developed to articulate and establish the relationships and processes for the exercise of power. However, going only by the visible expressions of such arrangements could be misleading. It becomes necessary to look below the surface to get a real grasp on the operations of social power. In order to do that I will attempt to shed some light on the psychological characteristics and motivations of significant wielders of power in Pakistan. Broadly speaking, 'significant wielders' mean middle-class and above, educated and urbanized males.

My argument is straightforward: There are traditional and institutional arrangements of power relationships in Pakistan. However, the outward forms of power relationships may or may not be revealing of what is really going on. To grasp the dynamics of power relationships we need to explore the inner worlds of the actors as that will give a more accurate picture of the prevailing situation. For example, in the history of Pakistan we witness a failure of the establishment of democratic and just relationships, and institutions, despite the fact that apparently the system of governance has been a parliamentary democracy since 1988. Notwithstanding other reasons for this failure, a significant problem is that the focal individuals in the country are psychologically authoritarian. As a result their behavior and relationships perpetuate and strengthen distortions of power, although formally they may be part of a democratic dispensation.

Stated thus, the problem of power may seem ubiquitous and rather difficult to address. It is easy to deal with tangible systems and processes but how does one go about addressing the inner worlds of people. I will not be providing any prescriptions in that regard but consider it absolutely essential that we recognize the psychological underpinnings of the problem of power in Pakistan. Such an understanding could be crucial to determining arrangements that may take us along the path of reducing the extreme distortions and imbalances in the body politic of the country.

Power-relations carry the weight of history, both material and psycho-social. My focus will be on the psycho-social determinants of power in Pakistani society. Social power is embedded in, and function in ways in which humans relate to each other, within the frameworks of the given institutional frameworks (Lukes, 1974). In the present analysis I will largely ignore the institutional structures that foster a particular (im)balance of power in Pakistan and focus on the psycho-social dynamics of power relationships. I will try to spell out how power is psychologically written into the prevalent social conditions.

A crucial and central aspect of Pakistani society is that the link between the individual and the social is dynamic and powerful. There is a flexibility (and fluidity) of the boundary between the self and other/s. 'The self and in-group have variable boundaries. The self does not relate to the in-group but is included in it'. (Sinha & Tripathi, 1994. p.136). Although Sinha and Tripathi are talking about Indians, I feel one can safely extrapolate this to Pakistanis also. Interdependence (Kitiyama and Markus, 1991) is the hallmark of social relations in Pakistan. Thus if one wants to understand social power in that cultural milieu it would be worth one's while to try to identify the psychological underpinnings of power at the individual level. From that one can reasonably extrapolate to power in its wider social manifestations.

Power relations are robust and tend to reproduce themselves. In their essence, power relations have changed very slowly, if at all. I will be making the case that this is so because of the particular psycho-social conditions prevalent in Pakistan and the likely psychological makeup of a person growing up there. Generally society is highly non-egalitarian and status quo oriented. Besides the biological, we believe in psycho-social inheritance. Such characteristics are 'in the blood', to speak colloquially. Social positions are inherited. Such social themes become a significant part of everyone's worldview because of child-rearing practices. Thus power-relations are part of the psychological architecture and not easily amenable to change. However, it needs be kept in mind that change inevitably goes on, along with continuity. Social processes are dynamic and it has to be assumed that power-relations are also in some sort of a flux.

A. Power and the Individual

A number of psychological theories have tried to come to grips with the power of an individual person. I will signpost those and try to formulate a synthesis which has ecological validity for Pakistan. Surprisingly, Freudian psychoanalysis does not give explicit attention to power, though its importance is indirectly recognized and dealt with. The infant's earliest experiences are said to be those of omnipotence; thus Freud referred to the infant as 'His majesty the baby'. The process of socialization is a movement from such a primary process of grandiosity to the development of a more realistic person functioning by secondary processes. In a sense, development is a progressive loss of narcissistic power, which has wide and important implications for personality and society (Freud, 1912; 1921). This shift is handled differently by each person but given the implication of society in the development of individual identity, there are particular sociocultural prescriptions in this regard (Erikson, 1959; Kakar, 1978). Thus one would expect that there would be ways of handling this shift which is socioculturally given and unique to a society.

For Adler, power and the striving for superiority were central. He said 'Behavior is determined by a goal of superiority, of power, of over-powering others. All psychological phenomena are united in an inseparable relationship; on the one hand they come under the law of society and on the other hand the striving of the individual for power and superiority.' (Adler, 1956, pp. 113–114). This understanding of power was later modified and in the normal person it was proposed to be a striving for perfection, a forerunner of Maslow's self-actualization need (1968). In Maslow's view the feeling of dominance is central to positive self-esteem, which in turn is essential for self-actualization. A negatively biased view of personal power is discernible in the authoritarian personality of Adorno et. al. (1950). All of the authoritarian person's behavior is connected to power. On the other hand the democratic person was said to have no need for power.

Karen Horney distinguished between a healthy striving for power and the neurotic's compulsive need for power, stemming from basic anxiety (Kelman, 1972). Thus she was a pioneer within psychology to recognize that power is not necessarily negative. White (1959) further developed the view that power is an essential need for the development of a healthy person. He proposed that besides primary drives humans also have the competence drive: the need to interact effectively with the environment. White later extended this notion to include social competence (White, 1963). He argued that humans and animals alike need to develop a sense of control and impact on themselves and on the environment, referring to this as 'efficacy'. This need was considered to be organic and independent of any tangible gains. Competence was seen to be intimately related to self-esteem and personality development. In a similar manner, de Charms (1968) talked about the human need to be the cause of producing changes in the environment. He proposed a distinction between a 'pawn' and an 'origin': The former feels that the locus of causation lies outside, while the latter feels that the locus is within. Pawns feel powerless, and origins powerful.

According to this view, powerlessness is detrimental to psychological health and development. There is some evidence to indicate that powerlessness is related to personal rage and violence, and psychiatric problems (May, 1972). Seligman's (1975) studies of learned helplessness are the most direct empirical articulation of the negative effects of powerlessness. When a person experiences lack of control, the expectation develops that outcomes are independent of his/her responses. In a sense there is a breakdown in the relationship between actions and their consequences. If learned helplessness is combined with a sense of low self-efficacy, then feelings of powerlessness become profound.

I submit that in Pakistan, the underlying sense of powerlessness of the individual is rather deep and consciously unrecognized. This manifests in a wide variety of social, political and cultural expressions. People are keen to associate themselves with someone currently and/or ancestrally powerful. This could very well be a way of overcoming feelings of being marginal and powerless. Thus one witnesses a somewhat poignant social habit of name-dropping. Discourse is marked by belligerence and machismo. The rule seems to be that you are by default weak and powerless, unless you can prove otherwise. Thus many positions are taken and postures adopted with the purpose of looking powerful. This is a complicated game and often results in adopting positions which make no sense whatsoever until one realizes the need to convey a message: I am not powerless! Such posturing has some very unfortunate pragmatic consequences. For example, there is a strong tendency for political brinkmanship. Alternatively, positions taken are rigidly and puritanically adopted because flexibility is construed to be a sign of weakness. The social positions taken, as defenses against feelings of powerlessness, are counter-therapeutic and a mutually reinforcing loop sets in.

Most relations could be understood as social manifestations of mechanisms of coping with the sense of powerlessness. Based in childhood experiences (see below), such feelings are strengthened by the pragmatic social reality that for the majority of people actions do not seem to have any relationship with their consequences (Gilani, 1985). By and large people do not experience themselves as 'Origins'. The sense of powerlessness is over-determined by family dynamics, history and politics.

B. Child-Rearing and Powerlessness in Pakistan

The average male child[1] in Pakistan has a privileged position for about the first 6–8 years. The child is considered to be an innocent *farishta* (angel) and can do no wrong. He usually has to leave this heaven on earth rather suddenly when it is considered that he is mature enough to step into the outside (male) world. He has to cope with the frustrations of the real world without adequately having experienced them earlier. Thus the child in Pakistan undergoes a rather different process of psycho-sexual development than would one in the West (Kakar, 1978). It is not feasible to detail those differences here but we must keep in mind that the structure of adult personality is a function of those early experiences, which in turn has ramifications for ways of relating.

More significantly, the boy's elevated position is maintained primarily by the mother[2] and other females involved in child-care. In the typical Pakistani family the father is an absent figure both emotionally and in terms of actual time spent with the young child.[3] At the societal level, large sections of society are functionally segregated along gender lines. Female/male roles are clearly defined and rather strictly followed. Further, in many cases the practicalities of earning for the family forces the father to be away from home for most of the day. In recent years large numbers of men have had to travel to the city, sometimes to another country, and may be away for prolonged stretches. Even when residing in the same house, typically the father is there only at mealtimes and sometimes in the evenings, watching television. As is obvious, on such occasions the family is engaged in parallel-social activities and any one-to-one contact is incidental. There is quite a lot of demographic diversity in this regard but we need not be concerned with those details. The central point is that the father is an emotionally distant figure. The consequences of the child's emotional growth primarily with females are profound.[4]

Psychoanalytic theory has made it amply clear that the early experiences of the child are affective, unconscious and powerful. Given the lack of a genuine affective experience of the father (male), the child starts developing a sense of maleness at a later stage of psychic development. Lacking the sensuous contact, this is a relatively more abstract construction which is largely based on fantasy. All early experiences have the quality of fantasy, but this fantasy doesn't go through correctives of reality. The strengths (and weaknesses) of the 'first sex' are thus not associated with their affective being but with their perceived (fantasized) position in society. In a sense the developing child inhabits two worlds: there is the early feminine world of sensuousness and feelings and the later more worldly one which is not drenched in so much affect. More often than not for the female child, there is no shift from one to the other but the male child has to leave one and step into the other. This shift has important consequences.[5]

C. Male 'Birth' and its Consequences

The young boy in Pakistan, unlike his western counterparts, spends his early years in great intimacy with his mother. It is not uncommon for boys to sleep in the same bed with their mothers until late childhood and through adolescence. Weaning is usually a relaxed affair and goes on at a pace determined by the child. Thus it is not considered unusual for a five to six year old boy to play with his mother's breasts and at times suckle her. Something similar is true for toilet training as toilet training does not usually entail a very strict regime of discipline and conflict. In a nutshell, the narcissistic tendencies of the boy remain unmodified for longer. It is not relevant here to discuss the differences in the rearing of boys and girls but suffice it to say that the girl-child does not have access to a similarly beneficent maternal bosom.

Nevertheless, the boy has to, in the end, step out into the outer (male) world. The lack of preparation for this transition does not make for a smooth journey. On the one hand the boy's affective connection with the maternal remains robust. On the other the lack of an affective relationship with the paternal results in an idealized construction of the male and maleness. This colors and determines later relationships, leading to invariant cultural patterns.

One manifestation is the proverbial, and often actual, tension between the wife and mother. The husband looks for mother in the wife but is bound to remain unsatisfied, because no substitute can ever be 'the real thing'. Reciprocally the mother resents the daughter-in-law's trespass into her boy's emotional world and jealously guards her boy from being ensnared by her (the daughter-in-law). This mother-son dyad is somewhat symbiotic and leaves the wife on the outside. There are a very large number of anecdotes about this uneven triangle, some of them rather comical. She (the wife) is thus thirsting for a deep and affective relationship with a male; therefore, the son is eagerly awaited. Once he (the son) arrives he is entirely hers. She opens up the rich bounties of her love to him. And so it goes from generation to generation. There are a host of social patterns of male-female relationships that can be fruitfully explored through this framework, but that is a task tangential to the agrument being made here. In many ways the male in Pakistan is perennially a son, and the female a mother.

The affectively barren relationship of the child with the father has important consequences. The father (and the male, and one's own self) becomes an idealized figure, remote, powerful and flawless. Processes of identification and projective identification seem to be at work (Freud, 1921; Klein, 1957). The child gains power by identifying with the powerful father. Projective identification is a more complicated process whereby the person projects his/her feelings onto the (idealized) other, and identifies with those (projections). If unaware of what is going on, the other is pulled into being the projection, and the circle gets completed. In other words, one sees certain (desirable) qualities in the other, which are in fact emerging from one's own needs, and identifies with them. The other unwittingly accepts the projected definition and plays the part. Thus idealizations keep gaining strength and are mutually sustained.

In the absence of an experienced affective relationship with the father, a fantasized father-image develops: this father inhabits the outside world, is perceived to be powerful, and the solver of problems. The archetypal worldly savior is male. At a more mundane level this gets expressed in the manner in which social hierarchies are formed and perpetuated. Thus patrilineage is deeply entrenched. For our purposes the more important reality is the manner in which men relate with each other. Most men have multiple allegiances to (male) mentors (*pirs*) and leaders of different ilk.[6] The nature, spread and depth of such allegiances are, in important respects, expressions of the early feelings towards, and later search for, father.

This strong pull towards idealized males is further strengthened by the unconscious need to try and break the feeling of the suffocating grip of mother. The early intimacy and love of the mother continues to retain its psychic power. Thus there is the need to break loose of the maternal influence. Socially this can be witnessed in the severe and ugly undermining of femininity, and a glorification of machismo. It is commonplace to ascribe failure, immorality, weakness, in short everything evil, to femininity. The average Pakistani male never tires of proudly proclaiming his total lack of need for, and independence from, woman. At best any relationship/s with women are described in terms of conquering and subjugating them, usually sexually: the boys' declarations of freedom. The only woman who escapes this treatment is the mother. Motherhood is glorified. In Pakistan the female as mother is the archetype of human perfection. Parenthetically, this also explains the need of the Pakistani female to become a mother because that elevates her psycho-socially. The worst insult for a male refers to his having sex with mother: defiling the pure. Motherhood seems to be split-off from femininity.

The early intimacy with mother also leaves its mark in another way. Namely, the Pakistani male has certain characteristics which could be labelled feminine in prevalent terminology. One is the intimacy men have with their male friends. For example, it is commonplace for men to be holding hands while walking. In Pakistan, men get together to talk about and share intimate details of their inner, and social lives, something the western male is unlikely to do. The nature of male-bonding is in certain significant ways different than what is observable in western men. Again, men have lesser problems in accepting their passivity (Kakar, 1989). This may seem like a contradiction of treating feminity as trash but it is not. Such behaviour patterns are labelled feminine only in the framework of the western discourse of polarities, including the male–female. They are not recognized in the same manner in Pakistan. Being male and being intimate (with other males) is not out of the ordinary. Feminine qualities are not abstractions; the woman is feminine, the male masculine, and it does not matter whether one has aspects of the other.

D. Power and Relationships

In the light of the above what can one say about the likely psycho-social contours of social power in Pakistan? The central need seems to be one for a savior/redeemer/leader. Fuelled by the not-very-well-modified narcissistic needs, each seems to look for someone to take care of things, to solve problems. The fantasized image of the father remains in play and gets projected onto the one who may be perceived as a redeemer. The need to 'escape from freedom' (borrowing from Erich Fromm) is strong and a social hierarchy of power a foregone conclusion. Thus in Pakistan almost everyone is a follower of some *pir* (mentor), leader, elder, etc. Further, social positions are inherited. It should be clear that such needs are not consciously recognized by the individual. Thus one witnesses that each finds faults with everyone else but self-observation and criticism are rare. There is constant complaint about having been failed or let down (by the other). Implicit in such a complaint is the power position of the other up to which he has failed to live.

A cursory look at illustrative leader-follower relationships in Pakistan can shed light on the points being made. M. A. Jinnah was a westernized barrister whose life bore no resemblance to that of his most devout followers. He spoke to them in English or Urdu, which most people did not speak as their native language and few understood. Still they adored and followed him, and have come to refer to him as the 'father of the nation', the Quaid-i-Azam. He was the pied piper who was to lead the people out of British and (anticipated) Hindu hegemony. Even today people feel the loss of that father deeply and believe that if he had not died so soon after 1947, Pakistan would not have the myriad problems it is facing today. A somewhat similar relationship emerged with Zulfikar Ali Bhutto (Gilani, 1995). What is notable is the nature of the followers' feelings towards these leaders. There is a lot of evidence to indicate that there was a feeling of intimacy, and intensity of emotions. Policies and such positions took the back seat and the person (of the leader) was all-important. They were perceived to be flawless and could do no wrong. The leaders were looked upon as saviors. Their deaths were widely and deeply mourned.

The above are illustrative of the widespread need amongst Pakistanis for a savior. Similar needs are also operative at micro-levels. I have argued that ways of child-rearing makes for a particular (male) personality type. Such a person is amenable to idealization and in search of a savior. These factors in turn reproduce social power hierarchies. However, a crucial element of the power dyad has been left untouched: how do we understand the psychology of the one who is the savior, the leader?

E. The Dynamics of Power-relations

In order to answer the above question we need to analyze the dynamics of the power-relationship. Here the boundaries of psychology cris-cross with those of sociology, culture, and history. As mentioned earlier, in the Pakistani view, social position in the world is largely inherited. On the one hand this is non-egalitarian and detrimental to social mobility. On the other it provides the sense of security of 'knowing one's place'. Thus, in Pakistan leadership potential is in large measure an accident of birth. But potentials do not make leaders. Ancestry is (in most cases) a necessary but not a sufficient condition for attaining social power.

An individual who attains leadership does so through capitalizing on projective identifications. The upbringing of the potential leader is, in its basics, quite similar to that of any other child. There is a crucial difference though. For one, the mother is likely to have a strong need for her son (and through him, herself) to attain greatness. It is not possible to make generalizations here but a certain theme seems to have a bearing on this. In Pakistan the only achievement a woman can have traditionally, is in her motherhood. If a woman has other capabilities they are not socially recognized, and this leaves her frustrated. In such a situation where there is no space for the direct expression of a woman's capabilities, the son becomes the most likely vehicle of her frustrated dreams. Thus the woman, as the mother of a son, can beat the system. The son is raised with a sense of destiny. Psychoanalytically speaking, the mother projects her fantasies on the son and identifies with them. The son 'accepts' those projections and is the ideal one. This gives a new meaning to the old saying that 'behind every great man stands a woman'. It is probably true that every mother wants her son to be 'great' but here we get into an interaction with another variable: ancestry.

Thus the would-be leader comes from a background where the males traditionally have an elevated social position. Witness the very high preponderance of socio-political leaders who come from 'good' families. The females (the mothering ones) are unconsciously actualizing their dreams through the son. The self-perpetuating nature of leadership running in families has been noted and commented upon. However, most of those have focused on the economic bases for that and have by and large ignored the psycho-social aspects. Raised in an abundance of projective identifications, the leader continues to seek and thrive in being idealized. To him, and to everyone else in that social framework, that is the natural order of things. The leader thus starts symbolizing the (unattainable) needs of the followers.

Although I have been talking in terms of leaders and followers, which gives the discussion a political bias, I must clarify that in my view projective identifications and idealizations are in play in most everyday relationships. The leader-follower relationship is just an exemplar of a widespread social phenomenon. The outlined pattern of relating is also quite robust. That is so because child-rearing practices and socio-cultural patterns dovetail. Further, these relationship patterns are firmly embedded in history and tradition.

F. Conclusion

I have tried to simplify the complicated intertwinement of the individual and the social, regarding power. It has been argued that the child is embedded in a tradition of child rearing, which has significance for personality development. The average Pakistani grows up looking for a father/savior/leader, and this search continues through life. The sociology of the country also provides certain people who are psychologically prepared to take on that role (of leadership).

In the post Zia ul-Haq period, we have witnessed a widespread social breakdown. The processes of dispersal seem to have set in at all levels of society. One contributing factor could be a breakdown in traditional power relations, without new patterns having emerged or been established. For political reasons, Zia tried to undermine Bhutto's symbolic appeal, and seems to have succeeded to a degree. But he failed to project himself as the new father. In my view this failure was a function of his non-nurturing persona, combined with the essentially negative positions (*vis-à-vis* the deposed father) which role he took. He was not good idealization material. In 1988 a majority voted for the daughter, Benazir Bhutto. However, she was too young, and a woman to boot, to fulfill the peoples' need for a redeemer, idealized as an older male. In addition, the significant minority which was building on Zia's legacy kept chipping away at the Bhutto image, resulting in a negative process gaining ascendancy. There was no one deserving to be 'father' and the credibility of even the previous one now came into question.

Such a process could prove to be positive for strengthening egalitarianism and democracy but there was a crucial ingredient missing: The psychological needs of the individual did not undergo any real changes. The need for the father remains, but the claimants to the title are now seen to have 'no clothes'. The individual still has no power and there is no one through identification with whom the individual can attain it. The result is anger and disillusionment with the leader culminating in a sort of 'free for all'. Most people feel profoundly powerless and apathetic. A sense of ennui pervades the social fabric.

This powerlessness has a number of other consequences which can only be touched upon here. There are widespread lamentations about the numerous social problems currently prevalent in Pakistan. However, there is a strong unstated complaint in these lamentations; the problems seem to be a result of others' faults. Everyone feels that problems cannot be solved by them but can be solved by others. Consequently each feels failed and let down by everybody. There is an increasing frequency of 'power bubbles' at the local level. An individual lays claim to leadership based on the promise of fulfilling needs. People accept him, but he fails and the bubble is burst. With each disillusionment, the credibility of claimants is further eroded and the sense of powerlessness gets deeper. Today Pakistan is in the grip of this deteriorating spiral. Consequently it is difficult to identify the centres of power. Such power anarchy is evidently detrimental to social stability and progress. This is not a very happy situation. As John Kenneth Galbraith aptly remarked, 'The exercise of power, the submission of some to the will of others, is inevitable in modern society; *nothing whatever is accomplished without it*' (1984:13, author's italics).

References

Adler, A. 1956. *The Individual Psychology of Alfred Adler* (ed. and annotated by H.L. Ansbacher and R.R. Ansbacher). New York: Harper and Row.

Adorno, T.W., E. Frenckel-Brunswick, D.J. Levinson, D.J. and R.N. Sanford. 1950. *The Authoritarian Personality.* New York: Harper.

de Charms, R. 1968. *Personal Causation: The Internal Affective Determinants of Behavior.* New York: Academic Press.

Erikson, E.H. 1959. 'Identity and the life cycle'. *Psychological Issues.* Vol I. Indiana University Press.

————, 1921. 'Group Psychology and the Analysis of the Ego' in A. Dickson (ed.) 1991. *Civilization, Society and Religion.* Penguin Freud Library, Vol. 12, pp. 91–178.

Freud, S. 1912. 'The dynamics of transference' in J..Strachey (ed. and trans.) *The Standard Edition of the Complete Psychological Works of Sigmund Freud.* Vol. XII. London: Hogarth Press and Institute of Psychoanalysis, 1958.

Galbraith, J. K. 1984. *The Anatomy of Power.* London: Hamish Hamilton.

Gilani, S.Z. 1994. 'Z.A. Bhutto's leadership: A psycho-social view'. *Contemporary South Asia.* Vol. 3, No. 3, pp. 217–236.

————, 1985. 'Drug abuse: Inner needs and outer reality'. *Proceedings of the First International Congress: World Islamic Association for Mental Health.* Lahore, pp. 67–70.

Kakar, S. 1989. 'The maternal-feminine in Indian psychoanalysis'. *International Review of Psycho-Analysis 16*, pp. 355–362.

————, 1978. *The Inner World: A Psychoanalytic Study of Childhood and Society in India.* New Delhi: Oxford University Press.

Kelman, H. 1972. 'Power: the cultural approach of Karen Horney' in J.H. Masserman (ed.) *The Dynamics of Power.* New York: Grune and Stratton, pp. 71–82.

Kitayama, S. and H.R. Markus. 1991. 'Culture and self: Implications for cognition, emotion and motivation'. *Psychological Review* 98, No. 2, pp. 224–253.

Lukes, S. 1974. *Power: A Radical View.* London: Macmillan.

Maslow, A.H. 1968. *Towards a Psychology of Being*. 2nd edition. New York: Nostrand.

May, R. 1972. *Power and Innocence: A Search for the Sources of Violence*. New York: Dell.

Seligman, M.E.P. 1975. *Helplessness: On Depression, Development and Death*. San Francisco: Freeman.

Sinha, D. and R.C. Tripathi. 1994. 'Individualism in a collectivist culture: a case of coexistence of opposites' in U. Kim, H. C. Triandis, C. Kagitcibasi, S. Choi and G. Yoon (eds.) *Individualism and Collectivism: Theory, Method, and Application*. London: Sage.

White, R.W. 1959. 'Motivation reconsidered: the concepts of competence'. *Psychological Review* 66, pp. 297–333.

————, 1963. (ed.) *The Study of Lives*. New York: Atherton Press.

NOTES

1. It is likely that what is being theorized about child-rearing in Pakistan is in many ways generally true. However, there are important reasons for detailing the specific Pakistani situation because there are certain peculiarities to the society and culture which has its particular consequences. The empirical basis for what is being said below is the data obtained from my working with patients over a period of sixteen years. The data itself, however, is not being presented here.

2. In all that follows, 'child' should be read as 'male child'. As the need arises, specific reference will be made to the female.

3. 'Mother' should be read as primary female caretakers who may or may not be the biological mother.

4. The relationship of the child with the father may not be as affectively intimate as with the mother in other societies also, but there are significant differences in detail which have important psycho-social consequences.

5. For a wider analysis of this phenomenon, *see*, Dorothy Dinnerstein's (1976) *The Mermaid and the Minotaur: Sexual Arrangements and the Human Malaise* (New York: Harper & Row).

6. Broadly speaking, the dynamics of child-rearing described here may be true for all humans living in different societies. However, cross-cultural differences in child-rearing have a significant and specific impact on personality development. Therefore the usefulness of a contextually embedded description of child-rearing practices remains.

7. Women also have such allegiances but with different motivational bases, the primary one being that such allegiances provide socially sanctioned ways of stepping out of the house and/or having an affective relationship with a male outside the immediate family.

4

GENDERED POWER RELATIONS: PERPETUATION AND RENEGOTIATION

Anita M. Weiss

Pakistan is undergoing unprecedented social dilemmas and challenges, and the implications these have for women are profound. At the same time when traditional views towards women's roles in society are being championed in many domains, changes—in social practices, orientations and values—are occurring throughout the country. Conflicting images regarding the place and power of women are having profound social, economic and political consequences. Issues which arise in this context have one thing in common: the dialectical question of a woman's access to power, to being able to follow her own aspirations or initiatives. A woman with access to power in Pakistan can decide for herself such things as whether or not to wear a veil; whether to seek employment and, if so, in what profession; and the number of children she will have. She can also decide if she wants to play a role to influence the state's actions at any level as well as if she wants to work towards expanding women's civil rights within the country. To gain access to power at any level, Pakistani women need to find a voice in both public and private spheres of life. While the participation of elite women has been gradually increasing in public institutions, women of all classes have had a harder time finding a voice in the most critical social institution of all: the family.

A resultant paradigm shift in women's access to power is occurring today in Pakistan, albeit slowly and in limited quarters, engendering conflicting notions regarding the status and power of women throughout the society. How this translates into motivating and facilitating women to move out of the vestiges of the home into the arena of social life outside of it is, for many women, one of the most daunting challenges of their lives.

This chapter interrogates the transmittal and manifestations of male and female perceptions of power—as well as the practical exercise of power—and places these in the context of larger social changes and power configurations occurring in Pakistan today. It explores the foundation of power relations within the home, within extended families, and how this is mitigated by the socialization process occurring in schools in Pakistan. It analyzes how it is possible that women are joining the ranks of new social participants in Pakistan's emergent civil society, a topic that will be addressed further by Khattak and Bari in Chapter 9 of this volume.

The gendered exercise of power within the family provides a foundation, often reinforced in schools, for socially accepted norms of women's participation in spheres outside of the home. I am arguing that women are encountering conflicting norms and roles, and the ways they perceive how to accommodate them vary, for the most part, from men's perceptions of how such conflicting norms and roles should be accommodated. The reallocation of obligations which is occurring, therefore, is resulting in a redistribution of gender-based rights and power. The combination of the demands of the new international division of labor and the global telecommunications revolution is fuelling this transformation. Where women fit into these changing social processes is pivotal, requiring a constant renegotiation of power relations within the social order. As a final example of this, I conclude by addressing the relationship between this renegotiation of gendered power and the on-going discourse on population planning and fertility choices that is occurring in Pakistan today as it affects and is affected by the family, education and choices that the state is making which affects Pakistan's nascent—yet emergent—civil society.

As a political entity, women[1] were powerless until the early 1980s, when their organized opposition to the state's imposition of an Islamization program compelled it to change course.[2] Since then, women have been seeking various ways to have a political voice. While formal political power plays a very minor part in this schema—most participation occurs within either a women's group or an NGO—in raising this voice, women are also contesting established boundaries within families and the larger social environment. That they are becoming an increasingly viable force as seen in recent state actions towards women, particularly in the massive follow-up project to implement the Beijing *Platform for Action* that has resulted in the *National Plan of Action*[3] as well as Pakistan's subsequent ratification of CEDAW, the UN Convention on the Elimination of all forms of Discrimination Against Women.

With women in Pakistan gaining a political voice, why don't we see broad changes occurring in women's status and their having a greater public voice? I am arguing that public and private spheres of power can no longer be separated in Pakistan because they have reached the stage of being intrinsically interrelated. Before a woman can act independently in the larger society, she must have some power within her own family. Women collectively can gain only a limited political voice and limited social power in the public arena until the Pakistani family, as a social institution, empowers its female members. In most instances, that is where the bottleneck remains.

A. The Gendered Division of Power within the Family

The gendered division of power within the family is due to a unique combination of economic and status concerns. Without question, the institution of the family plays a principal, central role in Pakistani social life. Access to many opportunities are often contingent on the connections which one's family has with others. Family interpretations of religious and social values and its own preferences and traditions are the greatest factors in affecting such things as whether or not daughters are sent to school, parallel cousin marriages are preferred, or whether women must wear a veil. Indeed, women can come from similar socioeconomic backgrounds where some will wear a veil, others will not. Some families will allow—and be proud of—a daughter to enroll in a college for higher education while others refuse to send a girl even to primary school. Until recently, these decisions were based more on family traditions than on any other factor.

Families provide a virtually complete package of economic and social support, provided that members abide by its norms. Individual members are expected to concede to the power of what is acceptable within *that* family, more than simply acquiesce to the power of any individual family member. Importantly, however, there is one domain where men wield power over women within a family: in their absolute control over women's mobility. In fieldwork I have conducted in a variety of locales in Pakistan, I have found that whenever a woman has been stopped—from going to school, from applying for government assistance, from travelling, from taking a job, even from walking down a street alone—the initiative for stopping her has always come from a man in her family.[4]

Indeed, while women are considered the repository of their family's respectability, the multi-faceted system of norms and controls which has served to constrain female activities and mobility in traditional society does not exist mainly out of concerns regarding female promiscuity. It is the *notion* of what is accepted as respectable and what is not—perhaps initially tied to matters of sexuality but no longer—that has become a form of social control. The fear of losing respectability is indisputably the driving force behind men suppressing women's actions. When a female seeks to traverse social boundaries, the objection raised seldom questions whether she will behave herself properly or what she might do wrong, but instead 'what will others think?' It is not the intrinsic value of the female's action but the social value placed on respectability—*izzat* and *sharafat*—that has long suppressed women's inventiveness in response to challenges. The fear of men losing control to a woman's domination is also associated with such male suppression, as such a man becomes an object of social ridicule. The result is a general consensus in mainstream values that any activity in which a woman engages outside of the home needs to be monitored. This also explains why conditions of high density in rapidly changing poor urban areas such as Faisalabad, Wazirabad, Multan, and parts of Lahore have become factors in strengthening the power held by families over their members, particularly power held by males over females.

When women who are now grandmothers were young, the norm was to place a girl into *purdah* before the onset of puberty. This decision was usually made by some close male relative who, at a certain point, decided that the girl's interactions with males should now be limited. One woman in the Walled City of Lahore recounted to me how one day when she was nine years old, her grandfather decreed that she was no longer to go outside and play with the other children in the neighbourhood.[5] There was no warning, no preparation for the event. He just decided that the time had come for her to be put into purdah, the formalized separation between the worlds of men and women. From that day onwards, she could only observe social life on the street from the roof of her home; she was no longer to partake of it. She could play within her house, but not outside of it. Interactions with males was now to be extremely limited and closely monitored. She was no longer a free agent who could decide whether she wanted to take a walk or play with a toy outside or inside. Invariably, whenever a woman has recollected to me how and when she was put into purdah, it was her father, grandfather, brother or mother's brother who had decided that the time had come.

Within families, while both boys and girls must be obedient in front of their elders (particularly in front of older men), I have never seen an instance of significant mobility restrictions being placed on boys. Rather, family pressure may be placed on boys to attend school, choose a certain career, or in marriage selection. Even so, parents and other elders are rather relaxed about enforcing the first two of these. I have heard many accounts that a boy stopped going to school because he 'wasn't interested in studying' or he 'didn't like to study.' Career options often become available through informal networks which may not require an independent decision on the part of a boy. It is only in the latter kind of pressure—to marry a spouse of one's family's choice—that it seems that both men and women generally submit to their family's will.[6] A generation ago, while it was possible for a boy to suggest a potential spouse and have his family then arrange his marriage with her, this was unheard of in the case of a girl proposing to do so. She would have disgraced herself and her family just to have voiced an opinion. Indeed, only a very limited number of sons and virtually no daughters in most families in the country have much say in spousal selection or in voicing a preference. Importantly, once a decision is made as to a marriage partner, it seems that both sons and daughters are unable to break the engagement without generating severe discord and antagonism within the family.

We find, however, that gendered power relations within the family is in the midst of flux. In most instances they are being renegotiated out of necessity: the incorporation of virtually all areas into the market economy requiring women to earn an income; schools and the media stressing civil obligations; and low-cost transportation enabling a woman to travel on her own. These strains, coupled with the loss of will to maintain the extended family (at least in urban areas), also have repercussions for women as victims of domestic violence.

Men's desire to control their wives—with physical violence if necessary—has a long-standing basis in many areas of Pakistan. People will often refer to Qur'anic verses for justification (generally cutting the given verse short and therefore not elaborating on the full meaning). Importantly, traditional society had a viable system of built-in checks and balances that ensured physical assault would not be allowed to go too far. First cousin marriage is widely practiced (and preferred) throughout this patrilocal society, resulting in a woman's father-in-law or mother-in-law (with whom she will live) often also being her paternal uncle or an aunt. Such a marriage to a girl from 'within the family' often implies greater power for the young wife as she has grown up around all her in-laws and no one is a stranger for her to fear. Another common practice is *watta sutta*, or exchange marriage: a daughter for a daughter-in-law. The assumption is that a male will treat his wife better knowing that his sister will face a similar fate from his wife's brother.

In villages, most people will interfere in domestic matters as the lines between nuclear families, extended families and fictive kin are, for practical purposes, nonexistent. While this interference usually quells domestic violence, on occasion it provokes or aggravates it as well. Relatives, friends and neighbors will allow the abuse to proceed only to a point, at which time they would feel both obliged and justified to intercede. The hyper-urbanization that Pakistan has experienced in the past two decades has inadvertently upset this social balance. I have found that the common urban stereotype that it is village men who beat their wives often and mercilessly is not substantiated by facts or field research. Instead, the highest incidents of domestic violence have been related to me in transitional cities, those places (e.g., Jhelum, Wazirabad, Mardan) where people move temporarily before moving on to a larger city and a permanent home. There, lacking the traditional support structures of the village as well as new fictive kinship networks, greater wealth, improved quality of consumer life, and civic mechanisms of the city, women are battered without the possibility of intervention. There is neither a social nor a civic force present which can stop a batterer.

While extended family members continue to intervene despite the shift to nuclear families in urban areas, the lack of relatives physically present within the household leaves open the possibility of increased domestic violence. This tends to be truer in those urban centers where traditional close-knit communities no longer exist; it appears to be less true within long-standing urban communities (generally poorer) where interconnecting kinship and other sociocultural ties replicate traditional relationships between groups, such as is found in the Walled City of Lahore.

Culturally sanctioned violence against women is pervasive in Pakistan, and the implicit threat of gender-based violence is particularly acute within the household in the form of domestic violence. However, domestic violence is seen as a private matter and therefore beyond the concern of the public spheres of policy making and legislation. Laws enforced during Zia ul-Haq's Islamization program exacerbate prevailing culturally sanctioned violence. Marital rape is not a punishable crime under Pakistani law at this time. Due to the tendency to censure the victims of domestic abuse, women are often reluctant to discuss violent acts of abuse. Indeed, in Pakistan today, a woman who claims to be a victim of rape but is unable to prove it can be charged with adultery (*zina*) and imprisoned. A common fear among women is that if they flee from their homes (as victims of abuse), they may be charged with *zina*. Additionally, they fear they will be separated from their children who, by law, are to be remanded to a father's custody under most circumstances. I have met many women who have told me of their struggles in enduring a range of abuses (beatings; cigarette burns) but they remained within their homes so that they could not be charged with *zina*. Some feared they might be condemned as a '*KaroKari*' who had illicit sex (and could well be subject to an honor killing) for no reason other than that they are defenseless in the face of such a charge. Perhaps because of this sense of powerlessness, I have found women tend to be quite open and frank in talking about one's own husband hitting her—there is no other outlet for condemnation, really—but less responsive in pinpointing who else in a household may be hitting or abusing her, especially other men.[7] I have found a great reluctance (as expected) in exploring personal details of sexual abuse, though many women volunteered accounts about *other's* experiences. When women—particularly better educated women—talk about 'mental abuse' (*zehni tashaddad*), they often relate it to a crisis of changing roles, values and social expectations.

When I tried to get statistics from the Punjab Police on the extent of recorded domestic violence, an official from a district Crimes Branch was only able to give me data on murder, attempted murder, kidnapings and abductions, and recorded rapes. Interestingly, it was his personal opinion that *recorded* rapes were usually instances of adultery; true rapes generally go unreported as a family usually seeks out its own revenge. Regardless, this data is not reflective of instances of domestic abuse. Other figures may exist in government records somewhere, but I have neither seen nor heard of them.

Violence against women within their homes is an extension of the subordination of women in the larger society, reinforced by religious beliefs, cultural norms, traditional practices, and—as is the case in Pakistan—actual laws. It is likely exacerbated by changing roles and expectations which men and women are experiencing coupled by the assumption held by men of the social expectation that they exert control over the actions of their women. The cultural structure of the family not only places women in a subordinate role, but also fosters gender-based violence and coercion. The prevailing family structure—particularly prevalent in Pakistan where a new bride moves into her husband's home with all his relatives—coupled with perceptions of women's dependent role within the family and in society, create an atmosphere conducive to violence against women.

In my discussions with women, two popular perceptions emerged as being the most responsible for domestic violence in Pakistan: lack of education among men and women alike (especially quality education and not merely rote memorization) and domestic quarrels resulting from inflation and financial pressures. People, overall, seemed to be frustrated by a perceived lack of jobs, especially for men. As one man told me, urban areas are full of men with BA degrees who remain unemployed, frustrated, and beat their wives. Other reasons given for domestic violence concern changing expectations that men and women have of each other. Women who are now better educated and more aware of their rights will not put up with men's infidelity as they did in the past. They will argue about the 'other woman' and deplore the double standard of sexuality that has prevailed here for centuries. Men, in turn, are increasingly suspicious of their wives' actions amid increasing mobility. Unrealistic expectations (often glorified) that both men and women hold of future spouses also contributes to manifestations of domestic violence. This is exacerbated by: i) the widespread prevalence of arranged marriages in villages and among working and middle class urban families; ii) the precipitous rise of a consumer-oriented culture; and iii) media portrayals (especially prevalent in satellite transmissions) of consumerism, ideal lifestyles and ideal wives and husbands. A final, important factor that has been offered is the rise in drug abuse.

Importantly, negotiations of gendered power within families do not consistently result in spiraling domestic violence. An alternative result is the family encouraging a girl's empowerment, the path towards which is seen to be the acquisition of a good education. As noted above, the lack of others physically present within a household leaves open the heightened possibility of escalated domestic violence. Increasingly, however, the absence of close extended family members coupled with the rise of female primary education is resulting in a significant shift to schoolfriends becoming a replacement support system. However, while a schoolfriend may have become a fictive kin for a woman, the friend cannot wield the same degree of influence over a woman's husband that a member of his extended family can. There is no longer any viable social control over men's attempts to subdue their wives by the use of physical (and/or psychological) force. Often, this fear of domestic violence has replaced the former willing acquiescence by women to male and familial control.

Indeed, *family* control over female mobility is significantly lessened in the 1990s, particularly in urban areas. Power issues between spouses is constantly being renegotiated: in many cases, women have indeed gained power by now having the right to make some of their own choices. In other cases—whose ranks are steadily shrinking—rigid tradition-based restrictions still apply to women. But in seemingly more and more instances, an ambiguity is now prevailing where before there was more clarity. Ambiguity, however, can be empowering in the family, especially if it means that it is a move away from a previous rigid conformity to norms.

B. The Perpetuation of Gendered Power Relations through the System of Education

Following through on the discussion of changing power relations in the family, I want to turn to the arena of education, namely how the system of education is both a cause of these changes, and is in turn responding to them. Pakistan's education system has expanded greatly since Independence, and the number of schools continues to grow. Education in Pakistan has long been considered an important institution for creating a sense of nationalism among the population. However, compared to other institutions, relatively limited resources have been allocated to education. In 1980, public expenditure for education was 2.7 per cent of GNP; this had only increased to 3.0 by 1996. That same year, however, military expenditures were 5.6 per cent of GDP.[8]

The overall literacy rate in Pakistan was estimated at 38 per cent of the adult population in 1995, though only 24 per cent of women. Successes to raise literacy rates have been limited: one of the government's responses has been to change its definition, from being able to read a newspaper and write a simple letter to being able to read the Qur'an. The latter definition commands higher female literacy rates than the former within a socially sanctioned context.

Despite Pakistan's low female literacy rates, there has never been a systematic, nationally-coordinated effort to improve female primary education in the country. Between 1970–1995, the percentage of children enrolled in primary education rose dramatically, from 40 to 74 per cent.[9] That of females rose less so—from 22 to 45 per cent—underscoring the reality that at least double the number of boys than girls were attending primary schools. The UNDP reports that the combined first, second and third-level gross enrollment ratio for male in 1997 was 56 percent, though it was only 28 percent for females.[10]

Primary school drop-out rates remained somewhat consistent in the 1970s and 1980s, at just over 50 per cent for boys and 60 per cent for girls. They began to decrease significantly in the 1990s, to 16 per cent.[11] Middle school drop-out rates for boys and girls had been similar, rising from 22 per cent (for both) in 1976 to just about 33 per cent in 1983. However, an interesting shift occurred in the beginning of the 1980s in the secondary school drop-out rate: while boys and girls had relatively equal rates (14 per cent) in 1975, by 1979—just as Zia was initiating his government's Islamization program—the drop-out rate for boys was 25 per cent while for girls it was only 16 per cent. However, by 1993, this trend dramatically reversed, and boys had a drop-out rate of only 7 per cent compared to girls' at 15 per cent.

Greater numbers of parents are allowing their daughters to acquire a secondary education, even though such mobility for a post-pubescent girl is antithetical to traditional mores. Indeed, men's diminishing ability to control the mobility and activities of women within the family is due in large part to the increase in female education and related access to mass media and other forms of information. It may not be what is actually learned in school but the experience of leaving one's home after puberty and attending classes—mixing with people from a wide socioeconomic spectrum—that exposes a woman to other students and teachers and, in effect, to the larger society from which she was once hidden and uninformed.

The Seventh Five-Year Plan (1988–93) envisioned that every child of age five years and above will have access to a primary or mosque school. However, due to financial constraints, this goal was not achieved. In the Eighth Five-Year Plan (1993–98), the Pakistan government reiterated the need to mobilize a proportionatly larger share of national resources to finance its educational efforts, but at the end of the plan period, there was little difference from the past in amounts allocated.

While it was once assumed that the reasons behind low female participation rates in schools were cultural, research conducted by the Ministry for Women's Development and a range of international donor agencies in the 1980s revealed that access was the most crucial concern that parents had. Indeed, reluctance turned to enthusiasm when parents in rural Punjab and rural Baluchistan could be guaranteed of their daughter's safety—and hence, of her honor.

Until the late 1970s an excessive amount of educational spending went to the secondary and tertiary levels. This was consistent with the pre-independence goals of education which were focused on staffing the civil service and producing an educated elite—unquestionably male—sharing the values of and being loyal to the British colonizers. It was unabashedly elitist and patriarchal, and contemporary education—reforms and commissions on reform notwithstanding—shares the same emphasis.

The planning process used to develop the Ninth Five-Year Plan bodes better than in the past for substantive advances in the arena of female education. The interactive process has resulted from efforts to develop a *National Plan of Action* to implement promises Pakistan made in becoming a signatory to the Beijing *Platform for Action*.[12] Discrete goals accompanied by realistic time frames at least make the promise that the above-noted figures will improve. The *National Plan of Action* contains some of the most ambitious plans, targets and implementation strategies ever proposed by the Government of Pakistan yet to tackle this problem.

Educators seem to be the most concerned about the quality of what is actually being taught in the curriculum. Shaheed and Mumtaz (1993:69) discuss how the prose used in most secondary education texts stereotype women by portraying them solely in their domestic roles. In my own evaluation of college-level teaching materials, I have found no mention of such things as women's roles in Pakistan's history, the women's movement in Pakistan and the creation of the Women's Action Forum, or the movement's objections to explicit policies towards women that threaten their legal status. Nor have I seen acknowledgment that low female literacy or labor force participation rates pose a problem for the country's overall social development.

The extension of literacy to greater numbers of people has enhanced working class aspirations to achieve middle class goals such as owning an automobile, taking summer vacations in the Murree hills, and providing a daughter with a once-inconceivable dowry at the time of marriage. While Pakistan has been a country that the landlords owned, the army ruled, and the civil service governed, in the past only male members of the elite comprised these three ranks. But including more girls in schools has resulted in the Pakistan civil service now enjoying a greater proportion of educated women than ever before. An unfulfilled 1993 election promise made by Benazir Bhutto was to reserve ten percent of all government appointments for women, and to try to ease more women into higher positions within the bureaucracy. The highest levels of the bureaucracy remain in the hands of men. A five per cent quota for women's employment in all government jobs does exist, but activists claim that these are being filled almost exclusively at peon and clerical levels within the federal government, and hardly at all in the provincial governments.

The former government of Nawaz Sharif launched its Social Action Programme in 1992 in an effort to ameliorate some of the extreme social inequities which had earned Pakistan a great deal of criticism from donors in the international development community. Many NGOs established their own schools, especially primary ones in poor areas for girls. Some long-standing women's organizations created their own NGOs which often targeted educating women about their legal rights, adult literacy or income generating activities. By the time Nawaz's government was dismissed in 1993, there was a massive proliferation of NGOs which, merely a decade earlier, had been a rarity in the country. The important consideration here is that this created many girls' schools which were independent—not run under the auspices of the government—

and which further opens possibilities for female empowerment through education.

Education is no longer reserved only for elite women, who have generally enjoyed greater degrees of freedom to begin with than women from poorer backgrounds. Most working class Pakistani adults would contend that certain activities that elite women have come to see as norms (e.g., entering a non-female domain profession, joining a women's political movement, or selecting her own husband) are outside the purview of female respectability, and that elites have become too westernized for their own good. Yet these same working class parents aspire for their daughters to receive higher education. Idealized norms have not yet caught up with the pragmatics of daily life which often require college degrees to arrange a good marriage or survival strategies for poor girls who may someday need to earn an income. In the same way, the issue of a separate women's university is raised without regard for the very real resource limitations existing universities must confront in these times.

I have found that the kinds of changes in perception once associated with elites are gradually making their way into those of girls enrolled in colleges, despite their class background. Aside from what is taught in classes, students are exposed to a lot of nationalist ideology and propaganda. This is exacerbated by the state's increased emphasis on Islamic and Pakistan Studies in the curriculum, local campaigns to collect clothes and raise money to help flood victims in rural areas, and the media coverage of demands for autonomy in Indian Kashmir. Participation in such activities have given these girls the sense that they indeed are Pakistanis and that there is a role for them to play to make a difference in these matters. However, most girls do not have the means or a direction in which they can channel this sense of newfound knowledge, awareness and sense of responsibility and citizenship. When asked about their occupational aspirations, most girls simply opt to write down that they want to become teachers or doctors. Rarely do they articulate occupations which culturally lie in the male domain, though some do consider them. Aspiring for any other occupations is antithetical to the mores and norms of what is most likely in store for their future, and what they would be allowed to do.

I found two different kinds of responses among men studying at colleges in Lahore regarding the merit of educating women. The majority from upper class families found it to be a good thing and would prefer a highly educated wife, while most men from working class families told me that there was no reason why women should occupy places in colleges that men could take or jobs that men needed. Despite the fact that women studied alongside them in their classes, they would not approve if it were their own sister or wife studying in their college. Clearly, the latter group felt more threatened by the prospects of educated women than the former.

C. Gendered Power, Participation and Ambiguity within the Larger Society

Ambiguity in the larger arena of power and participation in the external, public sphere, however, is more misleading. While elite women have a history dating back to the Khilafat Movement and the struggle for Independence from Britain, such activities did not entail a paradigmatic shift in women's access to political power. As a political entity, women as a group remained powerless.

Prior to women in Pakistan claiming a political voice for themselves in the early 1980s, there was no perceptible stance that the state took which opened channels either for women's increased input or as provoked reactions. For example, the passage of the 1961 Family Laws Ordinance, which sought to regulate marriage and divorce, was a critical juncture for women's rights, because the state was interceding fundamentally in power relations within the family. By law, men were no longer able to marry and divorce women hastily, discarding them at will. While the Family Laws Ordinance was a formal step to mediate power relations within the family, in practice little changed in the way men regarded marriage and their rights within it. Nor was its passage the result of women gaining new found power in the public political arena, but rather it was a way for the state—at that time—to assert its own priorities in the face of moderate Islamist opposition.

Khattak and Bari (Chapter 9) document how women's groups have been making a place for themselves within the emerging civil society since the 1980s. Importantly, however, the state has refused to recognize women's groups as viable actors, often hiding behind the strictures of tradition or religion when declaring they don't exist. In 1994, however, something unique finally happened: the state publicly declared that local interpretations of women's place in society was antithetical to Islam. The Commission of Inquiry for Women, established in 1994 while Pakistan was preparing its National Report for the Beijing conference, had the mandate to review the country's laws as 'a step towards ending the grosser iniquities against women.' Its resultant Report states that:

> There is a widespread misconception about the place Islam accords to women, which is not just a distortion spread in the West but it exists even among the intelligentsia in the Muslim World, including Pakistan. It is believed that Islam relegates women to an inferior status; it confines them inside the four walls of their homes; and it restrains them from taking up employment outside their homes or running their own business. This is wholly contrary to fact. Muslim scholars are agreed that Islam accords women virtually the whole gamut of rights, including the rights to property, to work and wages, to choice of spouse, to divorce if marriage does not prosper, to education and to participation in economic, social and political activity. These are guaranteed to Muslim women by Shariat.[13]

The Report of the Commission of Inquiry for Women identified certain areas—laws, customs, practices, criminal procedures— that are discriminatory towards women, and made lucid recommendations on how Pakistan can remove such discrimination. It made three important, albeit controversial key recommendations: 1) to legalize abortion; 2) to abolish the Federal Shariat Court as it is redundant and other courts can adjudicate the same issues; and 3) repeal the *Hudood* laws since they have not achieved their objectives. For example, it suggested that the government repeal the *zina* law relating to 'unlawful fornication' (e.g., adultery), which contravenes constitutional safeguards and various provisions of CEDAW, that laws do not discriminate between men and women. The issue of evidence—particularly as codified in the Evidence Law—was also taken up here, as a woman can be found guilty of *zina* by virtue of becoming pregnant while a man cannot. The report notes that since the *zina* law was promulgated, the numbers of women in Pakistani prisons has risen dramatically. While nearly two-thirds of these women have been accused of *zina*, hardly any of the charges have been proven and most women are ultimately released, underscoring that while in theory there are checks against false accusation of *zina*, in practice it happens very frequently. The Report also challenges prevailing power relations within the family when it argues for the amendment of the Pakistan Penal Code to make marital rape a penal offense 'and to impose a severe punishment for rape on a minor wife' (Government of Pakistan 1997:75).

Indeed, this and other recommendations made throughout the Report has prompted both private and public discourse about the position and power of women in Islam and in Pakistan. The Report has also drawn the state further into the discourse of defining women's human rights through the institutional structures it will support. Importantly, another example is seen in its consideration of the role of the *wali*, guardian. The Criminal Law Amendment Act (1997) passed as an Act of Parliament lays out the method for distribution of *qisas* and *diyat* (blood money) in the event of a murder. The Report interprets this act as making criminal offences 'a private matter rather than treating them as crimes against society.'[14] While the *wali* is defined in gender-neutral terms, in both language and examples the *wali* is always a male. For the state to contend that the *wali* need not necessarily be a man would be to invalidate longstanding local patriarchal interpretations of men's responsibilities vis à vis women. In addition, it would enter into the arena of women's honor, particularly men's perception of their responsibility for women's actions in preserving that honor which often leads to 'honour killings' (when the men of a family murder a woman of their family for betraying the family honor). The state does not prosecute such crimes in the way it prosecutes other murder cases, in practice seeing the jurisdiction for policing women's actions being within the domain of the men of a family. To now do otherwise and fully prosecute male perpetrators of such crimes[15] would be to transform the state's own understanding of the family unit and the responsibilities of its members, something which it has not claimed it is willing to do nor even willing to bring into the public arena of negotiation.

D. Discussion

That we now find greater numbers of educated, economically independent women is a direct outcome of what it is that women now are doing differently from the past. This is resulting in men relinquishing some of the powerful control they have held over women while also expecting women to hold different roles. Given women's increased proficiencies, men are also realizing that women do not need them as much as in the past, and that it is possible for women now to be self-reliant. Needless to say, this creates a great deal of confusion in a society where social norms still revolve around honor and respect. There is a discernible increase in men's fears of what uncontrolled, qualified women might do.

Men and women have very different visions of important changes regarding personal power and mobility. While men view women as being able to be more capable now than in the past, they also feel threatened by the potential of uncontrolled educated and/or economically independent women who may compromise their honor and therefore their status among other men. Interestingly, they tend to regard women as more honest than men in economic matters.

Men no longer appear to have the same level of genuine trust in other men, including biological and fictive kin, as they had in the past. This may be due to the acute rise in corruption in recent years which has, in the eyes of many of these working class men, favoured unscrupulous actions over integrity and has promoted an unprecedented regard for crass materialism.

Many women have expressed to me that they feel they can no longer rely on the men in their family with as much confidence as they had in the past. They have seen men abandon their wives, go abroad to work leaving a wife virtually on her own, increased usage of drugs among men, and the breakdown of extended families as relatives relinquish traditional obligations. One woman from the Walled City told me that the most viable survival strategy now for daughters is for them to acquire a good education, as gold and property can always be taken away by someone else. Many women feel that the education and work opportunities now available to women can help them take a tentative step towards independence.[16]

The most noticeable change seems to be in women's expectations of other women. Women realize that they are now more capable to conduct necessary worldly activities (e.g., pay an electric bill, take a child to a doctor and get the prescription filled). They are raising their expectations of which arenas of life women can be responsible, and of what they can achieve—especially what their educated daughters might achieve—to unprecedented levels.

That changes in gender relations will continue to accelerate is reflected in the opinion voiced by many women to me that few women will be wearing a *burqa*, a body veil, in ten years, despite it still being common today. However, while the physical restrictions on women's mobility by her own family may be lifting, this is being replaced by a new threat to her mobility: the rise in violence against women by unknown assailants, especially when women venture outside their own neighborhoods. In the past, rape was comparatively rare and generally effected as retribution against the property of an enemy. This has changed given the current level of frustration (political and economic) that many men experience in the larger society. The materialism which has pervaded most sensibilities stresses status, the assertion that one is powerful. Does the rise in violent crimes against women indicate that men perceive this as a way of being powerful, or are they punishing women who are acting outside of traditional norms which emphasize limited mobility?

An important outcome of the above-mentioned gendered changes in perception is that the nature of restrictions on women's actions are undergoing rapid modifications. Therefore, while in practice women's power over their own mobility and actions has increased, men and women alike continue to articulate the stereotyped view of women's place in the family and other traditional concepts of family dominion. This is perpetuated by a number of factors, especially repressive images of women which are periodically promoted and perpetuated by the state. The government of Zia ul-Haq, in particular, had idealized the image of women faithful to '*chador aur char diwari*,' wearing a veil and remaining within the confines of the four walls of one's home. The government had promoted this image despite the reality that women's lives were becoming increasingly integrated into the public realm.

These images are now promoted by Islamist parties, which are increasingly regarded as an alternative to Pakistan's cyclical crises of political corruption, military intervention and resurgence of democratic hopes. Events in the Fall of 1998 underscore the ways such perceptions were framing Nawaz Sharif's Pakistan Muslim League government support of the 15th Amendment, that all laws are to be *derived* from Islam. At issue, for many women are the provisions in the 1961 Family Laws Ordinance as well as policy changes resulting from Pakistan's accession to CEDAW, acceptance of the *Platform for Action* and the resultant *National Plan of Action,* and other policies to promote the empowerment of women that have been integrated into the Ninth Five-Year Plan. The resignation (or dismissal, depending on one's level of cynicism) of General Karamat Ali over the 15th Amendment reinforced the perception held by some that state policy which furthers Islamist paradigms will break the destructive political cycle in which Pakistan has been immersed. But the implications of this view regarding gendered power negotiations, especially within the family and the larger arena of civil society, are staggering.

There is an urgency associated with questions of education, family planning, and women having a political voice. Are there enough physical, capital, and human resources to have the postulate of equal but separate viably work? Can Pakistan's social development goals ever be met if it doesn't contain its population growth rate? What kinds of conflicts and compromises will emerge in the future within working class families where educated women who join unions, a political party, or an activist group are the norm?

There is a clear connection between the renegotiation of gendered power within the family, greater numbers of women becoming literate, the resultant expansion of women's labour force participation prospects, and women wielding greater power within civil society. Women and men are actively engaging in renegotiating power relations and access to power in unprecedented arenas. It is in this process that the greatest potential for positive, participatory outcomes lie.

References

Ahmed, Leila. 1992. *Women and Gender in Islam: Historical Roots of a Modern Debate.* Yale University Press.

Akhtar, Humaira. 1995. 'Women, Paid Work, Controls and Resistance' in Nighat Said Khan, Rubina Saigol and Afiya S. Zia (eds.), *Aspects of Women and Development.* Lahore: ASR, pp. 17–57.

Amnesty International. 1995. *Women in Pakistan: Disadvantaged and Denied their Rights.* New York: Amnesty International.

Ayub, Nasreen. 1994. *The Self-Employed Women in Pakistan: A Case Study of the Self-Employed Women of Urban Informal Sector in Karachi.* Karachi: Pakistan Association for Women's Studies.

Duncan, Ann. 1989. *Women in Pakistan: an Economic and Social Strategy.* Washington, D.C.: World Bank.

Government of Pakistan. 1998. *National Plan of Action (NPA) for Women* (Draft). Islamabad: Ministry of Women's Development and Youth Affairs.

————, 1995. *Pakistan National Report: Fourth World Conference on Women, Beijing.* Ministry of Women's Development and Youth Affairs.

————, 1997. *Report of the Commission on Inquiry for Women.* August.

Hussain, Maliha. 1989. *Women in the Urban Informal Sector in Pakistan: Productivity, Employment and Potential for Change.* Islamabad: Development Research and Management Services Ltd.

Ibraz, Tassawar Saeed. 1993. 'The Cultural Context of Women's Productive Invisibility: a Case Study of a Pakistani Village', *Pakistan Development Review.* Vol. 32, No. 1, Spring, pp. 101–125.

Jahangir, Asma and Hina Jilani. 1990. *The Hudood Ordinances: a Divine Sanction?: A Research Study of the Hudood Ordinances and their Effect on the Disadvantaged Sections of Pakistan Society.* Lahore: Rhotas Books.

Jilani, Hina. 1994. 'Law as an Instrument of Social Control' in Nighat Said Khan, Rubina Saigol and Afiya Zia (eds.), *Locating the Self: Perspectives on Women and Multiple Identities.* Lahore: ASR Publications, pp. 96–105.

Kandiyoti, Deniz. 1988. 'Bargaining with Patriarchy'. *Gender & Society.* Vol. 2, No. 3, September, pp. 274–290.

Kazi, Shahnaz. 1995. 'Rural Women, Poverty and Development in Pakistan'. *Asia-Pacific Journal of Rural Development.* Vol. 5, No. 1, July, pp. 78–92.

Khalid, Humala. 1990. *Education of Women and National Development.* Islamabad: National Education Council.

Mumtaz, Mumtaz and Farida Shaheed. 1987. *Women of Pakistan: Two Steps Forward, One Step Back?* London: Zed Press and Karachi: Vanguard Books.

Pakistan Commission on the Status of Women. 1986. 'Report of the Commission on the Status of Women in Pakistan'. Islamabad.

Pakistan People's Party. 1994. *People's Government Fulfilling an Agenda for Change: Social Sector.* November.

Planning Commission, Government of Pakistan. 1988. *The Seventh Five-Year Plan: 1988–93 and Perspective Plan, 1988-2003.* Karachi: Manager of Publications.

————, 1992. 'Eighth Five-Year Plan (1993–98) Approach Paper'. Islamabad.

Said Khan, Nighat, Rubina Saigol and Afiya S. Zia (eds.) 1995. *Aspects of Women and Development.* Lahore: ASR.

Shaheed, Farida and Khawar Mumtaz. 1995. *Women's Economic Participation in Pakistan: A Status Report.* Lahore: Shirkatgah for UNICEF Pakistan.

————, 1994. 'Women's Education in Pakistan' in Jill Ker Conway and Susan C. Bourque (eds.). *The Politics of Women's Education: Perspectives from Asia, Africa and Latin America.* University of Michigan Press, pp. 59–75.

United Nations Development Program. 1998. *Human Development Report 1998.* Oxford University Press.

————, 1991. *NISA: Database of Publications on Women in Development in Pakistan.* Islamabad: UNDP, July.

Weiss, Anita M. 1994. 'Challenges for Muslim Women in a Postmodern World' in Hastings Donnan and Akbar S. Ahmed (eds.). *Islam, Globalization and Postmodernity.* Routledge, pp. 127–140.

————, 1992. *Walls within Walls: Life Histories of Working Women in the Old City of Lahore,* Westview Press.

————, 1994. 'The Consequences of State Policies for Women in Pakistan' in Myron Weiner and Ali Banuazizi (eds.). *The Politics of Social Transformation in Afghanistan, Iran, and Pakistan.* Syracuse University Press, pp. 412–444.

Zafar, Fareeha. 1991. 'Women's Education: Problems and Prospects' in Nighat Said Khan, Rubina Saigol and Afiya S. Zia (eds.). *Aspects of Women and Development.* Lahore: ASR, pp. 125–132.

Zia, Afiya Shehrbano. 1994. *Sex Crime in the Islamic context: Rape, Class and Gender in Pakistan.* Lahore: ASR Publications.

NOTES

1. Here I am referring to women as a group, a discreet social entity, and not to individual, influential women.
2. For example, the state sidelined passage of the Shariat Bill given the women's movement's vocal opposition to it. Years later, the Nawaz Sharif government ratified a much watered-down version of the original Bill.
3. This is the final document that emerged from the United Nations' Fourth World Forum for Women held in Beijing in September 1995.
4. These locales have included social places as varied as Faisalabad, Islamabad, Khushab, Lahore, Peshawar, Pishin, Quetta, Rawalpindi, Sargodha, and Sialkot.
5. This and other observations based on the Walled City of Lahore are discussed further in Anita M. Weiss *Walls within Walls: Life Histories of Working Women in the Old City of Lahore* (Westview and Pak Books, 1992).

6. The only social group in which this is changing somewhat is among urban-based, generally English-speaking elites, a small minority of the total population of the country.

7. These acts were discussed using the Urdu and Punjabi terms *jasmani tashaddad* or *mar peet*, respectively.

8. UNDP *Human Development Report 1999* (Oxford University Press, 1999, p. 190).

9. These figures are based on World Bank *World Development Report 1994* (Oxford University Press, 1994, p. 216) and UNDP *Human Development Report 1998* (Oxford University Press, 1998, p. 153 and 162).

10. UNDP *Human Development Report 1999* (Oxford University Press, 1999, p. 140). The combined gross enrollment ratio is the percentage of males or females attending school, of all males or females of school-going age who could be attending school.

11. Federal Bureau of Statistics, Government of Pakistan *Pakistan Integrated Household Survey, Round 2: 1996–97,* 1997, p. 38.

12. Refer to Anita M. Weiss 'Women, Civil Society and Politics in Pakistan' *Citizenship Studies* 3(1)1999, pp. 141–150 for further elaboration on this.

13. Government of Pakistan, 1997, pp. ii.

14. Ibid., p. 56.

15. In may 2000, Pervez Musharaf vowed that his government will prosecute honour killings in the same way as any other murders. It is too soon to ascertain if this edict is being implemented.

16. For further discussion of women's survival strategies for their daughters, *see,* Weiss 1992.

PART THREE

Political, Economic and Legal Power Structures

5

BUSINESS AND POWER IN PAKISTAN
Imran Anwar Ali

The role and status of business in society has, in the modern world, become an important indicator of the degree to which any society has achieved, or is positioned to achieve, economic development. The major transitions in the shaping of the modern world, namely the rise of industrialization and the commercial and other sectoral transformations that accompanied it, were intimately linked with, and indeed relied upon, changes in business structures and practices. Every nation that has successfully industrialized, or otherwise achieved high standards of living for the large majority of its population, has endeavoured to reach this outcome only through a significant enhancement of its business performance. Such activity could have been aided and abetted by foreign business enterprise, and in the present age the degree of interaction between local and foreign, and indeed international, business operations has achieved a high level of symbiosis. Nevertheless, it has hardly ever been sufficient to place reliance simply on foreign enterprise for achieving sustained change within particular societies. Conducive internal developments in the business sector remain a necessary prerequisite for any society to experience broad and soundly based economic development

Of course, the one great exception to the above stated scenario has been the very real strides in industrialization among some of the socialist economies. Central planning and public ownership of the means of production were, in these societies, substituted for the goals that private sector business attempted to achieve in the capitalist economies. The rejection of capitalism and the incorporation of state socialism also appeared for some decades, from the mid-twentieth century, to provide an alternative set of strategic directions and policy options to the 'underdeveloped' or 'developing' nations. The viability of this alternative fell into serious abeyance with the collapse of the Soviet system after 1990. Subsequently the rapid, if at first only nominal, acquiescence in these regions of the need for capitalistic enterprise further eroded the political and economic structures of socialism. This is not to say that the latter might not return, if only as a reaction to the perceived amoralities, and very real failures in the distribution of wealth, of the 'free enterprise' system. Moreover, the continuance in China of, at the very least, a dual system, must militate for a reconsideration of capitalism as the only possible outcome at the 'end of history'. Nevertheless, China's economic future too is being seen within an emerging internal private sector, expanding foreign investment, and in the already extensive participation of Chinese export goods in the global economy. Thus, there is now a growing convergence internationally in the meaning and implications of the term 'business' and of its role in economic life.

In analyzing the role of business in Pakistan's political economy, therefore, both the external and internal dimensions in the development of business structures and operations ought to be considered. Internal developments need to be assessed in their own light, and these will take up most of the discussion here. They should also be related to, and compared with, the possibilities and potentialities that modern business has achieved and realized in the international context. The notion of 'power' should also be approached in the broader sense, and not simply be confined to denote politics or political activity. The latter is clearly a major operational outcome, or end product, of systems of power and authority, but it should by no means be taken to enfold all the parameters that these terms signify. A number of different factors are involved in making up the concept of power, and these will be alluded to during the course of this analysis.

We will also look a bit more deeply into historical factors that is invariably the norm with analyses of Pakistan. Too often, learned discourse on different aspects of Pakistani economy and society has suffered from a peculiarly a historical approach. Apart from superficial allusions to the period before 1947, mostly comprising some oft-repeated facts about Muslim nationalism, little effort is made to grapple with the nature of historical causation in this region, or with continuities and discontinuities in historical trends and structures. In such accounts, serious attention is reserved for the period not much earlier than the mid-twentieth century. Owing to this bias, there remain serious weaknesses in the analysis and understanding of the underlying issues and problems of business development that the country might be facing.

In an exercise of this nature and size, our intention will not be to provide an account or description of how and in what forms business has developed in Pakistan. Nor will it be practicable to explain in any detail how and when business elements have been involved in politics, or tried to 'exercise' political power. Similarly, any detailed account is not possible of the various interactions of business with political structures and state institutions, either at the level of individual businesses or of business oriented organizations, such as chambers of commerce and trade associations. Rather, the intention here will be to identify and explore some of the more significant parameters within which such developments and interactions have occurred. In a field that has traditionally been more or less bereft of systematic research and analysis, we will endeavour here to discuss some pertinent themes and issues. We will, therefore, be concerned less with providing answers than with raising questions, regarding essentially the relevance of what needs to be investigated. Let us start with some queries about the appropriateness of historical factors.

If history before Pakistan is to be seen as a significant determinant of the interrelationship of business with power, then the question arises as to how far back in time should this theme be pursued. Clearly, it could be argued, with some conviction, that the immediately precedent period of British colonial rule did have a major impact on the shaping and relative performance of the business domain in post-1947 Pakistan. But it might even be useful to push the analysis back somewhat further, into the eighteenth century and even to late Mughal times. This longer-term perspective could reveal the manner in which the relationship of business with power unfolded historically. Such perceptions could, in turn, help to better understand the nature of this relationship in the contemporary context.

The north-western part of the Mughal Empire, approximating roughly the Pakistan area, was clearly an important region in political and economic terms. Lahore was one of the three capital cities of the empire, a status it shared with Delhi and Agra. At its height it was said to have attained a population of around half a million. The extensive size of the Walled City of Lahore indicates that it was one of the largest preindustrial urban centres in the world. Moreover, satellite townships in the proximity, as well as the royal and elite overflow of villas and gardens, added significantly to the size of greater Lahore. There existed in addition several regional towns, such as Multan, which were centred on trade and manufacturing, but which also had significant administrative functions. These patterns indicated the extent and presumable buoyancy of the urban, or secondary, sector of the Mughal economy. Artisanal groups were concentrated in both the smaller and larger urban centres, and were also diffused through the countryside. They produced a great diversity of manufactured goods, spread over a large number of trades, albeit through manual production methods. Agrarian surpluses and specialized crop production had already created a quite extensive base for commerce in agricultural goods. Both shorter and longer distance trade routes were well established, and the sheer volume of commodity exchange represented sophisticated networks of transport logistics and mercantile enterprise. Banking and credit mechanisms for financing the trading systems were also said to be well developed.

Despite the extent of commercial activity undertaken in the Mughal economy and the considerable affluence of commercial groups that these processes represented, 'business' in this age suffered from several structural and institutional drawbacks. These were not so much inherent weaknesses or disfunctionalities in their own right. Rather, they appear as being anomalous in more relative terms, and specifically in comparison to the economic transitions and developments that were beginning to appear in parts of the European subcontinent.

For one, the military-administrative element of the Mughal Empire continued to be politically predominant. It remained essentially unchallenged by any European-type bourgeois ethos, with its revolutionary philosophical constructs, or by the ramifications for political economy of the commercial revolutions that eventually overtook incumbent structures in the West. The Mughal court continued to retain a feudal predisposition, as the ultimate recipient of rents and taxes generated from the rural economy. For these inflows it relied on an assortment of intermediaries, comprising either appointed functionaries (the likes of the *ijaradars*, *jagirdars* and *talugdars*), or various levels of land based magnates (the *zamindars*). This extractive pyramid depended on the acquiescence, though not without elements of coercion, of the upper peasant proprietary groups that organized agrarian production at the local level. The intermediaries exercised both civil and administrative functions, and also provided military and paramilitary levies. This integration of civil and military roles underpinned the power and resilience of the upper agrarian hierarchy in Mughal political economy. Here was a degree of entrenchment, of a continuum in the access to power, that those involved with trade, commerce and non-agricultural production were not able to contest.

Production systems, as well as the organizational structures and social milieu within which business operated, also appeared to lack innovation and change. While producers did not lack the capability of adopting new products, methods and materials, there was still a notable weakness of innovativeness in the manufacturing process. Tradition remained the general arbiter of technological levels and production techniques. Similarly, the social organization of production also retained major continuities throughout the Mughal period, as indeed they did even during later times. Though the aggregate levels of secondary sector output were clearly impressive, production itself was highly fragmented. Unit levels were predominantly micro sized; they remained within the established parameters of a division of labour based on hereditary occupations. Larger scale factory type production was said to exist, such as in state owned metallurgical works, but was by no means significantly diffused. Its rarity in the private sector was by no means surprising, as this was essentially a pre-industrial and pre-capitalist society. However, the significant question to be posed here is whether these systems of artisanal production ever witnessed a transition towards larger scale, more formalized manufacturing. In the urban centres, as in the rural economy, the caste system continued to determine occupational roles in manufacturing, services and commerce alike.

Moreover, even during the colonial period, any major discontinuity in these traditional structures was doubtful, at least in the Pakistan territories. Indeed, propitiation of the factory system through indigenous enterprise was neglected during foreign rule, in keeping with British imperialist antipathy towards fostering industrial capitalism in these regions. Thus the colonial economy, too, at least in the Pakistan area, continued to be characterized by the predominance of artisanal and small-scale production. These outfits were essentially geared to meet consumption needs in the domestic market. Furthermore, portions of the local demand were also beginning to be absorbed by the import of manufactured goods, largely from Britain itself. With time, the increasing volume of manufactured imports tended to further crowd out the development of larger scale indigenous industrial enterprise. Internal manufacturing capacity thereby remained confined within traditional patterns.

It remains problematic whether this situation has experienced any extensive transition, even after a half century of the independent existence of Pakistan. Does the real nature and predominant functioning of indigenous enterprise still lie within these traditional parameters, albeit overlaid by a veneer of modernized commerce and manufacturing? If this is true, then the interrelationship of business with power needs to be understood within a perspective quite different from one in which the formal sector is assumed to be the 'high ground' of the economy. Could it be that the real economy of the country is being marginalized in analysis, because it fits so little with the current firm-sector oriented concepts of business?

A further issue is the political role and authority, or influence, of the entrepreneurial sector over state and society. The Mughal economy certainly had substantial and affluent trading families and communities. Many of these were much richer, and their operations much more extensive, than their European contemporaries. Did these South Asian commercial groups attain the kind of political importance that the latter began to enjoy as the capitalist economy advanced in Europe? The answer is clearly in the negative. Power continued to be channelled through the royal court, and its military and administrative functionaries on the one hand, and the larger and medium *zamindars* on the other. These structures then interacted with the landholding peasant lineages, who held access to local authority. The degrees to which these relationships were cooperative or coercive provided much of the substance of history. Merchants and financial creditors might well have enjoyed individual influence and prestige, but in the aggregate they were not able to counter the collective, extended power of those positioned within state and agrarian hierarchies. Thus, authority in the past, and possibly in the present as well, emanated through those who lived off, in one form or another, the produce, revenue and rent from the land.

Of course, in Europe, too, the relative autonomy of the entrepreneurial class varied in different regions. The middle class clearly took a more subordinate position to the landed hierarchy in Germany than in Britain, even through the nineteenth century. However, either group was as intimately involved as the other was with the industrial revolution in their respective countries: the German variant with, if anything, more concerted proficiency. By contrast, the mercantile elements in South Asia were, as already noted, failing to make the transition to industrial capitalism. They were, in addition, also unable to recreate the systems and protocols, the new 'software' that comprised the vital institutional accompaniments to successful capitalistic industrialization in the West.

Indeed in the area that became Pakistan, the violence of post-Mughal transitions further impeded the development of 'business' as a politically significant societal force. Especially in the Punjab, the final stages and ultimate collapse of Mughal rule were accompanied, if not actually brought about, by widespread peasant rebellions. In the central Punjab, the rebel war bands coalesced within an increasingly militarized Sikh religion. This transition in Sikhism, from its earlier quiescent Khatri origins to a predominantly Jat composition, was a response to more unstable times. It created greater peasant cohesion in confronting, and ultimately overwhelming, the imperial adversaries. Moreover, the rebellious activities of Hindu and Muslim upper peasant groups were not dissimilar to the recalcitrant Sikhs. Their collective impact was the assertion of the autonomy of the peasant landholding lineages, or *bhai-acharas,* in significant parts of the Punjab.

Not only was central rule overthrown but, equally significantly, the extent and duration of this agrarian revolt was such that the old Mughal elite was also almost totally effaced in the Punjab. This social upheaval was more complete than in other Mughal territories at the end of empire. This regional differentiation was reflected in the very different constituencies with which the encroaching British had to deal in their advance through South Asia. In most other regions, continuities in social structure were much greater than in the Punjab. These successor states were aligned under autonomous rulers who were none other than the descendants of ex-Mughal governors, and incumbent agrarian elites that had survived the Mughal collapse. With these elements the British had to contend for control over administration and revenue, leading to military conflicts of which the most famous occurred in 1857–58.

The agrarian uprisings of eighteenth century Punjab were directed not just at emperor, court and rural magnates, but more broadly at urban culture and upper urban classes as well. For a pre-industrial economy, urbanization had reached impressive proportions in the Mughal Empire. Lahore became one of the largest cities in the world, even reaching a purported population level of half a million inhabitants. Compare this with a decline in Lahore's population through the Sikh interregnum to a mere 85,000 at the time of British annexation in 1849. Mughal urban efflorescence and the extent, richness and diversity of markets was attested to by European travellers. Yet the negative side of this apparent buoyancy was that the cities became repositories of the surplus extracted from the agrarian economy. Rather than returning to agriculture for reinvestment, these resources were seen to be expended on the burdensome, and increasingly unsustainable, maintenance of intermediary classes and state functionaries.

The eighteenth century agrarian revolts, therefore, hit at the sprouting urban economy by targeting the upper end consumers of secondary sector products and services. This in turn disrupted artisanal and trading networks, leading to a weakening of the business community of the time. Indeed, the resultant urban decline in the Pakistani area contrasted with the opposing trend of commercial upturns in regional towns in other parts of South Asia, where post-Mughal transitions were more orderly. The earlier structural weakness of the business sector was now replaced by a substantive contraction in its size, at least in the larger urban centres of the Indus basin. During the Sikh interregnum, up to the mid-nineteenth century, the pre-eminence of agrarian interests and ongoing political instability were hardly conducive for a deepening of trade and commerce, let alone for any major increments in manufacturing capability. With this reversal of urbanization, there was, then, presumably little room for the emergence of societal institutions that might have contained capitalistic potentialities.

During the British period, the century of political 'stability' certainly provided the basis for an enhancement in business activity. The most significant historical phenomenon during this time was the development of a canal-irrigated zone in the Indus basin. Stretching over the Punjab and Sind, this became perhaps the largest contiguous canal irrigation network in the world. It entailed an extensive process of agricultural colonization and of land settlement schemes, since these areas were either arid waste or only sparsely inhabited by semi-nomadic pastoralists The great rise in agricultural production that ensued made this a surplus agrarian region, supplying the South Asian and export markets with such commodities as cotton, wheat, oilseeds and rice. The accompanying rise of market towns reflected the expansion in trading activity as well as the beginnings of agro-processing with such enterprises as cotton ginneries and wheat flourmills.

The enhanced role of business in society, presaged by the new agrarian frontier, could have led to a greater exercise of influence and authority by this sector. However, several factors combined to seriously constrain such an outcome. For one, this area remained almost completely non-industrial during colonial rule. By 1947 Pakistan had only a single textile mill and a single sugar mill. The colonial authority, while it fostered extensive agricultural growth, did little or nothing to promote industrialization. Indeed, it did not see the commercial castes either as a major support group, or one whose interests should be propitiated. Rather than business development, at least of the indigenous variety, the British built up, through land distribution in the canal colonies, the social and economic power of incumbent landholding groups. Canal land was predominantly allotted to landholding peasant lineages, and to medium and larger zamindars. Commercial groups could only acquire land at auctions and at market rates, in contrast to the highly subsidized purchase prices extended to land grantees from the agricultural 'castes'.

In the Punjab, moreover, these castes were already being cushioned against the vicissitudes of the market economy through measures that were likely to further constrain the domain of business. Existing landholders were beginning to be protected from expropriation by non-agricultural castes, or more specifically by commercial money-lending groups, through a remarkable piece of paternalistic legislation. This major protective measure, the Punjab Alienation of Lands Act of 1901, forbade non-agriculturists from acquiring land owned by the agricultural castes. Neither in the open market, nor through mortgage foreclosure, could the incumbent castes now be displaced. The British strove to prevent such an outcome owing to its threatened political repercussions. By constraining the social market for agricultural land, the colonial authority in the Pakistan area succeeded in retarding the very process that had expedited the transition to agricultural capitalism in Britain itself. Thus, in rolling back the emergence of a new class of more vigorous, commercially oriented owners, and in retaining an already entrenched, caste-based agrarian hierarchy, the British clearly preferred to trade off economic development for political expediency.

Additionally, two other institutions also gained further authority through agricultural colonization. The first was the state bureaucracy, which exercised control over both the process of land settlement and the operations of the canal irrigation network. Through such leverage state officials obtained a much greater hold over the population. Compared to this nexus, in regions with rain-fed or *barani* agriculture, the relations of the cultivator with the state were almost tangential. With water at a premium in an arid zone and subject to more centralized control, the bureaucracy could now exercise much greater authority and coercive power. This relationship was certainly exploited to extract greater political compliance. It also led to manipulative alliances between canal officials and the more influential landholders, for inequitable water supply or local coercion. The subordinate bureaucracy, native in composition, was already well steeped in corrupt practices and rent seeking behaviour. These activities the British appeared unwilling to eradicate, again for purposes of political convenience. This negligence, indeed, laid the basis for quite another magnitude of misdemeanours, by the post-independence successors of the erstwhile native officials of the colonial regime.

The other institution significantly strengthened in this emergent hydraulic society was the military, which became a major recipient of canal irrigated land. This occurred in various forms. Substantial areas were reserved for land grants to military personnel who were either retired soldiers, or during the two world wars were veterans rewarded for war services. In addition, significant land grants were allotted for the breeding and maintenance of military animals, such as camels, mules and, on a much vaster scale, cavalry horses. The greater monopolization of economic resources by the military in the colonial era was clearly a precursor to its exercise of political authority after 1947. Moreover, the fact that the Punjab alone supplied over half the recruits to the British Indian army, and these overdrawn from the same landholding groups that obtained colony grants, further consolidated the linkages between military service, agricultural land and political power.

The nature of intervention of state institutions in the economy was bound to have an impact upon the domain of business. Metropolitan business networks were not adversely affected. Firms such as Volkart Brothers and Ralli Brothers were extensively involved in commodity trade in this region. The British Cotton Growing Association, based in Manchester, took large areas on lease for cotton production. These at one stage amounted to around 70,000 acres, mostly in Lower Bari Doab Colony in the Punjab. Metropolitan business was also served by keeping this region deindustrialised, under colonial fiat. Indigenous business remained small or medium sized, confined to mercantile activity, and to intermediate technology agro-processing at best. Colonial rule almost completely prevented any transition into large-scale manufacturing. Nevertheless, the very scale of agricultural expansion did create a sizeable commercial and professional middle class, providing perhaps the basis for an emerging bourgeois ethos. These developments were based on the rise of market towns to handle the large volumes of trade in agricultural commodities; and the rise of employment and service opportunities for the educated.

However, transitions in the mid-twentieth century, as in the eighteenth century, were to result in a further decisive rollback of the position and stature of business in society. The castes that traditionally practised a commercial and professional vocation in the Pakistan area were largely, if not predominantly, non-Muslim. At Partition in 1947 these groups were forced to migrate to India. Indeed, economic nationalism might well have been a significant factor behind the ultimate conversion of the majority Muslim population to the idea of a separate nation. Resentment undoubtedly existed at the growing economic hold of the minority Hindu and Sikh communities, with their much greater representation in the business sector. The fear of the moneylender, largely non-Muslim, had been institutionalized in British imperialist writings. Encroachments by non-agriculturist creditors were already being resisted through legislation. In the 1930s, however, this challenge became much more substantive, with the onset of the economic depression. Agricultural prices and rents collapsed, but consumption patterns among the agrarian elite and upper peasantry remained more inelastic. Had market forces continued to operate, a significant turnover, or rationalization in the traditional landholding structure could have occurred. Had such a process of expropriation been accompanied by the entry of more progressive, capitalistic farmers, a more rapid modernization of Indus basin agriculture could well have eventuated. The creation of Pakistan was undoubtedly the outcome of a populist Muslim upsurge. But it also provided timely relief to an economically beleaguered, but politically entrenched, agrarian hierarchy. Religious and economic nationalism coalesced in the fortuitous removal of the threat posed by the non-agriculturist trading and creditor segment.

The continued subordinate status of indigenous business during imperialist rule, and its further emasculation at its eclipse, was underscored by political configurations before and after Partition. A clear discrepancy existed in the development of political organizations between the Pakistan and Indian territories at independence. The implications and impact of this disparity have not been properly addressed by social scientists, with their neglect of historical structures and processes. In the Indian area by 1947, the Indian National Congress, under M.K. Gandhi's tutelage, had already become a mature political organization. It had expanded its presence to virtually all the Hindu majority areas of South Asia. It had also built up an impressive organizational structure, from the grassroots to an apex all-India level.

After independence the Congress enjoyed an extended tenure in power, during which it was able to maintain, at least ostensibly, the autonomy of the political domain. It could effectively resist unconstitutional incursions by the bureaucracy or military and it had already weakened landlord power through land reforms. While its major support group remained the upper peasantry, the Congress had never been 'anti-business.' In fact, it was closely tied to business interests and continued to propitiate business development after 1947. Through these arrangements, of course, the Indian masses continued to be deprived of any tangible economic gains from nationhood. Yet so pervasive is the impress that these realities have done little to deter local and foreign analysts from declaiming on that country's 'democratic' system.

In contrast to the Congress and India, Pakistan lacked any proper political organizations at independence. The Muslim League had made few if any organizational inroads in the Muslim majority areas, even up to the eve of Partition. Mohammed Ali Jinnah had not the time to work towards a structure even remotely comparable to the Congress, nor was he assisted by colleagues particularly in favour of such an agenda. The League had, in fact, appealed for support to the landed hierarchies of these regions. As the case of the Punjab showed, it had actually rejected the urban version of the provincial League, headed by the poet, Muhammad Iqbal. It had, in turn, become organizationally stifled through a disadvantageous accord with the landlord-based and British-backed Muslim component of the Punjab National Unionist Party, under Sikandar Hayat.

Muslim League advances in the Punjab only occurred when it was taken over by a malcontent Unionist group, led by Mumtaz Daultana, Shaukat Hayat and Iftikhar Mamdot. This faction used the League as a platform for expressing its resentment at the Punjab premiership passing, on Sikandar's demise, to Khizr Hayat Tiwana. The succession by Khizr was perhaps forced upon the British by the need, during the Second World War, for recruits from northern Punjab. It led, however, to the unravelling of the Muslim part of the Unionist coalition. Eventually this brought about the breakdown of the inter-communal alliances that had helped the British retain Punjabi unity.

By 1946, therefore, Jinnah's lieutenants in the Punjab were none other than these erstwhile Unionists, now reincarnated as Muslim nationalists. Similarly, in Sind and the Frontier, the landed hierarchy continued to adhere to and control the provincial Leagues. Only in the Frontier was this elitist control challenged by the Congress–inclined Ghaffar Khan, but after 1947 he was kept firmly in opposition. The outcome was the retention of landlord influence over the political domain in Pakistan, one to which the business sector, by contrast, had immeasurably less access. This imbalance of power was accompanied subsequently by the continued inability of the Muslim League to develop a sustainable political organization, in which channels might have arisen for incorporating more business as well as egalitarian concerns.

The personalization and continued deinstitutionalization of politics were to play a major role in Pakistan's political economy and business development in the subsequent half century. Significantly, the notion simply of landlord dominance, so faithfully adhered to by analysts from the social sciences, is insufficient in understanding the real roots of agrarian and political power. This actually lay in the continued support of the upper peasantry for its landlord nominees. In the Indian territories the Congress had succeeded in disengaging this nexus well before independence. The upper peasant economy in the new agrarian frontier of the Indus basin had remained less troubled and less nationalistic. This was a consequence of the dual but related mainsprings of widespread access to new canal irrigated lands, and the returns from commercialized agriculture.

We have reviewed above the historical parameters that defined the role of business by the time of the emergence of Pakistan. Some major conclusions can now be restated. As opposed to the deeply entrenched political status of the upper agrarian hierarchy, and the authority of the military and bureaucracy, the power of 'business' was seriously constrained. The post-Mughal rollback of urban society in the eighteenth century was repeated in the equally climactic reversal of the mid-twentieth century, through the emigration of non-Muslim business to Indian territory. The question arises, then, of how enduring has been the impact of these historical forces. Could the other half of this proposition be that this situation remained essentially unchanged in the second half of the twentieth century? Or would the alternative thesis, that there has been major qualitative change in the stature of business, be more accurate? For this, let us now turn to an assessment of developments since 1947.

In analyzing Pakistani business and its interaction with the systems of power and authority, we must first identify the themes that need to be examined. The nature of Pakistani business, its positioning and structure, has determined the role it has played in economy and society. We will concentrate on these broader aspects, rather than the minuscule activities of the involvement of business elements in political activity. It may be noted that many of these features are not unique to Pakistan. They are not only shared by other lesser developed countries, but may even be symptomatic of the concerns surrounding business in these regions.

The history of business development itself reveals the parameters and constraints of the interface of business and power in Pakistan. Commencing, as we have established above, from relative insignificance following the emigration of commercial groups to Indian territory at Partition in 1947, two broad groups emerged to fill the post 1947 lacuna. The first, which came to be based in southern Pakistan and especially in Karachi, comprised mainly Gujarati speaking migrants from western India. These were long-standing commercial castes such as Khojas, Bohras, Memons, and Ismailis. In southern Pakistan they remained quite distinct from the bulk of Muslim immigrants. These had moved from northern India, and especially the United Provinces, and their background was more in services and professions. Thus, these commercially dominant groups of western Indian origin comprised only a small ethnic minority in Pakistan. They held this status even within the province of Sind, and were a minority even in the metropolis of Karachi. What, then, were the repercussions of this minority status in the coming decades, especially in relation to the substantial economic assets obtained by these groups and the extensive business activities in which they were involved?

The second element benefiting from the exit of the non-Muslim trading castes was based upcountry in the Punjab province. These groups had formerly held a distinctly inferior position in business to their non-Muslim peers. They belonged to various artisanal and service castes, and after conversion to Islam had over time adopted such collective caste acronyms as Shaikh, Kakezai and Malik. Among them perhaps the most enterprising were the Shaikhs, originating from the area of Chiniot in the Jhang District. Some of these families had set up businesses in places as far as Calcutta, most commonly in such trades as leather tanning for which Hindus suffered from caste aversions. After 1947 these groups mostly returned to Pakistan, either directly or after operating business for some years in the then East Pakistan. In the ensuing decades the Punjabi mercantile groups were to become the backbone of the upcountry business structure. They also achieved substantial penetration in Karachi itself, most notably in the various segments of the cotton and textile value chain.

Over time there have been some other sources of entry into the business structure. One was the agrarian hierarchy. At the level of the upper peasantry and smaller landlords, there has clearly been an induction into agrarian trade and other entrepreneurial functions, in rural locations and market towns. This process has been a response both to market opportunities and the need for occupational diversification with the growing fragmentation of land holdings. At the upper end, large landlords have also attempted to set up industrial projects, mostly in related agro-processing sectors. For many, entry into business was little more than a perquisite for political support from the government of the time. In such cases, subsidized credit terms and other incentives had usually served as a major factor in securing business entry. While some landlord families have retained their business portfolios, most have over time made an exit from the sector. One method was by selling out with a mark-up to more established entrepreneurial elements, so that the sojourn with business became merely a rental exaction on society. Exit of an equally damaging nature has also occurred through the use of political connections, to have bad or non-performing loans rescheduled or even written off. Thus, both business entry and exit have served as reward mechanisms for politically manipulative elements. The net result has been that the landlord segment has failed to emerge as a major or a vibrant component of Pakistan's business structure.

A further avenue of entry into business has been through careers in state service, both civil and military. The extensive, and growing, incidence of corruption in Pakistan has led to a sizeable, albeit illegal, resource flow towards state functionaries. The declining levels of transparency and accountability have, over time, effectively removed constraints on wealth accumulation through the manipulation and misuse of public service. The almost complete lack of any effective punitive measures against corrupt functionaries has considerably emboldened this element to overtly display its misbegotten rents. Much of this wealth has been sent out of the country. Estimates of amounts held overseas by Pakistani citizens exceed $30 billion. A large part of the wealth kept internally has been put into acquiring property, against which the weak accountability systems have again failed to provide effective constraints. However, some part of the resource flow from official corruption has been reinvested in business enterprise. With the increase in foreign aid and loans in the 1980s, resource diversion by civil and military officials became rampant. In recent years, there have been some highly visible instances of business entry by such elements. Some have audaciously entered electoral politics and even been given positions of ministerial rank. None have yet been brought to book.

We need now to assess the kind of economic role that the groups involved in business have played, and thence the nature of their lien on state and people in Pakistan. For this, the actual trajectory of business development in the decades since 1947 can be analyzed. From its weak and limited base at Partition, the business sector, or at least certain segments at certain times, began to be provided incentives through state policy. From the very inception, the Pakistani government tried to promote industrialization, in order to create a more balanced economy and for import substitution. But throughout it had to contend with a scarcity of resources, especially foreign exchange. The early decision not to follow India in devaluing its currency had important ramifications. A stronger rupee did not help exports, but it did make the cost of imports cheaper, and thus encouraged the inflow of capital goods. An ensuing foreign exchange shortage forced the government to curtail imports, especially of consumer goods, through higher tariffs.

However, it was only through the profits generated from the Korean War boom that efforts to secure the transition from mercantile to industrial capital received their first major impetus. These surpluses were used for the first incipient industrialization in the private sector. Benefiting from government incentives, members of southern migrant trading groups, as well as some upcountry entrepreneurs, began to invest in the cotton textile and consumer goods industries. These had short lead times, and investors could soon hope for windfall profits. These projects did bring various bureaucratic controls and sanctions over business enterprise, a relationship that was to persist in the ensuing decades. In return, the new industrialists obtained subsidized project finance, protective tariffs, market monopolies and price controls over raw materials. The leading emergent industry, cotton textiles, benefited especially from controls over the price of raw cotton, an anomaly that persisted into the 1990s, and which has generated much debate over resource transfers from agriculture to industry. Individual business groups also benefited through industries set up first in the public sector, and then disinvested in their favour. These were usually projects in which the private sector was reluctant to invest, owing to longer lead times, greater capital outlay or slower returns.

These processes reached their fruition in the 1960s. The now famous emergence of the so-called Twenty-two Families in that period was the product of growing wealth and industrial concentration. This incentive-based investment policy led to the rapid accumulation of industrial assets by selected business families, belonging mostly to the Karachi-based immigrant groups or to the upcountry Shaikh community. Their strength was based largely on cotton textiles, which had emerged as the dominant industry, though some groups had begun to diversify. Leading groups also formed private banks and insurance companies, which brought criticisms about the misuse of funds. Public sector divestment of industrial projects, again to 'big' business, added further to industrial concentration. Finally, moves to create a political role for these families must have further disconcerted those who felt threatened by these rapid developments in political economy. Even deeper discontents did indeed lead to the fall of Ayub Khan's military regime, after a popular agitation, at the close of the decade. This transition was followed soon after by elections, and then the break-up of the country itself, with the separation of East Pakistan to form Bangladesh. On the basis of its electoral performance, the People's Party (PPP) government of Zulfikar Ali Bhutto took over in the rump Pakistan.

The factors behind these transitions were to have a fundamental impact on the issue of business and power in Pakistan. Large-scale industry, fostered through private wealth creation and concentration, had experienced rapid growth rates. In the absence of similar state concessions, small and medium enterprise had failed to prosper equally, and had felt increasingly neglected. The bazaar sector figured prominently in the agitations that shook the Ayub Khan regime in 1969. Its members provided strong local support to the Pakistan People's Party both in the cities and smaller market towns. Industrial labour had also been squeezed with the suppression of labour unions and lack of enfranchisement, and with little or no improvement in real wages. The concept of 'functional inequality' and a trickle down approach to wealth distribution were policies purportedly imposed on Pakistan by a now infamous group of Harvard economists, operating under the foreign aid mechanism. The business elite had hedged its bets with military rule and the upper bureaucracy. It had obtained major economic advantages from these linkages. Nevertheless, its political fragility had remained through its failure to forge any strategic alliances with a wider base of stockholders such as the agrarian order, smaller scale business and the working class. Big business paid dearly for this lack of political entrenchment but through outcomes that were almost predictable. Thus, the preference for expediency over these strategies resulted in the failure of big business to reach a consensus, over interests and ethos, with related segments and stakeholders.

Clearly, the most powerful of these interests lay, yet again, in agriculture. This sector presumably had good grounds for dissatisfaction with the expansion of big business. Agricultural growth rates had stagnated since the 1950s, accompanied by negligible state expenditure on agricultural development. The alleged squeezing of foreign exchange earnings from East Pakistani jute to finance West Pakistani industrialization was already beginning to foment Bengali nationalism. In the western wing, ongoing controls over cotton prices, in order to favour industrialists, continued to rankle the agricultural sector. In the 1960s, measures to achieve a green revolution benefited mostly larger and middle farmers, with their differential access to farm mechanization, input subsidies and softer credit terms. Weaker tenant rights, leading to easier expropriation of cultivators, and the ongoing ineffectiveness of land reforms, further alienated the middle and upper peasantry. These elements too sided with the People's Party in the elections of 1970, especially in the country's agrarian heartland, the Punjab. On the other hand, larger landowners also felt increasingly threatened by the growing stature of the emergent business families. The notion can by no means be discounted that Zulfikar Ali Bhutto himself, belonging as he did to the upper agrarian hierarchy, had as his real agenda a hostile feudal reaction to big business, for which his populist and socialistic orientation provided merely the rhetoric of power.

In the event, the reversal of private sector larger scale business in Pakistan in the 1970s was even more dramatic than its expeditious rise. Bhutto's nationalization policies extended over banks, insurance companies, and industrial plants in several sectors. While the core industry, cotton textiles, was spared, the state took over especially those industries and services into which the larger business groups had diversified, such as the engineering, automobile, chemical, cement and edible oil industries. These plants were placed under a dozen or so sector based state owned corporations. These drastic blows not only loosened the grip of the big business groups on the economy, but they also succeeded in deterring further private sector investment during the 1970s. Indeed, the investment shyness of indigenous business continued well into the 1980s. It was mainly within the public sector that investment occurred during this period. Meanwhile, the erstwhile tycoons, who did not seem to lack expatriated money, now preferred to seek business opportunities outside the country.

Who were the beneficiaries of this downturn in the private sector? The new state owned enterprises were brought initially under a Board of Industrial Management, to create some distance from the bureaucracy and provide a role for a managerial and technocratic cadre. The dissolution of the Board under Zia led to the effective transfer of decision-making for the SOEs to federal ministries. The public sector was thereby brought under direct bureaucratic control. This constituted a major extension of the space and authority of the public service, greatly increasing the parameters of corruption and rent seeking. The domain of private business experienced a commensurate decline. Privatization measures, not undertaken till the 1990s, diluted the bureaucracy's hold to some degree. However, to date privatization has extended only to the smaller industrial units, and not to the much more extensive parastatals and utilities.

Indeed, the full extent of Bhutto's nationalization in the 1970s revealed the depth of forces arraigned against private business. The state's interventionist policies went well beyond the take over of large-scale industry and financial services. Major inroads also occurred in the agribusiness sector, with the setting up of monopolistic state trading corporations. Virtually a sole procuring agency was established for wheat, the staple food grain; and this and other state companies also traded in the lesser crops. Similar corporations began to monopolize exports of the two major commodities, raw cotton and rice. These measures dealt a major blow to private sector agricultural trade, and further constrained the development of rural entrepreneurship. In its stead, public sector managers began to dominate agrarian trade and exports, again opening up new sources of malpractice.

The PPP government went even further. It undertook the extreme measure of nationalizing major parts of the intermediate agro-processing sector. Rice, flour and edible oil mills were taken over in the hope of severing, at a stroke, entrepreneurial control over the forward linkages of the agricultural value chain. This policy was probably designed to placate the larger landowners, whose agents and representatives now gained hold of these plants. After 1975, having by then exhausted his socialist credentials, Bhutto did indeed appeal for political support to this class, but had to pay the required price. As a consequence, the trading community also withheld its support for the PPP, and even actively opposed it during the agitation of 1977. Finally, these acts of economic irrationality were reversed with the denationalization of these agro-processing units by the Zia ul-Haq regime. The restructuring of the state trading corporations was much more retarded: they were to outlast Zia himself.

It might be claimed that to this day business has failed to recover from these adverse impacts on its potentiality for development. The larger business groups almost completely ceased to develop into corporate structures with diversified portfolios and deep managerial hierarchies. Instead, the major groups relapsed back into medium sized family operations. The consequences of the 1970s nationalization also impeded any significant moves into more capital intensive and technologically complex industries, whose emergence internationally was creating new growth accelerators. These international trends were not reflected in Pakistan's industrial performance. The rapid developments, for example, in electronics in the 1980s, failed to have any resonance in Pakistan. This shortfall was repeated later with the computer-related industries, and with information technology. The private sector was unable to avail these opportunities.

In the 1980s, several efforts were made during the Zia ul-Haq regime to attract investment. Various schemes were introduced to ease the legalization of black money, but these met with little response. When private investment did pick up after 1985, it was not in internationally leading industries but remained instead tied more to commodity-type agro-processing, such as yarn and sugar production. Nevertheless, investment patterns did remain relatively buoyant for a decade from 1985, spurred by a combination of new entrants and a return of some older business groups. Prominent among the former category were elements that had aligned or held public positions with the military and subsequent civilian regimes. By obtaining access to loans from the nationalized banks and financial institutions, some of these groups were not only able to accumulate industrial assets rapidly, but even enter politics at the highest levels. This pattern was more evident with some upcountry groups, which had forged a coalescence of political involvement with wealth expansion. The Karachi-based migrant commercial groups, by and large, refrained from further involvement. Reasons could be not only the lack of business confidence in the country, but the adverse climate created by the rise of the Muhajir Qaumi Movement, the MQM, and the serious law and order problems in Karachi.

The improved investment climate began to recede in the second half of the 1990s. A rise in the price of local raw cotton, a longstanding agrarian demand, rendered the subsidy-dependent cotton textile industry uncompetitive. The economic crisis among Pakistan's East Asian trading partners, the major buyers of yarn, also proved detrimental. The nuclear tests of 1998 and the freezing of foreign currency accounts further eroded business confidence. Fear of religious bigotry and terrorism, coupled with poor law enforcement, also deterred foreign investment. The ongoing moral and material commitment to the Kashmir struggle, as well as continued Indian hostility, increased the perception of this as a region of potential military, and even nuclear, conflict. Moreover, inept public management, if not gross financial malpractice, typified the governments of both Benazir Bhutto and Nawaz Sharif, further polarizing the political spectrum. The substantial rise in external debt, moving well beyond $30 billion, reflected the damaging agenda of the international money lending agencies, such as the World Bank, of inducting loans into a society with weak transparency and accountability systems. While these resources have been mostly absorbed by state functionaries and their sponsored business clients, severe local taxation is required for generating funds to meet onerous loan repayments. The collective impact of these trends has been to create a deep depression in the Pakistani economy by the end of the 1990s.

While much of this later malaise was caused by externalities, the nature of business operations also played its part. Much of the new investment was based on fragile financial ratios, the impact of which was strongly in evidence by the late 1990s. Because of political liens, and with corruption and the weakness of transparency in the nationalized financial sector, most new projects were over-leveraged and under-financed. They had little, and at times even negligible, financial commitment by the entrepreneur. Through the stratagem of kickbacks on over-invoiced imports of foreign machinery, these 'investors' could get their own equity transferred to foreign bank accounts. This left them with little remaining personal risk in the project. Moreover, over-leveraging, though initially attractive, meant that interest charges were often disproportionate to earnings.

The result has been a very large accumulation of non-performing loans, along with a large number of declared sick units. The scale of these bad debts is said to have crippled, if not actually bankrupted, the financial sector. The DFIs, or development financial institutions, are now bereft of both capital and liquidity. This problem has even affected the privatization of the larger nationalized banks, owing to negative net assets. Rescheduling of loans, with the financial institutions taking heavy losses, or the instigation of numerous legal actions, have begun to characterize the Pakistani business scenario. Yet the defaulters, while showing seemingly bankrupted industrial assets, are commonly believed to have been personally enriched, with capital and profits transferred overseas. Their effective resistance to any accountability process reflects the weakness of the legal and judicial systems, and the strength of the politico-rental mechanism.

If it is true that Pakistani business prefers to function in a deinstitutionalised environment, there are important economic reasons for this genre. Pakistani business, as opposed to the multinational sector, is composed of family firms in which equity is closely integrated with operations. While the owner-operator mode is justifiable for the small and medium enterprise segments, it also happens to pervade the so-called large-scale sector. From this structure of the dominance of family firms, there has been little or no transition towards the building of corporatized business structures, or towards 'managerial capitalism'.

There are several reasons for this lack of organizational innovation. The traumatic setbacks of the 1970s could have impeded this process, the seeds of which might well have sprouted in the 1960s. The culture of business might also be too personalized, acting against instituting systems and decentralizing operations. Tax evasion, and the ubiquity of the black economy, has worked against devolving authority to managerial cadres. The insufficient supply of good quality managerial personnel could be another disincentive, though this could be a function also of low compensation levels offered by Pakistani business to managers. Even the larger capitalists have preferred to establish distinct companies for separate projects or industrial units, rather than develop divisionalized entities with multiple managerial layers.

Perhaps one crucial reason for this structural phenomenon on is the very nature of the manufacturing process involved in Pakistan's major industry, cotton textiles. Higher volumes of production in this industry fail to achieve discernible economies of scale, which would make larger business organizations economically competitive. Consequently, the industry structure of textiles in Pakistan has remained highly fragmented. Moreover, the particularism of family-based equity has also prevented any learning curves through horizontal integration. Indeed, most Pakistani public limited firms have essentially inactive share transactions in the stock market. The founding families have steadfastly retained their majority equity shares. The real reason for seeking public listings was most probably not to corporatize operations, but because this was a requirement for seeking highly subsidized project loans from public sector financial institutions.

What, then, can we posit regarding the political power of business? Individual businessmen or groups continued to enjoy privileges through their access to state functionaries. The collective strength of the various components of the bazaar or informal sector also remained quite considerable, either for preserving group interests or to combine for purposes of tax evasion. However, despite playing a major role in modernizing the economy and the society, business has remained quite peripheral. Even after the return to civilian democracy in the late 1980s, any stimulus from the business sector to develop political institutions or democratic political organizations or to initiate effective institutional reforms remained weak at best. The ongoing recession in the Pakistani economy during the 1990s has further reduced the prospects of a dynamic and transforming role for business in society.

There are, nevertheless, several economic privileges enjoyed by the groups involved in business. They reflect the nature of the lien that this sector has exercised on the state and people in Pakistan. The main relationship remains in the age-old area of rent and revenue. Mutually beneficial links between business and bureaucracy have seriously depleted the state's revenue generating capacity. The resulting revenue losses are serious enough to have created endemic fiscal deficits. Through the 1990s, the continuing excess of government expenditure over revenue has threatened to undermine the contribution of public finances to national development. Government efforts to widen the tax base in the face of widespread tax evasion, mostly by the business community, have yet not succeeded. The other means of achieving fiscal stability, through institutional reforms and curtailing expenditures on state functionaries, has also not been seriously attempted, indicating the state's unwillingness or incapacity to control incumbent stakeholders.

Thus, if one indicator of power is economic benefit through unequal resource disposals, then the business community is, along with state functionaries, very much a beneficiary of this substantial but highly questionable process of resource transfer. De-institutionalization is a function of this structure. In the shorter term, this lack of systems facilitates the kind of elite operations and activities that have burgeoned in Pakistan. In the longer term, it could well be a major factor in depriving the country of a favourable economic positioning, even among the lower income countries internationally.

References

Ahmad, Viqar and Rashid Amjad. 1986. *The Management of Pakistan's Economy, 1947–82.* Karachi.

Alam, Muzaffar. 1986. *The Crisis of Empire in Mughal North India: Awadh and Punjab, 1707–48*. Delhi.

Ali, Imran. 'Malign Growth? Agricultural Colonization and the Roots of Backwardness in the Punjab', *Past and Present* (Oxford), No. 114, February 1987.

————, 'Relations between the Muslim League and the Punjab National Unionist Party, 1945–47', *South Asia* (Australia), No. 6, 1976.

————, 1975. *Punjab Politics in the Decade before Partition*. Lahore.

————, 1980. 'The Punjab Canal Colonies, 1885–1940', Australian National University Ph.D. thesis.

————, 1988. *The Punjab under Imperialism, 1885–1947*. Princeton, NJ.

————, 1991. 'The Punjab and the Retardation of Nationalism', in D.A. Low (ed.), *The Political Inheritance of Pakistan*. London.

————, 1992. 'Emerging Role of Private Sector in Agricultural Development and its Imperatives for Agricultural Education,' in P. Amir et. al. (eds.), *Reforming Agricultural Education in Pakistan*. Islamabad.

————, 1996. 'Sikh Settlers in Western Punjab,' in Pritam Singh and Shinder S. Tandli (eds), *Globalisation and the Region: Explorations in Punjabi Identity*. United Kingdom, Association for Punjab Studies.

————, 1997. 'Telecommunications Development in Pakistan', in E. Noam (ed.), *Telecommunications Development in Western Asia and the Middle East*. Oxford and New York.

————, 1997. 'Canal Colonization and Socio–Economic Change,' in Indu Banga (ed.), *Five Punjabi Centuries: Polity, Economy, Society and Culture, c. 1500–1990*. New Delhi.

————, 1996. 'Equity, Exclusion and Liberalization: Pakistan and the Threats to National Sustainability,' Paper at 'SEPHIS Conference on Equity, Exclusion and Liberalization: a Debate among Historians', Zanzibar, September.

————, 1995. Land Market in Pakistan: The Role of Institutions' unpublished paper presented at 'Conference on Privatization of Agricultural Services', Lahore, October.

————, 1998. 'Past and Present. the Formation of the State in Pakistan,' Paper at 'Conference on Pakistan', Maison des Sciences Del Homme, Paris, June.

Ali, Tariq. 1970. *Pakistan: Military Rule or People's Power*. London.

Amjad, Rashid. 1982. *Private Industrial Investment in Pakistan, 1960–1970*. London.

Andrus, J.R. and A.F. Mohammed. 1958. *The Economy of Pakistan*. London.

Barrier, N.G. 1966. *The Punjab Alienation of Land Bill of 1900*. Durham, NC.

Baxter, Craig (ed.). 1985. *Zia's Pakistan: Politics and Stability in a Frontline State*. Boulder, Colorado.

Bayly, C.A., 1983 Rulers. '*Townsmen and Bazaars. North Indian Society in the Age of British Expansion,*' 1770–1870. Cambridge.

Burki, S.J. 1980. *Pakistan under Bhutto: 1971–77.* London.

Burki, S.J. and Craig Baxter. 1991. *Pakistan Under the Military: Eleven Years of Zia ul–Haq.* Boulder, Colorado.

Choudhury, G.W. 1974. *Last Days of United Pakistan.* Bloomington.

Griffin, L.H. and C.F. Massy. 1940. *Chiefs and Families of Note in the Punjab.* 2 vols. Lahore.

Habib, Irfan. 1963. *The Agrarian System of Mughal India.* London.

Jahan, Rounaq. 1972. *Pakistan: Failure in National Integration.* New York.

Kessinger, T.G. 1974. *Vilyatpur, 1848–1968.* Berkeley and Los Angeles.

Kochanek, S.A. 1983. *Interest Groups and Development: Business and Politics in Pakistan.* New Delhi.

LaPorte, Robert, Jr. and M.B. Ahmad. 1989. *Public Enterprises in Pakistan.* Boulder, Colorado.

Latif, S.M. 1981. *Lahore.* Lahore, 1892, reprinted.

Low, D.A. (ed.). 1977. *The Congress and the Raj.* New York.

Noman, Omar. 1988. *The Political Economy of Pakistan.* London.

Papanek, G.F. 1967. *Pakistan's Development: Social Goals and Private Incentives.* Cambridge, Mass.

The Cambridge Economic History of India, 2 vols. 1982. Cambridge.

van den Dungen, P.H.M. 1972. *The Punjab Tradition.* London.

White, L.J. 1974. *Industrial Concentration and Economic Power.* Princeton, NJ.

Ziring, Lawrence. 1971. *The Ayub Khan Era: Politics in Pakistan, 1958–1969.* Syracuse.

————, 1980. *Pakistan: The Enigma of Political Development.* Boulder, Colorado.

6

POLITICS OF POWER AND ITS ECONOMIC IMPERATIVES: PAKISTAN, 1947–99

Shahid Javed Burki

A. Introduction

Pakistan's 52-year history is marked by exceptional turbulence. Unlike India—born a day after Pakistan's birth and with the same inheritance in terms of traditions and institutions—Pakistan has as yet to settle down politically. India had a constitution in place within four years of its birth. On many occasions it has seen transfer of power from one set of leaders to another without political trauma and within the framework of the constitution. By coincidence when, in October 1999, while a military regime was establishing itself in Pakistan—the fourth government in forty years under the leadership of the army—India was concluding another massive general election in which some 600 million voters had cast their votes. Is there an answer for the obvious question this comparison poses? Why has it taken so long for Pakistan to find a political structure acceptable to its people and why, even after half a century of trying, there is still no light visible at the end of the tunnel?

In this chapter, I will search for an answer to this question. On the surface, there could be a simple explanation for Pakistan's travails. The country has remained in political flux since its birth. The social groups that have held power in the country for three and half decades, from the mid-1960s to the late 1990s, did not allow the rest of the population to enter the political system. Those excluded from power sought to enter the system by means other than politically legitimate. At times, these incursions took the form of military *coup d'etats*. At other times presidents, under the cover of the constitution, removed errant regimes from power. The regimes that were thus removed had lost their representative character in the eyes of the people who had originally elected them. In other words, Pakistan has not been able to politically accommodate diversity. On the face of it, this does not seem a good explanation, especially when we continue to compare Pakistan with India. If anything, India is even more diverse than Pakistan. Its people speak many more languages, subscribe to many more religions, are formally divided into a rigid system of castes, and live in geographical regions much more diverse than those in which the people of Pakistan reside. India, by all accounts, is considerably more diverse and yet politically more stable. What makes Pakistan different from India is that its social diversity has come quickly as a result of the developments that have no parallel in India. Its society has been—and continues to be—constantly churned over. It happened in 1947 with the arrival of eight million Muslim refugees from India that replaced six million Hindus and Sikhs who moved in the opposite direction. The refugees represented the social forces that had spearheaded the movement for the creation of Pakistan and, naturally, became the original leaders of the new state of Pakistan. It took the indigenous forces more than a decade before they were able to reassert themselves. Once they did, their control over the political system became total and exclusionary. At the same time, Pakistan's social transformation continued unabated, fuelled by two other waves of migration. One of them took the form of a massive movement of people from the country's villages to its rapidly growing towns and cities. The other involved the movement of some three million workers to the Middle East. Both movements had dramatic economic and social impact.

But the political system remained impervious to this change. Some accommodation was made in the early 1970s as a result of the civil war between East and West Pakistan. This war itself was the consequence of the inability of the system to bring in the Bengalis of East Pakistan into the political fold. However, the system proved to be inflexible and, within half a decade, the political culture reverted to its original form. The reassertion of the old system happened at a time when Pakistan was proceeding through another social transformation, this one caused by the large-scale migration to the Middle East. The migrants, by sending billions of dollars as remittances to their families in Pakistan, changed the social and economic landscapes but had no visible influence on the political structure. This tug of war produced the 'great divide' in Pakistan's history: the inability of the political system to remain in touch with the remoulding of the society that was constantly happening as a result of social and economic developments. The coup—or the counter-coup— of 12 October 1999 is yet another attempt to fix the political system so that it becomes fully representative. I describe these changes in greater detail in Section B of this chapter.

I continue with this story in the third section of the chapter, using the military intervention of 12 October 1999 as the backdrop. It is my contention that this intervention should not be looked at as an isolated event. It is, in fact, one more episode in a long list of developments that took place with a view to closing the great divide between the state of economic and social development on the one side and the structure of politics on the other. The events leading up to the coup of 12 October 1999 are described in some detail in order to illustrate an important point. Societies with poor institutions have to resort to unorthodox measures to restore what they consider to be the state of equilibrium. If the events of 12 October seem bizarre—and they are—it was because of the collapse of the institutional structure that has made it virtually impossible for the various groups in the society to communicate with one another. This section places the army move of 12 October 1999 in a proper context. It also provides a description of the way the Pakistani society has corrected itself on various occasions to obtain an equilibrium between socio-economic forces on the one side and the political structure on the other. The fourth section suggests an agenda of reform for the regime currently in power. This is done not to construct a blue-print of reform but to illustrate what kind of economic actions need to be taken to restore the balance between socio-economic forces and the political structure. I conclude the chapter with a short section that looks at the future.

B. A State of Constant Social Flux

As indicated above, the first social shock to the Pakistani system was given by the massive movement of people that accompanied the birth of Pakistan as an independent state. I have described the social, political, and economic consequences of this event in greater detail in some earlier works (Burki, 1999a and 1999b). Here I will offer a quick summary of the earlier analyses.

The migrants from India to Pakistan were able to quickly dominate the economy and the political system of the country they had created. It is the great paradox of the realization of Muhammad Ali Jinnah's dream for the establishment of an independent homeland for the Muslims of British India that it was created in the parts in which the Pakistan idea did not have great support. The leaders of Punjab, Sindh and the Frontier Province were at best lukewarm—if not openly hostile—to the idea of Pakistan. These people, therefore, could not be trusted with managing the new country. It was easy for the refugees from India to dominate Pakistan socially, economically, and politically.

In 1947–58, the refugees constituted no more than 25 per cent of Pakistan's population.[1] This was the main reason why the governing elite was not in any great hurry to give the country a constitution and hold elections as was done across the border in India. For eleven years, the Pakistani political system was in a state of disequilibrium, dominated by a minority, which sought to exclude the majority. The majority—the indigenous people of Pakistan—continued to be led by traditional elite groups. In keeping with tradition, the landlords of Punjab and Sindh and the tribal chiefs of Baluchistan and the Frontier Province continued to dominate the populations of their provinces.

The first wave of Pakistan's industrialization began to change the socio-economic composition of the majority. Some two to three million people migrated from Punjab and the Frontier Province to provide manpower for Karachi's construction and economic booms. This movement and the associated capital flows from the workers who had gone to Karachi to their families began to loosen the hold of the traditional elite in some areas of the country. This change manifested itself profoundly in the areas from which most of the migrants were drawn. The areas subject to this change were in central and northern Punjab and the Frontier Province.

The first military intervention in Pakistan's history—in October 1958 under the leadership of General Ayub Khan—was welcomed for the reason that it sought to restore the political equilibrium that had been lost by the events that followed Independence. However, it is ironic that the process of 'indigenization of politics'[2] launched by Ayub Khan took hold when the correction of the disequilibrium had begun to take place. Pakistan's industrialization and rapid urbanization—in particular the rapid expansion of Karachi—had begun to shift the centre of gravity from the landlord and tribal chiefs dominated areas towards the modernizing parts of the country.

The appointment of Amir Muhammad Khan, the Nawab of Kalabagh, as governor of West Pakistan—today's Pakistan—quickened the process of indigenization and turned the society back by decades. The Nawab was a large landlord from Mianwali, a remote area in the Punjab province. He had been lukewarm to the idea of Pakistan since he had correctly sensed that the landed aristocracy would lose some of its power in a country created by the urban classes. Once installed in the governor's mansion, the Nawab went to work with a vengeance, using personal authority rather than institutions and the rule of law to govern. Under his powerful leadership, the political pendulum swung way back towards the landed aristocracy and the tribal chiefs. The new classes—the refugees from India and the beneficiaries of the first wave of industrialization—that had come to share power following the birth of Pakistan were now relegated to the back seat. Ayub Khan probably did not want the process of indigenization to go to that extreme. Politically weakened by the war with India and a debilitating illness, he let Kalabagh distort the system. By the end of the 1960s, Pakistan was ready for another correction.

This time a combination of several political events—the elections of December 1970 and the civil war between East and West Pakistan—set the stage for the restoration of the equilibrium between the socio-economic forces and the forces that dominated the political system. Zulfikar Ali Bhutto and his Pakistan People's Party won handsomely in the elections as a result of the support of the people Kalabagh's 'reverse revolution' had excluded from the political system. But it took the defeat of the Pakistani army in the civil war, to bring Bhutto and his party to power.

Bhutto's initial populism was in response to the demands of the constituency that had brought him to power and which now demanded inclusion in the political and economic systems. This constituency had been excluded by the reversal to old social values and to the old political system under the guiding hand of Governor Kalabagh. The working class in the urban areas and the new middle classes felt excluded. Nationalization of large-scale industries, commercial banks, insurance companies, and of trade in rice and cotton were all directed towards increasing the economic power of the state in order to redirect to the poor income from the acquired assets. Bhutto also put new labour laws on the books to provide additional benefits to the working classes. With the help of these reforms he was hoping to deliver on his promise of *roti, kapra, aur makan* (bread, clothing and housing) for all. These were economic reforms; however, they did little to expand the political system to bring in these constituencies, in particular the middle classes. In fact, by the time Bhutto called elections in February 1977, he had put the political system squarely in the hands of the old elite—the landlords and the tribal chiefs. Instead of correcting the Kalabagh-induced disequilibrium, Bhutto merely perpetuated it.

Bhutto brought about another change in Pakistan's governing culture, which was to have a profound and lasting effect. He went beyond Kalabagh and borrowed the mode of governance the landed aristocracy and tribal chiefs had practiced for centuries for conducting the business of the state. All those institutions that stood in the way for making this transformation were levelled. The civil service was reduced in stature, independence of the judiciary was compromised, and the planning apparatus built by Ayub Khan was destroyed. These moves were made at the time the size of the middle class had begun to increase significantly and its composition change quite dramatically. The migration of Pakistani workers to the Middle East and billions of dollars of remittances sent by these had altered the economic and social landscape. The families receiving flows from abroad used it to establish new businesses, educate their children, provide better access to health facilities for the families, and improve the quality of their shelters. Millions of recipients of remittances climbed out of poverty and joined the ranks of the middle class.[3] This new social class began to look for a political home once it had secured an economic and social place for itself. It was attracted to Bhutto's Pakistan People's Party since it was Bhutto's close relations with most Middle Eastern governments that had made these people welcome in those countries. Also, the Bhutto administration had facilitated the migration of Pakistani workers by freely issuing passports to them. Had Zulfikar Ali Bhutto wanted, he could have changed the Pakistani political scene quite dramatically by creating space within the system for this class of people, as well as for the people who had earlier dominated politics. That was not to be the case. Bhutto, instead of opening the system, closed it by allowing the landed aristocracy and the tribal chieftains to continue to rule over it.

These moves thoroughly alienated the middle class. Apart from being denied full participation in the political system, this group of people was very troubled with the values that surfaced as a part of the culture of governance during the Bhutto period. Intolerance for opposing views, the use of the state apparatus for silencing criticism, award of favors for associates and inflicting material harm on those who refused to become camp followers were alien values for the middle class. It was their resentment which provided the opportunity for a long movement against Bhutto's rule and ultimately led to the military intervention by General Zia ul-Haq.

Zia sensed intuitively that the political system developed and presided over by Bhutto lacked the equilibrium that could sustain it for very long. He could have corrected the default by widening it; by making it possible for the millions of people who had been left out in the cold during the latter part of the Bhutto period. Instead, it offered a new sop to the alienated—Islamization. Being a devout Muslim himself, Zia believed that by formally introducing the tenets of Islam into the economy and the polity he could win over the classes that had been alienated by Bhutto's style of governance. That was not what the people wanted, however. The fact that Zia was able to survive for a long time was the extraordinarily high rate of economic growth which, as we will see in Section D, was the consequence of a large flow of foreign capital into the country. By keeping the lid on the political system, Zia let a lot of steam build up which resulted in the return to power of Bhutto's PPP—this time under the command of his daughter, Benazir.

Whether consciously or instinctively, Benazir Bhutto followed the footsteps of her father in the sense that she allowed the same elite—the landed aristocracy and the tribal chieftains—and the same style of governance to dominate the political system during her two terms in office. Her two dismissals brought Mian Nawaz Sharif to political power, the first time in 1990 and the second time in 1997, but he also failed in closing the great divide between the socio-economic forces and the political system. By October 1999 the political system was ripe for a major correction. 'The people here aren't really concerned with democracy any more. They have seen what kind of democracy there is here. What we want is stability,' said a prominent journalist a few days after the coup (Constable, 1999). What were the circumstances that led to the military take over and how did these compare with the previous military incursions into politics? I answer this question in the section that follows.

C. October 12, 1999 and the Preceding Military Take-overs

On 12 October 1999, General Pervez Musharraf, Chief of Army Staff (COAS), removed Prime Minister Mian Nawaz Sharif from office. The army was said to have acted spontaneously in response to a series of bizarre events that concluded with an attempt to keep the Pakistan International Airlines (PIA) plane carrying General Musharraf from landing at Karachi Airport. The general was returning from Colombo, Sri Lanka, after having represented Pakistan at an official function. The plane landed at Karachi after the army commanders in Islamabad, Pakistan's capital, and Karachi had moved against the government. By the time the PIA plane landed in Karachi, Prime Minister Sharif; his brother Mian Shabaz Sharif, the Chief Minister of Punjab, Pakistan's largest province; Information Minister Mushahid Husain, a close confidant of the Sharif brothers; Saifur Rahman, the head of the Ehtesab (Accountability Cell) in the Prime Minister's Secretariat; and Saeed Mehdi, the Prime Minister's Secretary were in the hands of the army. The army had also taken into custody Khakan Abbasy, the Chairman of PIA, who had gone to the air-control tower at the airport in Karachi to prevent the general's plane from landing.

The 'drama in the air' was the subject of many press reports in Pakistan as well as abroad.[4] In an interview given to a news agency several days after having dismissed the Prime Minister, General Musharraf gave his own account of what had happened.[5] On being told by the plane's pilot that permission to land at Karachi, the plane's destination, had been denied by the control tower and that the pilot was told to fly instead to an airport in India, General Musharraf had taken command of the aircraft. He told the pilot that the plane would fly to India 'over his dead body.' Finally, when the word came to the cockpit from the commanders in Karachi that the army had secured the airport, the plane landed with only seven minutes of fuel to spare.

There were reasons why Prime Minister Sharif and his colleagues wanted to prevent the general from landing at Karachi. They had dismissed him as COAS while he was en route from Colombo to Karachi, installing in his place Lieutenant General Khawaja Ziauddin, the head of Inter Intelligence Services (ISI). Government controlled Pakistan Television and Pakistan Radio had broadcast the news to the nation and General Ziauddin had gone to the General Headquarters (GHQ) in Rawalpindi to take command of the army. That the Prime Minister may make such a move had been anticipated by the military high command. General Ziauddin was stopped at the GHQ gate and turned back. He was told that it was the army's tradition to have the command pass from one general to the other when both were present. Humiliated, General Ziauddin went back to Islamabad and met with the Prime Minister and his associates. It was decided that since the army generals in the GHQ had refused to comply with the government's orders, there were legitimate grounds to arrest their chief, General Pervez Musharraf. His plane could be diverted to India or to some other place not too far from Karachi and the news would be given that, fearing arrest, the General had hijacked the plane that was bringing him back to Karachi. Or his plane could be diverted to a small airport in the interior of Sindh, the province of which Karachi is the capital. It would be easier to arrest the General in a small Sindh town where the army did not have a significant presence. An arrest of a defiant commander of the army in Karachi, which was also the headquarter of a large army corps, would be difficult.

Why did the Prime Minister act the way he did and why did the army, having pledged allegiance to the political government, defy the Prime Minister? The second part of the question is easier to answer. The immediate reason for the army's move was the plane incident. In a short speech to the nation at 3 a.m. on the night between 12 and 13 October, General Musharraf spoke of what had happened while he, along with more than two hundred passengers, was still in the air. 'On my way back the PIA commercial flight was not allowed to land at Karachi but was ordered to be diverted anywhere outside Pakistan, despite acute shortage of fuel, imperilling the lives of all the passengers. Thanks be to Allah, this evil design was thwarted through speedy army action,' said the General (*Dawn*, 1999a).

It was clear from the way the events unfolded on 12 October that the army had plans to intervene in case the situation in the country continued to deteriorate. This was clear from General Musharraf's brief address on 13 October and a more detailed one a few days later. On both occasions he spoke of colossal corruption and economic mismanagement which had brought the state of Pakistan close to a collapse. It was not the incident in the air that was played up by Sahibzada Muhammad Yaqub, General Musharraf's special envoy to the western countries as an explanation for the army take over. It was the fear of a general collapse. In an interview with William Safire of *The New York Times*, Yaqub said that 'his country was in a terrible mess. Bribery was rampant and taxes were routinely evaded. Banks were lending huge sums to politicians without collateral. Legislators were intimidating judges... The very moral fibre of the nation was damaged by its political leadership... Now, he says, a group of non-political technocrats has been appointed to root out the corrupt practices, reviving the rule of law, devolve power to local constitutions.' (Safire, 1999). According to this explanation, for the fourth time in Pakistan's 52-year history, the army had intervened to stem the wrought created by politicians.

It is important to answer the question about the Prime Minister's reason for seeking a change in the army's command, since an explanation will provide a clue as to the way the old establishment in the country sought to maintain power in its hands. To do so, it was prepared to use whatever means were available. If there were institutions in the way they had to be brushed aside. In that sense, what Nawaz Sharif did was not too different from the way Zulfikar Ali Bhutto had conducted himself in office. Bhutto and Sharif belonged to two different social classes; the former was a landed aristocrat, the latter an industrialist. But both had one thing in common: they were opposed to the opening up of the political system by letting in the classes that were clamoring to be accommodated. Sharif's methods were crude and, ultimately, exhausted the patience of the people. Since taking office in February 1997, he had worked diligently to remove all obstacles to the consolidation of political power in his hands. He had started by reducing the power of the President under the amended constitution of 1993 to dismiss the Prime Minister and dissolve the national assembly. This power had been acquired in 1985 by President Muhammad Zia ul-Haq under the eighth amendment. That was President Zia's price for taking the military out of politics and bringing back a limited form of democracy. The presidential power had been used repeatedly to dismiss prime ministers. Sharif was anxious to remove this constraint on the exercise of executive authority. The attack on the judicial system was quite literal since the Prime Minister's associates masterminded the storming of the Supreme Court when he, Nawaz Sharif, was being tried for contempt of the court. The dispute between the Prime Minister and the judiciary was settled in the former's favor. Both President Farooq Ahmad Khan Leghari, who had refused the Prime Minister's request for removing Chief Justice Sajjad Ali Shah, and the Chief Justice himself, resigned. Sharif had Muhammad Rafiq Tarar, a friend of the family, elected president. The senior-most judge of the Supreme Court was appointed its chief justice.

With a vast majority behind him and with support also of the opposition in the national assembly, Sharif moved quickly but surreptitiously. The national assembly, summoned on 13 March, was presented with the Thirteenth amendment to the constitution deleting most of the changes made by the Eighth amendment, was allowed a few hours to debate the issue and then asked to vote. President Farooq Leghari was out of Islamabad at that time. With the national assembly's vote in his pocket, Nawaz Sharif went first to call on General Jehangir Karamat, the chief of army staff, and then took a plane to Choti, the native village of President Leghari. 'A highly agitated Nawaz Sharif was brought into my living room. He told me of the action the national assembly had taken and asked if I could sign the amendment to make it law. I calmed him down by saying that I had no problem signing the bill. After all it was the unanimous wish of the national assembly.'[6]

With the presidency and the judiciary tamed, it was the turn of the military. This was a much bigger target, one no civilian leader since Muhammad Ali Jinnah, Pakistan's founder and its first governor-general, and Liaquat Ali Khan, Jinnah's lieutenant and the country's first prime minister, had dared to touch. A number of confrontations between the civilian and military leadership had occurred in the past and, with one exception, all of them had been resolved in favor of the latter. In October 1958, General Ayub Khan, then the commander-in-chief of the army, had carried out a straightforward military coup against the civilian authority. Ayub's reason for bringing in the army into politics were simple and explained at length in his *Autobiography* (Khan, 1967). He had been studying Pakistan's political situation for some time and with increasing concern. By the time he decided to move against the civilian authority, he was convinced that the political system was not representative of the people. As discussed in the previous section, this was a correct diagnosis since the system, as operated since the birth of the country, had been dominated by the refugees who had migrated from Pakistan into India. It had kept out the old establishment. Ayub Khan's coup was welcomed by the people who had become tired of the machinations resorted to by the politicians trying to maintain themselves in power. The coup was also not unpopular outside the country. Such coups were common occurrence in those days in the postcolonial world and not a great deal of notice was taken of them by the countries with democratic systems. The imperatives of the Cold War demanded quick recognition of the new leadership on the part of both Washington and Moscow. The failure to offer accommodation could be costly since the offended coup leader would happily take his country into the more welcoming arms of the opposite camp.

The second military intervention occurred on 27 March 1969 when General Agha Muhammad Yahya Khan encouraged President Ayub Khan to leave office. For several months, Ayub had tried to resolve his differences with the opposition, which had come to resent the increasing domination of the system by the established oligarchy. The opposition, smelling blood, had become more and more intransigent. The military, always fearful of prolonged instability, stepped in and asked President Ayub Khan to read a speech on the national radio. The speech had been drafted by the military. The transfer of power was gentlemanly; it lacked the drama that attended the military take-over of either 5 July 1977 or 12 October 1999.

The third major confrontation between the military and politicians took place in March 1972. It was provoked by President Zulfikar Ali Bhutto, who had taken over the reins of the government following the defeat of the Pakistani army in East Pakistan. Bhutto's own ascent had been inspired by the army. This was the only time in the history of the Pakistani army that a group of young officers stood up and defied the military high command. In normal times such behaviour would have led to a court martial followed by serious punishment for the dissidents. But December 1971 was not a normal time even for Pakistan, a country that had seen a great deal of political, social, and economic turbulence. The army had been humiliated by a combined force of the Indian army and Mukti Bahini (Bengali's Freedom Fighters). East Pakistan was no longer a part of Pakistan, the country's eastern wing. It was now an independent country called Bangladesh, the land of the Bengalis. This was the first time in modern world history that a civil war had led to the break-up of a country and a quick recognition of the seceding country on the part of all major powers. It was understandable that Pakistan—or what was left of it—had been seriously traumatized by these unfolding events. When the regime of General Yahya Khan sought to maintain its control over West Pakistan—now Pakistan—it was challenged by the younger officers. There was a showdown on 17 December 1971 between the regime and the younger officers of the army. Yahya Khan resigned and the charismatic Zulfikar Ali Bhutto, who had already captured the imagination of his people a few days earlier by walking out of a UN Security Council meeting, assumed control of a demoralized country. The Security Council had been deliberating a resolution sponsored by Poland that asked for the cessation of hostilities between India and Pakistan in the on-going war in East Pakistan. With his eye cocked on the audience in Pakistan, which he knew would see the televised proceedings of the Security Council meeting in New York, Bhutto tore up the Polish resolution and stormed out of the chamber. A few days later a grateful but humiliated nation turned to Zulfikar Ali Bhutto to lead them out of the chaos left by the civil war and to construct a new Pakistan.[7]

Bhutto was a clever politician but not a wise one. He followed the course that was taken later by Nawaz Sharif—he wanted to bring into his hands all the levers of power. He started with the military. The counter-coup of March 1972 involved the virtual kidnapping of Lieutenant General Gul Hassan, who was commanding the army, and Air Marshal Rahimuddin, who was the head of the air force. The two officials were brought to Bhutto's temporary residence on the pretext that they were to participate in a meeting, ushered into two waiting cars and driven to Lahore by Ghulam Mustafa Khar and Ghulam Mustafa Jatoi, two of the most trusted lieutenants of Zulfikar Ali Bhutto. While Hassan and Rahim were on their way to Lahore, Radio Pakistan announced that General Tikka Khan had taken over as the chief of army staff.[8] General Tikka was to stay in office for four years and was replaced by General Zia ul-Haq. This was the only time in the turbulent history of military-civil relations that a civilian leader was able to prevail over the leaders of the armed forces.

The next episode in this story was to occur on 5 July 1977 when General Zia ul-Haq, taking his cue from the intervention of General Yahya Khan, staged a coup against the regime of Zulfikar Ali Bhutto. Zia's move—as was the case with the move by Yahya Khan in 1969—was prompted by a deepening tension between Bhutto and his opponents. The impressive victory of the Pakistan People's Party in the elections of February 1977 was unexpected and therefore resented by the opposition. The opposition probably exaggerated, as oppositions are wont to do, the extent of the official bureaucracy's role in helping the PPP. The military intervened after months of street agitation by the opposition but the conflict between the military and the political forces did not end with the removal of Zulfikar Ali Bhutto from office on 5 July. It ended on 4 April 1979 when Bhutto, after having been sentenced to death by the Lahore High Court and after his appeal had been denied by the Supreme Court, was hanged in Rawalpindi's central jail.

In 1989, ten years after her father's execution, Prime Minister Benazir Bhutto tried to bring the military under her control. Her plan was to move General Aslam Beg, who had taken over as the chief of army staff after the death of General Zia in a plane crash on 17 August 1988, to the largely ceremonial position of the Chief of Joint Staffs (CJS). Admiral Iftikhar Sirhoey was the CJS at that time. The Prime Minister requested President Ghulam Ishaq Khan to make the appointments. The President, carefully reading the powers bestowed on him by the Eighth amendment, refused to accept the Prime Minister's advice. This led to what is generally known as the Sirhoey Affair (Burki, 1999b). Ishaq refused to oblige and Prime Minister Bhutto had to abandon the effort. It is believed that she wanted to replace General Aslam Beg with Imtiaz Ahmad, a retired army general who had served as the military secretary to her father while he was the Prime Minister.

The next clash between the military and the civilian authority occurred in the fall of 1998. Its protagonists were Prime Minister Nawaz Sharif and General Jehangir Karamat, Chief of Army Staff. Jehangir had spoken strongly about the poor performance of the Sharif government in terms of getting the economy to revive and reducing the level of violence among various groups who were shedding a great deal of blood settling ethnic or sectarian scores. The general's remarks, made at the Naval War

College at Lahore, attracted a great deal of comments both inside and outside Pakistan. Karamat's suggestion that the army should be formally inducted into the decision-making process did not sit well with the Prime Minister and his advisors. 'I had a difficult meeting at which we agreed that I will resign,' Jehangir told me in a conversation in Lahore in July 1999. The general was replaced by General Pervez Musharraf although it was widely known that General Khawaja Ziauddin would have been the Prime Minister's choice. Ziauddin was appointed, instead, to lead the Inter Services Intelligence (ISI), an agency staffed almost entirely by army personnel but responsible to the Prime Minister. The outcome of this episode was half a success—it was not complete since the army leadership was now alerted to the fact that the Prime Minister was inclined to move impetuously. This is the reason why the senior leaders of the armed forces were not prepared to accept another forced change in command when it was attempted in October 1999. When the Prime Minister moved, they were ready and implemented a plan for taking over the country's administration even when their commander was incommunicado, high up in the sky in a PIA plane *en route* to Karachi from Colombo. The Prime Minister could not be forgiven this time. In the words of Sahibzada Yaqub Khan, General Musharraf's emissary to the west, 'the Prime Minister tried to subvert the army's loyalty to the nation, subjecting it to political intrigue, attempting to murder the commander-in-chief.' (Safire, 1999).

An important question still remains unanswered. Having appointed General Pervez Musharraf in the fall of 1998 and having worked with him to restore law and order in the violence prone city of Karachi, and having also used a large number of army personnel to conduct the census and to collect bills for the Water and Power Development Authority—Pakistan's public power utility—why did the Prime Minister suddenly turn on General Musharraf? And why did the general, suspecting some move by the Prime Minister, prepare a counter-move that succeeded so well in putting the army back in the saddle without resulting in bloodshed and violence? Could the failed Kargil expedition in the disputed state of Kashmir be the reason for the souring of relations between the head of the government and the head of the armed forces?

The Kargil expedition was the brainchild of General Muhammad Aziz Khan, a close associate of General Musharraf. It was conceived to keep intact the public's trust in the army's ability to safeguard the national interest. Without such trust the army knew that the public's willingness to let the military claim such a large part of the country's budget would begin to dissipate. The army had been smarting for many years as the Indian army had improved its strategic position in northern Kashmir by constantly nibbling at the territory beyond the Line of Control (LOC). The LOC was the de facto border between the Pakistani and Indian held parts of Kashmir. It had been agreed upon by Prime Minister Zulfikar Ali Bhutto and Indira Gandhi at their summit held in Simla in 1973. The Indians fully expected that in course of time the LOC would become the international border between India and Pakistan in the area of Kashmir. However, the entire LOC had not been fully demarcated. The Indians had taken advantage of this ambiguity and had acquired some territory on the other side of the LOC. This included a large part of the Siachen Glacier. Pakistanis had fought back and the battle over the glacier had lasted for many years with a significant loss of life on both sides. Some time in the late winter and early spring of 1999, patrols mounted by the Pakistan army along the LOC discovered that the Indians left the high points of Kargil unoccupied during winter but came back to their positions when the snows melted. The Pakistanis saw an opportunity in this. They occupied the Kargil heights with the help of some *mujahideen* (freedom fighters). The *mujahideen* were involved to give the operation a sense of legitimacy since the Kashmiris had been fighting for a decade against the Indian occupation of their state. When the Indian forces returned they found the Kargil heights already occupied. A bitter battle ensued. The Pakistanis were surprised by the ferocity of the Indian response; the Indians used everything they had at their command—fighter aircraft, helicopter gun ships, heavy artillery—to punish the Kargil intruders. A nervous world—made more nervous by the fact that only a year before the two countries had tested nuclear weapons—watched the battle of Kargil escalate. It was only after an unexpected visit by Prime Minister Nawaz Sharif to Washington on 4 July 1999 and a three-hour meeting with President Bill Clinton that Pakistan acknowledged the involvement of its regular troops in the Kargil operation. Once it took that step, it was in a position to promise withdrawal from Kargil. The only comfort Pakistan received in return for the Kargil withdrawal was the promise by President Bill Clinton that he would get personally involved in finding a solution to the Kashmir problem.

Prime Minister Nawaz Sharif returned to an unhappy Pakistan after signing the 4 July declaration. His spinmeister, by suggesting that the Prime Minister's courageous visit to Washington had pulled Pakistan from the brink to which the trigger-happy generals had taken the country, created enormous tension between the civilian and military leaders. The army did not like to be blamed for what the Pakistani press had come to call the Kargil fiasco. Its continuing claim on resources was contingent on people's trust and confidence. It could not afford to lose these. The claims by the Prime Minister's associates and counter-claims by the army high command made it clear that the two sides were on a collision course. General Musharraf made a statement to the press in August that he was going to serve his full term of three years, until December 2001. It was a strange statement since, according to the constitution, the military chiefs served at the pleasure of the civil authority. Nawaz Sharif ignored the obvious implication in the General's statement. He appointed him, instead, to yet another job, that of the Chief of Joint Staffs. In retrospect, it is clear that this appointment was to win the Prime Minister some time before his next move.

The military take over of 12 October 1999 was not entirely unexpected nor criticized in the country but it was not treated with great warmth outside. The Pakistani army had challenged the belief that democracy, no matter how faulty it was, remained the best system. Editorial commentary in the United States and in the United Kingdom took cognizance of the political and economic mess created by the administration of Prime Minister Nawaz Sharif but condemned the general's move. The Commonwealth —a collection of fifty-four nations that were once affiliated to Great Britain, most of them as colonies—went to the extent of suspending Pakistan's membership and by withdrawing its invitation for the biennial summit which was held in Durban, South Africa. India, Pakistan's nemesis, would have liked the Commonwealth to go further. It pressed for reprisals but on the eve of the summit, there was consensus forming among the major players that no further punitive action was required.

The situation in Pakistan posed a real dilemma for the people who wished to see the world unambiguously subscribe to the notion of governance by democracy. As *The Times* (London) put it in an editorial: 'The easing of pressure on Pakistan marks Commonwealth awareness of the uncomfortable truth that its current rules on what constitutes democracy are inadequate. Pakistan's ousted civilian Government was elected, and therefore automatically deemed a worthy Commonwealth member. Yet it behaved in an outrageous fashion, suppressing the very things— press freedom and judicial independence—that democratic governments are prepared to encourage. By contrast, the country's current leader, General Pervez Musharraf is not elected; yet his pledge to uproot corruption, calm religious strife, and restore democratic freedoms are believed at home, making him more popular than his predecessor.' (*Times*, 1999)

While General Musharraf and his colleagues won the first round, they found themselves on a slippery slope once they decided to begin proceedings against the deposed Prime Minister. By the time the commonwealth heads of state met at Durban on 12–13 November 1999, the western world was not prepared to shed too many tears at the demise of a highly corrupt democracy whose institutions had been thoroughly mutated to serve a small group of people who had Pakistan's political system in their strong grip. This grip had to be loosened but not by replacing one type of authoritarianism with another variety. The rule of law administered by a set of institutions that had the confidence of all people, and not dominated by a few groups of influential persons, was the only way to get Pakistan out of the difficult situation in which it found itself half a century after its birth. The western powers were prepared to give General Musharraf the benefit of the doubt when he dispatched Prime Minister Sharif in a bizarre set of circumstances. However, when the announcement came out of Islamabad on 10 November that Nawaz Sharif and some of his associates were to be tried on charges that could carry the death penalty, the west's nervousness increased once more. Sharif was accused of 'hijacking and kidnapping for what military officials said was his treasonous refusal to allow a plane carrying the army chief to land in the port city of Karachi.' (Dugger, 1999). He was to be tried by a specially constituted court. Western concerns were articulated unambiguously once the announcement was made from Islamabad. Robin Cook, the British Foreign Secretary, warned that 'a show trial will do nothing to encourage confidence that the military genuinely intends to restore democracy. Mr. Sharif must have proper representation in an open trial, observed by the international community.' The same sort of sentiment was expressed by Washington. 'We have continued to raise our concerns with Pakistan authorities about former Prime Minister Sharif's well being and our concern that he be accorded due process,' said James Foley, a US State Department spokesman.[9]

By putting Nawaz Sharif on trial, was General Musharraf following the long established practice in Pakistan of blaming all the ills on the government that had fallen or had been forced out of office? In October 1958, General Ayub Khan included in his martial law proclamation a long list of misdeeds by the civilian governors that preceded him. The same approach was followed by Yahya Khan when he took over from Ayub Khan in March 1969, when Zulfikar Ali Bhutto took over from the military in December 1971, when Zia ul-Haq displaced Zulfikar Ali Bhutto in July 1977, and when five prime ministers, all of them popularly elected, were either fired by the presidents under the cover of the constitution or—as was the second removal of Nawaz Sharif in October 1999—sent packing by yet another military intervention, the fourth in the country's history. Or was the general aiming at discrediting the established oligarchy that governed for so long by refusing to broaden the political base and by not allowing the creation of modern institutions? Was the military leader undertaking a thorough cleansing of the old systems in order to create space to accommodate the social and economic forces that had been kept outside for three decades?

An important point needs to be emphasized for all the forced changes in governments in the last forty years, from 1958 to 1999. With the exception of the changes in October 1958, July 1977, and October 1999—all three involving the military—all other changes in administrations were in the nature of sibling rivalries. Benazir Bhutto's quarrel with Nawaz Sharif, and his with her, was not on account of ideological differences or because of the pursuit of interests and objectives that could not be reconciled. Put bluntly, the quarrel was about who controlled the family's assets. The change over from Ayub Khan to Yahya Khan was also of the same nature.

As against these, the three military interventions—those in 1958, 1977, and 1999—constituted serious attempts at social engineering. They sought to broaden the political base and close the great socio-economic-political divide. The authors of these changes may not have recognized what they were attempting to accomplish. That was certainly the case with President Zia ul-Haq.[10] Ayub Khan had intervened in part to bring political power into the hands of the indigenous groups who had completely lost out to the bureaucratic, industrial and business groups dominated by the *muhajir* community. By the time Zia ul-Haq moved against Zulfikar Ali Bhutto, the political pendulum had swung too far in the direction of the landed aristocracy and tribal chiefs. The middle class—the *shurafaa* (those who respected family values) as I called them in an earlier book (Burki 1989)—found that they had little place left for them in the political system. That had happened in spite of the palpable increase in the number of people who could be counted as belonging to the middle classes and the amount of economic wealth controlled by them. Zia's intervention was an implicit effort to bridge the great divide that had developed between those who had political power (the old, rural based leaders) and those who commanded both social influence and economic wealth (the several components of the middle classes, many of whom had acquired great economic wealth on account of the pronounced changes that had taken place in the economy over the last several decades).

An efficiently performing political system assures that social groups as they gather strength find a place within the structure of politics. However, as even foreign observers recognize, Pakistan's political system was not functioning well; it did not have the elasticity demanded of all resilient structures. By the fall of 1999, the socio-political divide had widened to such an extent that the military was once again 'required' to intervene. I use the word 'required' advisedly; I don't believe the takeover of October 1999 by the military was on account of the commander's ambition. He was forced to act on account of the rapid unfolding of events on 12 October 1999.

The Sharif case will not only be one of the several touchstones the world will use to judge the initial intention and the eventual performance of the Sharif regime. It will also indicate whether the new rulers of the country were finally prepared to start the slow, difficult but highly necessary process of institution building in the country. This was recognized by several observers who watched the developments in Pakistan with intense interest. 'How this case is handled is a real and important test for the general,' wrote the influential *Financial Times* in an editorial. 'For too long, it seems that governments in Pakistan have lived above the law. Real change means that they must set an example of living within it. It is doubly incumbent on a regime that has taken power by undemocratic means to set high standards of governance.' (*Financial Times*, 1999). In other words, the question being asked was whether General Musharraf and his colleagues will succeed in finally bridging the gap that had grown between those who dominated the political structure and those who possessed a great deal of social and economic power.

What could General Musharraf do in the next few months and will he succeed? This question is answered in the last part of this Chapter. It looks at the agenda of economic reforms the new administration should follow to do more than only revive the economy. They need an economic agenda of the type described below in order to broaden the political base as well.

D. An Agenda for Economic Reforms to Restore Political Equilibrium

Psychiatrists tell us that the patients who recognize that they are ill are half way down the road to recovery. A bit of medicine and a great deal of counsel takes them the rest of the way. Could the same criterion be applied to nations? If so, Pakistan should have been on the path to recovery for some time. After all, for more than a decade, we have talked unabashedly and at considerable length about our afflictions.

The trend started with President Ghulam Ishaq Khan, who issued two orders of dismissal of prime ministers, both elected by a restored democracy. The Presidential Order of 1993 that dismissed Prime Minister Nawaz Sharif covered virtually the same ground and provided more or less the same list of misdeeds as the order of August 1990 that dispatched Prime Minister Benazir Bhutto from office. It was clear that Mr Sharif had not learnt much from the fall of Ms Bhutto.

This failure to learn from history was even more puzzling on the part of Ms Bhutto who, in November 1996, was sent packing by a president who, once upon a time, was a friend and a loyal supporter. The Presidential Order of 1996 could have been written by the same scribe who produced the orders of 1990 and 1993. President Leghari accused Prime Minister Bhutto of the same economic crimes attributed to her six years earlier by President Ghulam Ishaq Khan. And then, in October 1999, Prime

Minister Nawaz Sharif's second term in office ended not with a presidential order for dismissal—for such a thing was not allowed by the amended Constitution—but by a military proclamation. General Pervez Musharraf's list of accusations was issued in more stark terms. They were probably not drafted by a legal hand but by those whose patience had clearly run out.

General Musharraf found the economy in a state of collapse, the country's institutions destroyed. In a later and more detailed address to the nation, he found the country faced with a grim crisis. It had hit the bottom and had to be brought back to the surface, he told the nation and the world.

If so many senior leaders of Pakistan have been so acutely aware of the country's problems, why have they not succeeded in finding a solution? The public has done its bit; it has laboured hard to make democracy work. The people have gone to the polls four times in the past-decade, each time with the hope that the representatives they sent to the national and provincial legislatures would work to improve the lives of citizens. Each time the people were disappointed. In 1988, 1990 and 1993 they split their mandate between two political parties, not ready to place all power in the hands of one politician and one political party. This was an understandable reaction to long years of dictatorship. In 1997, they reversed themselves. Troubled by corruption in the divided national and provincial legislatures, as votes were bought and sold for money, the people returned the Muslim League with a massive majority in the national legislature and in the Punjab assembly. There was an expectation that the leaders of the Muslim League, provided with a stable political environment in which to operate, would concentrate their attention on solving the country's economic and social problems. These problems were becoming more acute by the passing of each day and threatened to bring about the collapse of the economy. The Sharif government turned a blind eye towards the economy, persuaded that it had first to consolidate itself politically. In doing so, it hastened its own collapse, if not that of the economy.

This dismal record leads one to ask the obvious question: why has democracy failed so miserably in Pakistan? Why have democratic institutions failed to serve people? Why has democracy not succeeded in setting Pakistan on the course to economic prosperity? The answers to these questions can be provided only after a careful study of Pakistan's history.

However, before pointing to the lessons that we should draw from history, it would be appropriate to dispel one notion: that Pakistan's economy does better under the management of the military. Such an impression is created by a comparison of the rates of growth in gross domestic product (GDP) during the days the military was in power with the growth rates achieved by political managers of the economy. In 1960–70, the average annual growth rate was 6.7 per cent. With the population increasing at the rate of 3 per cent a year, the period of Ayub Khan ended in 1969 with an average Pakistani 44 per cent richer than he (and she) was in 1958. The annual rate of growth was a little lower during the Zia ul-Haq years (1977–1988) with the GDP having increased by 6.3 per cent and per capita income growing at the rate of 3.5 per cent. By the end of the Zia period, an average Pakistani's income had increased by 41 per cent.

These were impressive gains but they do not necessarily point to the superiority of military management. During the periods of military domination, Pakistan had access to large amounts of concessional foreign capital flows. That had happened because of the strong links the governments of Presidents Ayub Khan and Zia ul-Haq had forged with the United States. If anything, the availability of foreign finance during these two periods delayed the much-needed structural change in the economy. This delay in transforming the economic structure also inhibited the modernization of the political system.

Let me now return to history, some of which was covered in Sections B and C. It has become customary in Pakistan for an incoming regime to blame the one it has replaced for the country's ills. This kind of criticism goes well with the people who, by the time the change occurs, have become thoroughly disenchanted with the people in power. But the frequent changes among the people who have governed political affairs has led to an excessive preoccupation with the present, with very little attention paid either to the past or to the future. This is unfortunate. It should be recognized that the basic problems the country faces today have been around for a long time—they have certainly been in evidence from the time of the country's birth and will remain if no attempt is made to bring about structural changes in both political and economic systems. It is my belief that the change must begin simultaneously in both economics and politics. Both the political and economic systems must be reformed at the same time. Moving on the two rails at the same time will generate the momentum that is needed. It is necessary for the military regime that is now in control to recognize this important point.

One important insight history provides is that Pakistan never fully developed the social and political environment in which democratic institutions could work and evolve. Democracy was forced on a social structure which was thoroughly undemocratic, dominated as it was by large landlords and tribal chiefs. The immensely powerful tribal chieftains and the landed aristocracy mutated the political system to work for their benefit rather than become representative of the people at large. That is the reason why these forces would not allow population censuses to be conducted at regular intervals. Had that been done and constituencies appropriately re-demarcated, the focus of power in the national and provincial legislatures would have begun to shift from the countryside and move towards the rapidly expanding towns and cities.

There was an expectation in 1997 that such a shift would occur. The Muslim League had won a massive victory under the direction of urban leaders, and they could finally challenge the rural oligarchy that had governed the country since the mid-1960s—since the days of Nawab Kalabagh. The Sharif brothers and some of their close associates were from the urban areas. They were also fully aware of the contamination of the political system by the social values to which the tribal chiefs and landlords subscribed. It came as a surprise to most of the people who had voted the Muslim League back to power when its leaders continued to govern in the same way as had the landlords and *waderas*. The election of February 1997 did not bring about a change in the country's social structure and is the reason why the demise of the Sharif regime was treated with such relief by most people.

If this diagnosis of our political system is correct then the first order of business for the new rulers is to take steps to reform and overhaul it. For a system to be credible with the people it must allow them a sense of participation and must cater more fully to their aspirations. The system that evolved since the restoration of democracy, however, suffered from many problems. It was not representative of all segments of the society and it was very distant from the people. In recent years economists have begun to recognize the importance of economic decision-making that is fully participatory. They have also begun to focus on bringing government closer to the people. A re-engineered political system must, therefore, be fully representative and must provide for the devolution of power from the center to sub-national levels. These changes are essential for the revival and recovery of the country's economy and, at the same time, for maintaining social and political stability.

One important structural change that is needed for overhauling both the political and economic systems concerns the distribution of land. In spite of three efforts at land reform in the late 1950s and the 1970s, asset distribution in Sindh and South Punjab remains extremely skewed. This needs to be corrected. Only with a significant redistribution of land in these two parts of the country will Pakistan succeed in modernizing its political structure and lay the base for the commercialization of agriculture. Land reforms need not necessarily involve expropriation of large landholdings. In fact, reforms based on expropriation can be expensive and difficult to manage. There are other ways of handling this problem. Market–based land distribution is being implemented successfully in Brazil, with large landlords encouraged to sell their holdings to a land bank which sells them back to small land-holders and peasants. Those acquiring land are given credit on easy terms and are also provided with technical assistance to improve agricultural productivity. This is an approach that the new government would do well to study and implement if found practical for conditions in Pakistan.

Let me now turn to the restructuring of the economy.[11] There are several structural problems in the way Pakistan's economy functions that need to be resolved quickly. Four of these need immediate attention. They are a very low rate of domestic savings, a low level of human development, poor quality of institutions, and a state that has become increasingly dysfunctional. None of these structural weaknesses appeared overnight, or over the last decade. Pakistan was born with them and continues to live with them. Some of them became acute over time but their roots are to be found in history. As such, to take these roots out will require time and a great deal of political energy. Some of them can be attended to only if the political system is restructured; some of them will contribute to the overhaul of the political system itself.

First,[15] the problem of persistent low rates of domestic savings. That the Muslims of India saved little and spent a great deal was recognized by the British administrators who governed the part of the subcontinent that is today's Pakistan. Malcolm Darling (Darling, 1934), in his seminal work on the peasantry of Punjab, worried about this problem and explained how the Muslim agricultural class was becoming progressively indebted to Hindu moneylenders. Kingsley Davis (Davis 1943), in the report on the population census of 1941, noted the difference in the saving habits of Hindus and Muslims in Punjab and Sindh, and attributed the relative backwardness of the Muslim population to its extreme extravagance.

This propensity to spend and not save would have translated into low rates of investment—and hence a low rate of economic growth—had foreign capital flows not come into the country in generous amounts. Over its first fifty-two years, Pakistan had received about $150 billion of foreign capital (measured in today's prices). Of this some $55 billion, or 37 per cent of the total, came in by way of the remittances sent by the Pakistanis living abroad, $75 billion (50 per cent) as foreign aid, $26 billion as bank borrowings, and $14 billion as foreign direct investment. In other words, 87 per cent of the amount that came into the country from abroad was accounted for by foreign aid and workers' remittances. Both sources of finance have virtually dried up now and the country has become increasingly dependent on commercial finance. This is why Pakistan is now so heavily indebted to foreign creditors and why a significant amount of export earning is being spent on servicing external debt. But for as long as non-debt creating foreign flows are not forthcoming, Pakistan will have to rely on expensive commercial flows. This type of finance will be available only if the country is seen to be creditworthy. Currently, Pakistan has the lowest credit ranking of any country evaluated by the rating agencies.

The country's new economic managers, therefore, confront a Herculean task. They face two challenges: one immediate and the other long-term. The immediate can be addressed by strategic planning; the long-term problem will need a change in the political structure. The immediate problem is posed by the large debt-overhang. Servicing of debt does not leave enough resources to invest in development. Pakistan needs a breathing space which it may get from its creditors if it is able to convince them that the country has finally begun to address the structural problems it has brushed under the carpet for so long. Pakistan may be able to get some kind of debt relief in exchange for a well-formulated program of structural reforms. The longer-term problem concerns a very low rate of domestic savings. In order to revive growth, Pakistanis must increase investment. In order to increase investment, they must increase domestic savings. But a low level of domestic savings is embedded in their culture. What are the options available to them?

My suggestion would be to proceed simultaneously along three parallel tracks: generate savings in the public sector, create institutions to encourage private savings, and invite long term investment capital from overseas Pakistanis.

To get the public sector to become a net saver will require a number of difficult decisions including reducing the burden of public debt, constraining military expenditure, downsizing the government, and raising tax revenues. There are many assets on the books of the state that can be—and should be—privatized. The receipts from privatization should be used for writing down government debt. The military leaders should be encouraged to reflect on how they can adequately defend the country while reducing defense expenditure. Non-development public expenditure needs to be curtailed by reducing—if not altogether eliminating—subsidies on the provision of services and supply of goods and commodities. The size of the government also needs to be reduced quite dramatically. The proliferation of ministries and departments at the central and provincial levels has resulted in an explosion in the number of government employees. By rationalizing the distribution of responsibility between the center and the provinces, by privatizing public sector corporations and by out-sourcing to the private sector some of the functions performed by the state, it should be possible to reduce government expenditures.

There are powerful constituencies that have stood in the way of doing any one of these four things. Privatization has been opposed by the workers employed by public sector agencies, many of whom will lose their jobs once these agencies move into private hands. Just to take one example, Pakistan International Airlines has one of the largest employee-to-plane ratios in the airline industry. Placed under private management, there is no doubt that thousands of PIA employees will lose their jobs. That will also happen with the privatization of commercial banks, investment banks, public utilities, gas companies, the Water and Power Development Authority, the Railways, etc. Only a government that has the confidence of the working class—such as the government headed by Carlos Menem in Argentina—could deliver such a shock. The Menem government carried out massive privatization that resulted in larger-scale lay-offs since it had very close links with the labor movement in the country. The same is true of government downsizing since that too will result in the loss of jobs by tens of thousands of people. The two Bhutto and the two Sharif governments, dominated by the landed aristocracy and economic oligarchs, did not have the political will or the nerve to undertake privatization and a reduction in the size of the government. Had they done so they would have inflicted pain on the classes that were excluded from the political system.

Pakistan has had a problem raising tax revenues for a variety of reasons, some of them political and some related to poor public sector management. Only 1.1 million people out of a population of 140 million are on the tax rolls. The powerful landed aristocracy has not allowed agricultural income to be taxed. Small businesses and the service sector, not represented in the political system for the reasons described in Section A, could not be persuaded to come on the tax role. 'No taxation without representation,' held for these classes.

Finally, a reduction in expenditure on the military also involved complex political issues. The long-term conflict with India had made military expenditures subject to little political scrutiny. No government headed by a civilian authority had the courage to confront the military on budgetary issues. The political base of all democratic governments—with the possible exception of the one headed by Zulfikar Ali Bhutto and that also for a very brief period—was too narrow to give it the confidence to face down the armed forces.

Reform of the financial sector and development of capital markets should provide instruments to attract private savings. A number of developing countries have allowed the private sector to set up pension funds. Properly regulated, pension funds normally result in increasing private savings, particularly in the countries going through demographic transition. The census of 1998 suggests a significant reduction in fertility rates in the country, which means that households are now ready to save for old age rather than rely entirely on their children to provide this kind of security. They should be encouraged to use privately managed pension funds for saving for old age. Establishment of pension funds, in turn, will contribute to the development of capital markets.

But the part of the financial sector that needs immediate attention from the new set of policy-makers is commercial and investment banks. To the best of my knowledge, no country anywhere in the world has succeeded in reforming public sector banks by keeping them with the government. That was the reason why I, during my brief tenure as the finance chief in the interim government of 1996–97, established the Resolution Trust Corporation (RTC) for taking over the non-performing assets of the banking system and privatizing the cleaned-up banks. The Sharif Government that took office in 1997 chose not to take that route. The reason for this was the same as why Zulfikar Ali Bhutto had nationalized the banks in the first place: banks are the source of enormous patronage for clients and are, therefore, immensely useful for the regimes that have a very narrow social base. When it was elected in 1997, the Sharif government had a broad base but its instincts were those of the people who had presided over narrow systems. Accordingly, the Sharif government placed its faith in professional bankers' ability to reform the system, without placing it in private hands. By most accounts these managers were able to arrest the decay of the system but, for largely political reasons, they were not able to restore health to it. There were some $4 billion worth of bad loans on the books of the banks, equivalent to 7 per cent of the gross domestic product at the time of the military's intervention.

I have subsumed a great deal of the reform effort under the subject of increasing domestic savings. This way of looking at structural change underscores an important point—the linkages that exist among various components of an economic system. The same is true of the second cluster of proposed reforms— human development. So much has been written on this subject that I have the impression that it has now entered the mainstream of economic discourse in the country. It is now recognized that without a major effort in the fields of education and health, Pakistan will not be able to lift its economy out of the slump into which it has fallen. Empirical evidence from around the world points to the close relationship between the level of education and the health of the citizenry on the one hand and economic growth on the other. This relationship is particularly strong in the case of women. By educating women and improving their health, Pakistan will not only accelerate the recently noted decline in fertility and thus hasten demographic transition. They will also make it possible for women to contribute to economic growth. If the country continues to neglect the education and health of women—as it has done in the past—it will be condemning itself to perpetual backwardness.

Promoting education—once again particularly that of women—will have an enormous political payback. It will inevitably broaden the political system by making it difficult for the landed aristocracy and tribal chieftains to exercise total control over the people in their areas. Democracy's life-blood does not come from elections no matter how frequently they are held. That has become clear from Pakistan's experience since 1985, when its people have been called to the polls every two to three years. What gives life to a truly representative system is the flowering of civil society, but that cannot happen without education. Pakistan has a long way to go before it reaches that stage.

While the importance of primary education and basic health is now recognized in Pakistan and elsewhere in the developing world, it is equally essential to focus attention on the development of modern and sophisticated skills. As I pointed out in the article published in *Dawn* in which I compared Pakistan's performance with that of India, our neighbour has done extremely well in creating a software industry (Burki 1999e). The basis for India's extraordinary performance was laid in 1951 when Prime Minister Jawaharlal Nehru decided to establish six Indian Institutions of Technology (IIT). The IITs are behind the extraordinary performance of the Indian software industry. They have also contributed to the wealth of the Indian expatriate community in the United States. Pakistan has been left way behind in this area. Could it play catch up?

Pakistan could take the Indian route since it has demography on its side; it also has the language—English—which is the lingua franca of information technology. A crash program to train software and computer engineers launched with the help of the private sector should bring large dividends by making it possible for the country to participate in the on-going information technology revolution in the industrial world.

There is one other sector which holds great potential for a country in Pakistan's situation which should receive the government's attention. This is biotechnology, which is bringing about changes in the more advanced countries in the sectors of health and agriculture. Again, biotechnology—as in the case with information technology—is short of manpower and Pakistan, with a reasonably good infrastructure of medical colleges, could leapfrog into this area. A partnership with the private sector could lay the basis for turning out people with skills who will have a large market in the industrial world. By advocating attention to the development of information technology and biotechnology, I am advocating an approach that treats population as an asset to be developed for both domestic use and export. It will not take a great deal of public resources to produce these results as long as the private sector is prepared to come forward and make investments. What is required is a strong leadership commitment and a strong association with the private sector. Not only would such a strategy earn the country foreign capital, it will also develop close links between one part of the economy—the information sector—and the world outside. Such links are enormously helpful in the process of modernization. They change the indigenous culture and modernize it.

There are two aspects of the reforms I am advocating in the sector of education that should be underscored. One, they will cost more resources than the government has at its disposal at this time. Two, they call for a more prominent role for the private sector. At less than 3 per cent, Pakistan commits a smaller proportion of its gross domestic product to education than most developing countries. However, given the precarious nature of public finance, there cannot be a significant increase in the flow of government resources to tertiary and technical education. Therefore, resources available to the public sector will have to be more carefully deployed. Primary education and education of women are the two obvious areas of priority for government action. Without the possibility of a major increase in public expenditure, the country will have to turn to the private sector for taking care of other priorities, in particular improving the quality of secondary, tertiary, and technical education and making it available to a larger segment of the population.

This brings me to the question of the regulation of the private sector. How to make sure that private entrepreneurs get involved in education not just for turning a profit? How to get the private sector deliver social good even when it is pursuing profit? These questions are being asked in the country (*Dawn*, 1999) and need to be answered.

I don't believe the answer lies in government intervention. The right approach is to make the private sector regulate itself. An accreditation council should be set up in the private sector to provide certification to all institutions and, if possible, grade them on a scale of competence and excellence on the lines that credit agencies rank countries and enterprises. That way parents will know the quality of the institution to which they are sending their children. All institutions operating in the private sector should also be required to establish scholarship funds, which should receive deposits of a set proportion of the fees they collect. This fund should be used for aiding students whose families need assistance.

Institutional development is the third cluster of reforms that needs to be undertaken. There is awareness in the country that several generations of its leaders have allowed institutions to atrophy—even to die—all across the board. Wherever one looks one sees institutional graveyards, economic, political and social. The list of institutions that are dead or in decay is a long one. It includes the civil service, the police, the legal system, public sector colleges, universities, and hospitals; government regulatory agencies; public utility companies; public transport; and local government institutions. These and other modern institutions were killed by the governing elite for they offered a challenge to their exercise of total authority. It did not suit Kalabagh, the Bhuttos, nor the Sharif brothers to have their power constrained. By attacking these institutions, these political leaders inflicted a heavy economic cost on the country. Economists now understand that institutions are important for promoting development and for distributing the fruits of growth equitably among different segments of the society. Dysfunctional institutions impose a heavy cost on the economy and the society. Institutions that work will reduce transaction costs and add to economic efficiency. A society with a poor institutional base is inefficient and, often, corrupt. Pakistan obviously belongs to the latter category.

Institutional reconstruction is a long-term task but a start needs to be made. Pakistan cannot let the decay of the last three decades to continue. The new leaders should begin by setting in place institutions to guide the economy towards efficiency. Banks, insurance companies, public utilities, public transport, the state airline, and airports should be put in the hands of the private sector. At the same time, public sector regulatory agencies should be organized to oversee the private sector in all these areas. The regulatory agencies should work within a strictly defined framework and should be staffed by well-paid and well-trained people.

The state must give up the assets it cannot manage efficiently and without corrupting its officials. A massive program of privatization should be launched and its scope should not be limited for reasons of keeping the state involved in what are sometimes described as 'strategic interests.' Concerns about privatization have been articulated in the past mostly by the people who have vested interests in keeping assets and enterprises in the hands of the government. It is understandable why workers employed in state enterprises would oppose privatization. It is also understandable why bureaucrats managing these entities do not want to see them transferred to private owners. The opposition of these groups has been effective in the past but should not be allowed to stop a movement in that direction.

The fourth set of problems that the new administration must face and deal with urgently concerns a state that has ceased to provide even the most basic functions to its citizens. In a recent article published by *The Globe and Mail*, a Canadian newspaper, the author describes Pakistan as 'the dysfunctional adolescent of South Asia—a dysfunctional teenager with a gun.' (Stackhouse 1999). Such descriptions abound in the western press. There is an urgent need to re-establish Pakistan's dignity in the eyes of the international community.

What has made Pakistan—once a pride performer in the developing world—earn such epithets, such ridicule? The answer is a simple but depressing one; it has been the main theme of this discourse on the country's history. For three decades, the apparatus of the state was dominated by leaders and leadership groups whose principal interest was self-perpetuation and plunder rather than providing service to the people. That having been said, there is little to be gained by dwelling on the past. The need of the moment is to think about the future. This thinking must include the design of a new 'state' for Pakistan.

As in the case of other clusters of the reform effort—in increasing savings and generating domestic resources for development, in developing the quality of human resources, in revitalizing the economy's institutional base—the work on reforming the state will also have to proceed simultaneously on several fronts. I have already mentioned some aspects of the reform effort in this area when I discussed the first three clusters. Let me now deal with some other issues that have not received much attention in the on-going debate in the country.

First and foremost, a serious effort should be made to move as much of the government as possible out of Islamabad and relocate it in the provinces and districts. There is a good economic case for breaking up the provinces into smaller administrative units. These will be more manageable and economically more efficient. Punjab could be split into four provinces, Sindh into three, and the Frontier and Baluchistan into two each. Karachi and Lahore could be administered separately as cities with the status of provinces on the lines of

Beijing and Shanghai in China. Likewise, a system of local government with powers to tax and spend should be established with elections held on a regular basis. This may also be a good time to transfer such services as primary education, basic health, policing, and management of local road networks to local bodies.

Second, a well functioning government has many roles to play. It has to be active on many fronts. In a developing country—in particular for a country such as Pakistan, which has lost the growth momentum—it must act to activate the economy. This should be done by creating the right environment within which the private sector must work. The private sector must also reform its institutional structure. The various Chambers of Industry and Commerce are active in protecting the privileges they have been granted over time by the government. They do little to improve the competitiveness of their members. In comparison, the Federation of Indian Chambers of Commerce and Industry has played a significant role in advancing the technological base of their members. The FICCI has acquired PROBE, a software developed by the London Business School in conjunction with the Confederation of Business Industry, which has data on the technical competence of leading European enterprises. The FICCI is using this information to develop a benchmark to compare the performance of the Indian industry against it.

Third, the state in Pakistan must move expeditiously to improve two real sectors of the economy—agriculture and industry. In both sectors, lack of government attention has resulted in running down the asset base. Agriculture, once the mainstay of the Pakistani economy, is no longer pulling its weight. Averaging about 5 per cent a year in the first half of the decade, growth of agricultural output has declined to an average 1.4 per cent in 1997–99, one-half of the rate of increase in population. There are two consequences of the loss of growth momentum of this vital sector. It adds to rural poverty, pushing more and more people into the already crowded cities. It also increases the country's dependence on foreign suppliers of such important commodities as wheat and oil-seeds.

Of the many roles the state could play in reviving agriculture, two are very important: re-establishing the productivity of the vast network of irrigation, and two, improving the capacity to undertake crop research. Both functions were given a very low priority by a long series of past administrations. This needs to be reversed. The government needs to launch a crash program for the revival of agriculture which should center around the rehabilitation of the irrigation network, provision of quality input (seeds and chemicals) and market prices for agricultural output. The possibility of launching a large rural public works with the twin aims of rehabilitating rural infrastructure (irrigation channels, roads and bridges) should be investigated by the government.

Similarly, the administration that has taken office now should assign a higher priority to industrial revival. The ownership of industry must remain in private hands. However, a significant part of Pakistan's industrial assets, created with the help of public sector banks, remains idle and is often referred to as 'sick.' Some numbers will help to clarify the picture. There are more than 2000 sick industrial units spread across fifteen industrial sub-sectors. Some 920 of these units are large but only half of these can be revived. Of the 448 units that could be brought back to production, 284 were operating on 31 December 1998. Nearly two-thirds of sick industrial textile units have some potential, while only 10 per cent of those producing sugar have any life left in them. The point I wish to emphasize here is that a concerted effort needs to be made by the state to get the non-performing industrial assets back on track. To do this will need the involvement of the owners of these units, the banks to whom they owe money, people with higher levels of technical skills that would be required to upgrade and restructure the units, and government functionaries who understand the role industry must play in reviving the economy.

Before concluding this section, I would like to refer to one other neglected function of the state—upgrading the technical base of the economy. Once again, some numbers will help to underscore this point. In 1990—the last year for which this kind of information is available—expenditure on research and development (R&D) in Pakistan was only 0.3 per cent of the country's GDP. At 1.1 of GDP, India was making an effort four times as large as that of Pakistan. Pakistan could count only 6,626 scientists, engineers and technicians involved in R&D compared with 128,000 in India. Put another way, Pakistan had 54 science and technology persons for every one million of its population, compared with 142 for India, 173 for Sri Lanka, 3078 for Singapore, and 2645 for Korea. The numbers tell a depressing picture. Pakistan has fallen way behind East Asia and has a long way to go before it catches up with its South Asian neighbours.

E. Conclusion

To sum up, this is now the time to both diagnose the country's economic and political ills and to find cures for them. There are a number of areas that need action—urgent action—but this should be launched on the basis of a thoughtful analysis of what has gone wrong and how it can be put right. Any concerted action to bring about change should also look at the short-term costs of moving forward. There is enough experience around the globe to indicate how some of the pain—especially for the more vulnerable segments of the society—can be taken out from the effort to reform the economy. The scope of the effort required is considerably larger than the one undertaken by President Ayub Khan in 1958–62. Pakistan's problems had not then reached the stage where they are today. Ayub Khan established a number of commissions to report to him on a variety of structural issues. The present government could take the same route. It could, for instance, set up commissions in the four clusters of reforms identified in these articles—savings and domestic resource generation, human development, re-establishing the institutional base, and redefining the role of the state. These four areas cover a wide area and there is also some overlap in the ground covered. This is as it should be since it is not possible to neatly compartmentalize issues and problems in economics. If this is the route to follow then the new administration should have the courage to implement the programs the commissions will develop. That was the problem with the approach followed by Ayub Khan. By the time his commissions reported back to him, he had become a captive of a number of vested interests who were not interested in bringing about change. The military government of today should not let its degrees of freedom be reduced once again.

As pointed out repeatedly in this analysis, politics, economics and social change proceed in step. The failure to move in one or two of these fields produces disequilibrium which cannot be sustained. For most of its history, Pakistan has had to deal with these disequilibria. For most of the time the leadership groups sought to block the development of the political system while the country's social structure was being transformed. For some of the time, Pakistan's economy also moved fast creating wealth in the hands of the people who sought accommodation in the political system. They were denied this and that is why, without exception, they welcomed change as an unpopular regime was dispensed with by constitutional means or by the periodic intervention of the army into the country's political life.

References

Burki, Shahid Javed. 1999a. 'Crisis in Pakistan: a Diagnosis of its Causes and an Economic 'Approach for Resolving It'. Islamabad: Pakistan Institute of Development Economics.

————, 1999b. *A Historical Dictionary of Pakistan*. Lanham, Md.: Scarecrow Press.

————, 1999c. *Changing Perceptions and Altered Realities*. Washington, D.C.: The World Bank.

————, 1999d. *Pakistan: Fifty Years of Nationhood* Boulder, Colo.: Westview Press.

————, 1999e. 'Have We Lost the Race' *Dawn*, 12 September 1999 and 13 September 1999.

————, 1980. *Pakistan under Bhutto*. London: Macmillan.

Darling, Malcolm. 1978. *The Punjab Peasant in Prosperity and Debt*. Columbia, Mo.: South Asia Books.

Davis, Kingsley. 1943. *Indian Population, 1941: Punjab*. New Delhi: Government Printing.

Dawn, 1999. 'COAS records speech at Corps Headquarters' 13 October 1999.

Dawn, (Karachi), 'Free with university charters,' 28 October 1999.

Dugger, Celia W. 'Sharif faces charges of hijacking in Pakistan: Military cites refusal to let general's plane land, risking 200 lives,' *International Herald Tribune*, 12 November p. 1.

Durrani, Tehmina. 1998. *Blasphemy*. Lahore: Ferozsons Press.

Financial Times (London), 'Pakistan on Trial' November 12, 1999.

Hassan, Lieutenant General Gul. 1993. *Memoirs*. Karachi: Oxford University Press.

Khan, Muhammad Ayub. 1967. *Friends not Masters: A Political Autobiography*.

Niazi, Lieutenant General A.A.K. 1998. *The Betrayal of East Pakistan*. Karachi: Oxford University Press.

Safire, William. 1999. 'The Patience to Foster Democracy,' *International Herald Tribune* 9 November p. 8.

Salik, Siddiq. 1977. *Witness to Surrender*. Karachi: Oxford University Press.

Stackhouse, John. 1999. 'Pakistan: a dysfunctional adolescent' *The Globe and Mail*, Toronto, 15 October 1999.

Times, The (London). 1999. 'Pakistan on trial,' 12 November 1999.

Zaheer, Hasan, 1994. *The Separation of East Pakistan: The Rise and Realization of Bengali Muslim Nationalism*. Karachi: Oxford University Press.

Ziauddin, Muhammad Ihtasham ul Haque. 1999. 'Musharraf hints at referendum,' *Dawn*, 2 November 1999.

NOTES

1. When I refer to Pakistan I mean the country that goes by that name today. Bangladesh—erstwhile East Pakistan—is not included in this discussion.

2. I used this term for the first time in my first book on Pakistan (Burki 1980).

3. I explored the impact of the migration to the Middle East on the Pakistani economy in a number of articles published in the late 1980s. *See*, Burki (1984, 1986, 1988).

4. *The New York Times* provided a detailed account of the events surrounding the plane episode. *See*, Celia, W. Dugger 'Coup in Pakistan: the Overview' 13 October 1999.

5. General Musharraf's interview was carried by most Pakistani newspapers. *See*, for instance, *Dawn*, 7 November 1999.

6. The quote is from a conversation between President Farooq Leghari and the author in Lahore in November 1998.

7. The fall of East Pakistan and the emergence of Bangladesh as an independent country has received a fair amount of attention in Pakistan. Of the many people who made contributions to the analysis of this subject the more notable ones are Niazi, 1998; Sadik, 1986, and Zaheer, 1996.

8. The best source of this incident is the autobiography of Lieutenant General Gul Hassan published in 1996. (Hassan 1996).

9. Both quotes are from stories by Dugger (1999).

10. When I presented him my view that one reason why he chose to throw Bhutto out was his fear of the total eclipse of middle class social values by the value system of the landed aristocracy, Zia's response was that he had not thought of it in those terms but had no problem in accepting that this fear may have been in his sub-conscious. *See*, Burki (1989).

11. I have written previously on this subject for *Dawn* (Burki 1999e).

7

An Uncivil Society: The Role of Shadow Privatization, Conflict and Ideology in the Governance of Pakistan

Omar Noman

Pakistan's recent economic performance is not determined by economic policy. Indeed, amongst the many influences shaping the economy, the direct impact of economic policy is negligible. This is so because the environment within which economic policy is embedded is disturbed by a dysfunctional social structure. Economic policy instruments cannot function, and do not have the desired consequences, if the wider governance framework is not conducive to economic development. Three elements of this *political economy*, or *governance*, in the current development parlance, are shaping the economy. These are: (i) *Persistent conflict* (ii) *Shadow privatization and* (iii) *Ideological distortions*. Collectively, as will be discussed below, this triumvirate is manifested in an institutional catharsis and a breakdown in social trust, inimical to economic development.

These underlying factors are examined in the third part of this chapter, after the first and second section examine Pakistan's economy in a changing international environment, and provide a summary of recent economic performance, respectively. The final section provides prescriptions within which civil society can prosper.

A. Pakistan–US Relations in a Changing International Environment

A visit to Pakistan reveals the ubiquitous presence of the Bretton Woods institutions. Almost all prices of common interest appear to be influenced by them, ranging from electricity to bread, which depend on negotiations related to the subsidies given to utility companies or to agriculture. Virtually all public spending appears to require the approval of the World Bank and/or the IMF. All governments send their delegations to Washington D.C. A ritual of pleading, begging for understanding and the announcement of each agreement as an endorsement of the economy's health follows. Prime Ministers frequently refer the press to such World Bank-IMF support as an indicator that they are managing the economy well. All of the above convey a sense of lack of autonomy, a loss of sovereignty and reinforces perceptions, amongst some, that Pakistan's economy is governed from the outside.

A visit to Washington suggests a very different and more complex picture. For simplicity, one can divide perceptions towards Pakistan into two broad categories. The first views the country as a 'failed state', a country that is already ungovernable with the future promising further disintegration. Pakistan is viewed as having a potentially dangerous alliance with the Taliban and, as a result, the US's post-Cold War interests would dictate a wider strategic concern in South Asia. Thus Washington's interest in Pakistan has shifted away from Pakistan being a vital anti-communist ally to one where its relationship with Pakistan has to be balanced with other foreign policy demands. The primary concern now relates to the consequence of a disintegrating nuclear power. In brief, in this view, Pakistan has shifted decisively from being a country which promotes US interests to one where Washington has a relatively low priority. Supporters of this wary view can be found in the State Department, the CIA, as well as in the Bretton Woods institutions.

The second view in Washington is not as pessimistic as the failed state analysis. Under the 'techno-fix' scenario, Pakistan's deep-seated problems of governance can be solved by a technocratic fix from former and present World Bank-IMF staff. What is to be done is as clear as the instrument of delivery. A team of technocrats goes in for a brief period, takes corrupt politicians to task through an accountability process; the team also fixes the institutional decline, restructures the financial sector to mobilize savings and channel investments more effectively, controls the fiscal deficit by a wide ranging tax reform which vested interests cannot block, while public spending targets are not to be compromised by the electoral whims of populist politics.

No one questions the motivations of Moeen Qureshi et al. but there always was a fundamental flaw with the government-in-exile prescription. It was always inconsistent with parliamentary democracy and this tension was cruelly exposed. Each time that a techno-fix government was imposed, its refreshing disclosures were tempered with the knowledge that its interim nature made it impossible for it to pursue any substantive restructuring. By highlighting the issues and making corruption and rent seeking very transparent, the governments-in-exile assisted in the general process of showing how badly the elite has governed Pakistan. But they had no mandate for their task, and in a period where the legitimacy of government was also a concern, the periodic importation of distant power to execute the will of the military was destined to fail. As a result, the faith in the techno-fix view has all but disappeared in Washington.[1]

The net result of the above divergence of perception is that no group feels in control of economic management. After two decades of continuous structural adjustment, the World Bank and the International Monetary Fund complain about fiscal deficit targets not being met and quibble about failure to implement tax reforms, knowing full well that the underlying causes of the persistent economic crisis are getting worse not better. In other words, the structural reform programme after twenty years has not succeeded in tackling structural problems.

Successive civilian governments, on the other hand, have felt that they have been in power for too short a period to take charge and responsibility. During the 1990s, most governments have spent the first year blaming their predecessors and the second or third have been spent in crisis management before dismissal. The former regime of Nawaz Sharif, however, was the first with a strong and clear parliamentary majority, yet its economic record was appalling. It staggered from one crisis to another as the economy failed to revive from its decade–long slump. During its tenure, the balance of payments situation varied from weak to critical, and the country avoided bankruptcy simply through periodic bailouts.

The vulnerability and dependence of the economy was severely exposed at the time of the nuclear explosion in 1998 and the more recent Kargil adventure in the summer of 1999. Each episode was followed by desperate dashes to Washington by the economic managers. If it were not for the World Bank-IMF and assorted aid donors, Pakistan could not meet its external debt obligations. Further, with the new military government, it remains doubtful that the domestic debt-servicing situation is sustainable. Overseas Pakistanis, as well as residents, have also been burnt by the fiasco of having their foreign currency deposits frozen, as far as withdrawal in the designated foreign currency was concerned. The Diaspora has lost confidence and the residents are in despair.

B. A Disintegrating Economy—The Statistics of Despair

After receiving over $50 billion of aid, Pakistan still has one of the lowest literacy rates in the world. Relatedly it has the highest population growth rate in the world.[2] These fundamental shortcomings impose a crushing burden of unemployment and illiteracy on the economic system.

Many of the underlying shortcomings were glossed over by some fortuitous developments in the 1980s. All of the positive stimuli had an external cause—(i) the boom in the Middle East which became the source of vital remittances, (ii) the Afghan war–related aid inflows which provided a demand stimulus and (iii) the boom in East Asia which created markets through expanding regional incomes.

Towards the end of the 1980s, the underlying weaknesses became apparent as some of the external stimuli turned sour. The Middle East went into recession and the Soviet withdrawal from Afghanistan left Pakistan with endless post-conflict problems while net aid inflows became meagre. It was at this time that the costs of external and internal conflict began to be felt. Karachi exploded and the economy has never recovered from the conflict in the principal financial centre and port city of the country.

The depressing state of the country's economy is captured in the following data. The 1990s had been a period of sluggish growth. Indeed, over the decade as a whole, Pakistan stood still in terms of income as the average growth rate had been marginally higher than the population growth rate. The stagnation in per capita income was largely due to the worst performance in the manufacturing sector that Pakistan has ever witnessed, in any decade since its creation. This is directly attributable to the conflict in Karachi. Indeed, it is interesting to speculate on what may have happened to manufacturing growth in Pakistan if Karachi had not erupted.

The late 1980s and early 1990s was the period when foreign direct investment (FDI) flooded into Asia. One of the countries where it was noticeable by its virtual absence was Pakistan. This is not because the country provided poor returns to investment. On the contrary many sectors provided attractive avenues for capital investments, but FDI does not go to countries in conflict.

Conflict and economic stagnation combined to generate other problems of governance. Political patronage and rent seeking led to a sustained deterioration of financial and economic management institutions. Tax collection was poor, the elite groups failed to repay loans and the cost of this plunder was borne largely by the poor. Inflation soared and was, on average, double that witnessed in the early to mid-1980s. What was even more troubling is that the sensitive price indicator, which measures the basket of commodities of most importance to the poor, rose more than the general consumer price index.

The squeeze on the real incomes of the poor was accompanied by trends in public spending which further undermined human development. In the first seven years of the structural adjustment programme, the spending on education and health, as a percentage of GNP, actually *fell*. This occurred for a country with one of the lowest literacy rates in the world. Education and health spending was squeezed out by a combination of the burden of defence spending and, even more importantly, debt servicing. Indeed, by the mid-1990s, debt servicing alone was twice as much as the *combined* public spending on education and health. The mismanagement of the 1980s, which caused a mountain of external and domestic debt to be accumulated in a period of a booming economy was felt a decade later. Now a stagnant economy is facing a severe contraction of real resources available for vital investments in human development, as conflict and debt eat into the core of public spending.

The main source of increased debt servicing has been the accumulation of domestic debt in the 1980s. The phenomenal rise in debt servicing shows a pattern of servicing obligations, which almost doubled as a percentage of GDP, over a decade. The amount by which debt servicing increased during the decade was twice as large as the total amount spent by the government on health.

With half of its export earnings going into debt servicing Pakistan has grown increasingly reliant on external sources of finance for meeting its debt obligations. The inability to expand exports is not unrelated to conflict and law and order problems, which undermine the confidence of entrepreneurs. Again, the failure was not due to shortcomings of economic policy since numerous financial incentives were available for exporters. Indeed large scale smuggling of consumer goods, as well as tariff liberalization, had reduced the bias towards production for the domestic market. In principle these economic reforms would shift production towards exports. However, changing incentives in the context of conflict and insecurity did not lead to desired changes in production structure. Economic policy reforms, in a framework of deteriorating governance, do not work for the simple reason that potential exporters do not invest in new equipment and training.

Other adverse external developments further accentuated the domestic causes of poor performance. The best news for the poor during the 1980s—migration to the Middle East and the sending of remittances to families at home—proved to be a temporary stimulus, particularly on the scale evident in the 1980s. These remittances fell dramatically, from a high of 10 per cent of GNP in 1983 to around 2 per cent by the mid-1990s. Since the beneficiaries of these inflows were primarily poor families, the decline in remittances compounded domestic problems of unemployment, underemployment, high prices, and declining education and health services.

Adding to the above mentioned causes of social tension and poverty was the pattern of inequality: Pakistan was becoming a more unequal country. Indeed, Pakistan was more unequal in the 1990s than the infamous period of the Twenty-Two Families, which became the symbol of inequality in the 1960s. In sum, the 1990s have been a period of economic stagnation, worsening poverty and inequality, disintegrating institutions, the further running down of social services, and a serious erosion in social trust.

C. The Causes of the Economic and Institutional Deterioration

The explanations for this poor economic performance have deep structural roots which, as argued earlier, have more to do with three non-economic factors than traditional economic explanations. A conventional approach is to blame the poor performance due to a mix of domestic policy failures and exogenous shocks. In the case of Pakistan, the exogenous shocks in the 1990s include bouts of weather adversity, which have affected agriculture as, floods, droughts and pests have affected agricultural output in a few years. Similarly the downturn in the Middle East have affected remittances, while the East Asia crisis towards the late 1990s has contributed to a global downturn which has not facilitated export growth.

Allied to this are domestic economic policy shortcomings, the most obvious of which are: the continued failure to reduce the fiscal deficit, the slow pace of privatization to reduce the domestic debt burden, the lack of progress in diversifying from a narrow export base, the slow movement towards a privately run financial sector, and distortions in the political granting of credit in the public sector which hamper efficient allocation of capital.

The above explanations provide a very limited part of the underlying causality of what ails Pakistan. Many of the explanations point to symptoms of the real problems—the inability to expand taxation or to reform the financial sector or to diversify the export base are themselves due to deeper weaknesses. We now turn to the examination of the three core reasons and the manner in which they have jeopardized economic prosperity, social advancement and institutional development.

The first of the underlying causes is *conflict*. Pakistan has been at war for two decades. Since 1979 it has been deeply embroiled in the Afghan conflict. The effects of the Afghan war have been devastating, and Pakistan has suffered the most, apart from the Former Soviet Union and Afghanistan. In addition to the Afghan conflict, the effects of which are documented below, Pakistan has been entangled and exhausted by violence generated in Karachi and, to a lesser extent, from sectarian groups. On top of this, the 1990s have also witnessed Pakistan's deep involvement in the escalating Kashmir conflict. As a result, the last decade has seen heightened insecurity of life and property due to these multiple conflicts. This insecurity lies at the core of undermining the economic foundations of the country. In this environment, people do not make long term investments no matter how good the purely economic incentives may be.

These conflicts have militarized civil society. This has been tragic particularly because the country started from a strong militaristic tradition, built partially on the notion of martial races, which translated into a disproportionately high level of representation in the Indian army during the colonial period. There has, however, been one major crucial difference. Prior to the onset of the current spate of conflicts, Pakistan had a disciplined militarism. There was a disciplined formal army, which was largely the custodian of arms and ammunition. Much of civil society was unarmed and lacked any means to settle disputes through weapons. Only at the margins—in the so-called tribal areas—did weapons circulate with relative ease amongst civilians. In the aftermath of the Afghan conflict, the basic equation between the Pakistan military and society has been altered. Society now contains organized groups with access to a plethora of light weapons. Previously Pakistan had a strong army—now Pakistan is a militarized society.

The unfortunate evidence of this came when Karachi began to come apart in the late 1980s. The civilian protagonists in the sad destruction of this city have been equipped with sophisticated weapons. These were either bought in the open market from parties involved in the Afghan war, or provided by State agencies to particular factions that they chose to support in a seedy and murky battle for supremacy in Karachi. The MQM's fortunes have fluctuated from alliance partner in government to one which gets treated as a terrorist force. After a decade and a half of turbulence, Karachi does not seem to be any closer to revival. There are temporary respites but Pakistan's principal port and financial center has been devastated by sustained conflict.

The disintegration of Karachi has a resonance, which is far deeper than the fate of a city. No other city offers diversity which remotely parallels that of Karachi. Indeed, Pakistan's other cities are largely mono-ethnic. One of the most extraordinary features of the second largest city, Lahore, is its lack of ethnic diversity. The same can be said of virtually all the other major urban centres of Pakistan. Karachi is a mosaic of Pakistan's multi-ethnic character. The second largest Pushtun city of Pakistan, it has strong representation of virtually all ethnic groups though does not belong to any individual one. The city is a symbol of the ability of the various ethnic groups to live together.

The breakdown in Karachi is most importantly, a national tragedy, not solely a provincial mess. What has been most disturbing is the lack of urgency or care to resolve the Karachi conflict. However, the links between a debilitated Karachi and a disturbed Pakistani economy have long been evident to foreigners. For example, all recent Prime Ministers have held major investment conferences across the world to try and woo foreign direct investment. In each of these, virtually the first question raised by foreign firms concerned the violence in the principal port and financial city of the country. Many foreign investors expressed incredulity that a government was seeking private investment from abroad in a country wrecked by internal violence. The conflict in Karachi was also one of the major reasons why the major inflows of FDI into Asia during the 1990s went past Pakistan and into more distant but less violent lands to the east. Businessmen being kidnapped, prominent public figures being shot, cars being stolen and private houses being looted—this is not a social structure conducive to private capital accumulation, diversification of exports or closing of the fiscal gap.

In addition to Afghanistan and Karachi, two other sources of conflict have undermined human security or intensified fiscal distortions. The militarization of society took a menacing form in the rise of sectarian terror groups, particularly in the province of Punjab. Again the State was confronted with well armed civilians whose violent activities were not only leading to losses of life but were also contributing to an environment where citizens felt insecure about their lives and property. Without a reasonable law and order environment, the basic precondition for economic development has been missing. Added to this is the engagement in Kashmir and resulting tensions with India. This has forced an arms race and continued commitment to higher levels of defense spending.

The net result is a tragic downward spiral that has enveloped Pakistan. Those in power are consumed by the management of different aspects of conflict. Their priorities and energies are concentrated on actions which relate to these conflicts—more financial resources are required to combat a militarized society and for military involvement outside its borders. Many of these actions and policies have accentuated domestic and international conflicts, as evidenced recently in the dangerously misplaced Kargil adventure. The ultimate irony is that Pakistan has become a highly militarized society with a large formal army. A large professional army should have created a sound law and order environment for economic development, if it could not support the expansion of civil liberties. Unfortunately this is not the case as a militarized polity frequently confronts a well-armed army. The latter are also involved in regional conflicts. Collectively the economy collapses and it becomes that much more difficult to generate the fiscal resources to sustain the past levels of military spending, let alone the increased demands for defence. It is in this context that previous Chiefs of Army Staff have publicly stated that the primary threat to human security in Pakistan are a collapsing economy and social order, and not an external enemy.

To state the obvious, across the world economies in conflict do not do well, no matter what the economic policy regime. Pakistan is no exception.

The second structural cause of institutional breakdown is 'shadow privatization'. This is not a process of selling state assets into private hands. Shadow privatization is a far more destructive force—it involves the subjugation of state institutions to the private and political agendas of those in control of the executive branch of government. Virtually all major public institutions were affected including the judiciary, the financial sector and the tax collection machinery. Loans are given on the basis of political alliance, judges are intimidated into making favorable decisions, and the tax machinery had been used to punish political opponents or those out of favor for any other reason.

Shadow privatization is a process through which public institutions serve the interest of the chief executive. The judicial system is unable to prosecute those allied to executive authority, no matter what crime they commit. The tax system is unable to collect direct taxes from those in positions of power. The financial sector is unable to enforce the law with regard to defaulters, because they are protected by the executive. The police are unable to arrest those exempt from the rule of law. It is in this sense that public institutions in Pakistan are referred to as being 'feudal'—an extension of personal power. In other words, public institutions are not a mechanism to control the arbitrary exercise of power. On the contrary, public institutions have become the symbol of arbitrariness and the whimsical exercise of power. The result of this 'shadowy privatization' is the institutional breakdown so evident in Pakistan.

In principle this is the vacuum which civil society institutions can fill. To some extent they have done so but, as I shall argue later, the growth of civil society institutions cannot compensate adequately for the wider institutional breakdown.

The third cause of institutional confusion and social fragmentation is the *puritan onslaught* on public institutions. Since the 1980s there has been a half-baked attempt to convert Pakistan into a theocracy. Shariat Courts have been established and an attempt made to ban interest from the economic system. Issues related to a theocracy were revived again in the late 1990s with an attempt to pass another Shariah Law which was, however, unacceptable to the Senate. The attempt at bringing the judicial and financial system in conformity with religious injunctions has occurred during a period where the gap between *piety* and *morality* has widened. Pakistan has increasingly become a more pious society where the rituals of religion appear to be more widely practiced. At the same time there is little doubt that this piety has been accompanied not by simplicity but by fierce consumerism and a dangerous deterioration in public morality. Corruption is widespread, as is the extensive involvement in the drug trade, frequently in regions which are considered to be the most pious in the country. The gulf between piety and morality has contributed to a widespread cultural disillusionment. Those in power and espousing a puritanical Islam are frequently viewed as corrupt and immoral. As a result, a number of civil society institutions have emerged which seek to close this gap. Frequently they seek a greater puritanism as the means of closing the gap between piety and morality. The religious orientation of some of these civil society groups, typically galvanized through *madrassas*, leads to fears that Pakistan may experience a Taliban or Iran style puritan revolution if these groups acquire a more political agenda and become allied to some key levers of power in the civilian or military authority. Such possibilities, however unlikely, add to the sense of insecurity about the country's direction. There are fears that the crumbling current order will be replaced by a radically different one, through means other than democratic change.

The proponents of an 'Islamic economic system' argue that Pakistan should create an alternative economic institutional structure with no interest. The issue is not one of mere academic interest, since all banking and finance laws of the Government of Pakistan have been under threat from the Shariat courts. Various legal appeals have prevented these actions from taking force. It is, of course, possible to design many alternative economic systems. If a society so wishes it can go back to barter and eliminate money altogether. The issue is not whether one can conceptually design and practically implement an interest–free economy. That is possible. The real question is whether such an economic system can allocate resources efficiently, achieve high rates of growth, reduce poverty and advance human development. On any such criteria, the so-called Islamic economic system envisioned by its proponents, would simply not measure up. The only effect, therefore, of such pressure is to increase uncertainty and divert attention from the real causes of the economic downturn and institutional breakdown.

D. The Needed Macro Policy Response

In the face of such a comprehensive institutional breakdown, the policy reform agenda is daunting. Small, micro, incremental changes will be ineffective within the present context. It is very important for agents in civil society to press for and participate in these macro changes, rather than carve a separate and comfortable niche of community based activity. The structural reform agenda has to have priority objectives in three areas:

1. *Governance*: the reduction of conflict and use of arbitrary power,
2. *Human Development*: reducing illiteracy and curbing the population explosion
3. *Economic management*: generating employment, reviving growth and diversifying the export base.

In pursuit of these fundamental structural reforms, I am proposing a 6-point agenda, as follows:

i. The Government of Pakistan (GOP) should utilize the Pakistan Development Forum (previously the Aid-to-Pakistan consortium) to advance the case for *a debt-mandatory primary education swap*. This would kill two birds with one stone. It is quite clear that Pakistan is effectively bankrupt and is unable to service its loans without increasing volumes of assistance from abroad. Like many countries in Africa, Pakistan needs relief from an excruciating debt burden. In July 1999 the G8 countries made progress on advancing the Highly Indebted Poor Countries (HIPC) initiative by writing off increasing amounts of debt. Pakistan's economy is in such deep trouble that a similar major relief effort is required. But the relief on debt servicing needs to be linked to social programs. It would be a travesty if the reduced debt is substituted by higher defence spending.

In Pakistan the investment with the greatest rate of return is primary education. A literacy rate of 30 per cent, high incidence of child labour, poor social status of women, high fertility and a population explosion is a menacing vicious circle. Accordingly, the debt write off should be linked to a basic human right—the right of Pakistani citizens to read and write.

The GOP has made several commitments at the international level—at UN conferences such as the Copenhagen Social Summit and the Jomtien Conference on Education for All—to introduce universal primary education. It is time to honor this basic human right, in return for a reduction in debt. A phased introduction of mandatory primary education, which is not expensive, should be partially financed by a debt swap. Resources saved for debt servicing would go into the mandatory primary education scheme. Previous fraudulent schemes, such as the Iqra tax in the 1980s which raised money for education but which got diverted to other uses, must be guarded against and the commitments on education spending monitored.

ii. The **privatization of the financial sector** should be accelerated, and the proceeds used to retire domestic debt. Otherwise, public finances will not improve and the GOP will keep insisting on new taxes, at the insistence of the IMF, in an environment of a recession and where the business community is very hostile to public institutions. The government neither provides security through law or order, nor an appropriate infrastructure to support market transactions. Yet in this environment, it keeps pushing for increased taxation. It is not surprising that every budget is followed by hostile protests from groups who view the government as rapacious and not conducive to creating a helpful environment for business.

The privatization of the financial sector will also reduce the political patronage in the granting of credits, through the 'shadow privatization' process referred to earlier. Instead of this shadow privatization, what the economy needs is a real one.

The level of savings and investment will rise over the longer run, as will the efficiency with which capital is used. The main reason for the reluctance to move forward with greater speed is shadow privatization, whose beneficiaries are fearful of criminal cases against them, as well as legal demands for payment of loans on which they have defaulted. An amnesty against criminal proceedings may have to be given in order to facilitate real privatization. In sum, the privatization of the financial sector will reduce domestic debt sharply, raise the levels of savings and increase the efficiency of capital utilization.

iii. **Controlling light weapons proliferation** is vital for containing the rise of an uncivil society. The first test should be Karachi, where a major operation should be launched to eliminate weapons. Since the army and the police are no longer trusted due to the various politically motivated operations in Karachi, the control of light weapons proliferation in Karachi has to be internationalized. A UN agency should be involved to ensure 'the rules of the game' and to see that the process is not viewed as an attempt to eliminate any political party. In collaboration with the UN, the Pakistan army should play a professional non-partisan role in a serious attempt at de-weaponisation of Karachi. After a major operation in Karachi, the effort should be repeated elsewhere in the country.

iv. **Restoring Karachi** has to be at the heart of a national political and economic strategy. Diversifying the export base, opening the economy, and attracting FDI will remain pipe dreams as long as the principal port and financial centre remains in such a mess. A major political investment in Karachi is more important for Pakistan's human security than the pursuit and energy demonstrated in Islamabad for the conflicts in Afghanistan and Kashmir. A country which cannot get its own house in order will have few supporters for its foreign policy ambitions, as recent events have demonstrated. A country that is not able to manage its four provinces, and one which is economically bankrupt, does not enjoy credibility in the international community. A critical part in restoring credibility to Pakistan's image is to revive Karachi's economy, which has strong multiplier effects on the rest of the country.

Karachi's symbolic value as a melting pot for Pakistan was mentioned earlier and cannot be overstated. It must become a city which welcomes Pathans, Baluchis, Punjabis, and Sindhis from rural areas, while acknowledging its historic affinity for the erstwhile *muhajirs* from India. In addition, it must take pride in its Christians and Hindus, and through it show a more tolerant face of Pakistan. For a liberal, democratic Pakistan, the reconstitution of Karachi is a vital indicator of progress.

v. The process of **parliamentary democracy has to be deepened, not abandoned,** due to its many obvious shortcomings. This is not only because an important principle of civil and political rights is at stake but also that the alternative, military rule, has been such an unqualified disaster in the past. Both of the two long periods of military rule undermined social cohesion and long-term human security of the country. The danger for parliamentary democracy does not come from fear of a military take-over alone. The civilian government is as great a potential obstacle. It should be noted that no elected government in Pakistan has ever handed over power to another civilian elected regime. In order to facilitate trust in the electoral process, the UN should be involved as an honest broker, in the way that it has become involved in many electoral campaigns across the world. The involvement of the UN is by no means a guarantor of success but it can play a potentially much more important role than international monitors. These monitors are too weak and often have too superficial an understanding of the process. The next general election should be held in collaboration with the UN's electoral support branch.

Another aspect of the continuing deepening of democracy is the commitment for the independent media and NGOs. Further, independent policy institutes, such as the Sustainable Development Policy Institute, and semi-official think tanks, such as the Pakistan Institute of Development Economics, have an important role to play in collaboration with civil society institutions. There have been several attempts at muzzling the press and NGOs engaged in expanding civil and political rights. For the next election, pressure should be brought on all political parties to break the government monopoly on the electronic media, which is another instrument in the nasty process of shadow privatization.

vi. The shadow privatization of the judiciary has to be reversed, if property rights and rules resembling law are to be restored. The **separation of powers** enshrined in the 1973 Constitution has to be enforced by reducing the arbitrary powers, and manipulation, by the executive. While religion will play an important role in the private and social life of Pakistan, a theocracy has strong totalitarian, fascistic tendencies built into it. The 1973 Constitution should also be adhered to in this respect.

Needless to add that not all elements of the above agenda can be implemented as rapidly as the others, and not all elements are equally important. A move, however, on some of the key points for improved governance, social investments and economic liberalization are the necessary precondition for reviving the uncivil society that the country has become.

This is an agenda for fundamental structural reform in the context of Pakistan, not a tinkering with price incentives and institutional change at the margin. Pakistan's current structural reform programme, with the Bretton Woods institution, has been accompanied by a deteriorating economy, mounting debts and growing underemployment. This is not because many of the economic reforms contained therein are at fault. The problem is that these programs do not address the structural causes of Pakistan's poor performance—as argued above, issues of governance are the real hindrance to economic revival, not poor economic incentives.

E. Civil Society and Power within the Context of Severe Problems of Governance

The rise of civil society institutions in Pakistan has to be viewed in the above context of uncivil society. The emerging civil society institutions are connected to these dynamics of power. Some institutions have emerged which raise fundamental issues of human rights abuses, environmental degradation and gender discrimination. These should be active agents in the changes proposed above. At the same time a number of civil society institutions are engaged in the opposite—sectarian bigotry and indoctrination of extreme religious views. Allowing this fertility of views, even unpleasant ones, is part of the process of building a civil society. There are obvious caveats of control when civil society institutions instigate or preach violence or hate against any particular group. Clearly some extreme sectarian organizations, for example, would need to be outlawed.

A mix of circumstances and abuses of power have created an uncivil society. In response to these, numerous civil society groups have emerged, which seek to extend a wide array of economic, social, political, and civil rights. Such civil society groups, analyzed elsewhere in this volume, play a critical role in advancing the human rights agenda in Pakistan. But they operate in a hostile economic and political environment. This chapter has attempted to outline an agenda of reforms required to address these fundamental structural problems, and pointed to some of the external and national actors who must shape this agenda to tackle the menacing rise of an uncivil society.

NOTES

1. There has, however, been a revival of another related idea. This takes the form of a National Security Council, a mechanism to provide a more sustained institutional role for the military under a democratic government.
2. This statement applies to Pakistan when compared with any major country, defined as those with a population greater than twenty million.

8

THE MILITARY

Hasan-Askari Rizvi

The long years of direct and indirect rule have enabled the military to spread out in the civilian administration, semi-government institutions, the economy and the major sectors of the society. Its clout no longer depends on controlling political power. It is derived from its organizational strength and its significant presence in the polity and the society. The military has acquired a formidable position and role over time. It is the crystallization of the importance and centrality it has enjoyed in the state structure from the beginning. Pakistan came into existence under extremely difficult circumstances and faced serious problems in the formative years. A new state structure was to be created against the backdrop of the partition-related communal violence, influx of refugees, problems of internal security, and a paucity of experienced civil and military officials. Its external problems were no less intimidating with strains in its interaction with Afghanistan, deterioration of relations with India, and especially the war in Kashmir.

The survival of the state became the primary concern of the rulers of Pakistan who equated it with an assertive federal government, strong defence apparatus, high defence expenditure, and a state–directed monolithic nationalism. The imperatives of state security and survival gave primacy to state building over nation building. The emphasis was on building state apparatus and institutions rather than the creation of participatory political institutions and processes that could accommodate diverse regional, ethnic-linguistic identities in pluralist and responsive parameters.

The military was a major beneficiary of such an approach to politics and society because it was viewed as integral to state survival and state-building. It was in a way an extension of the role the military had played under the British Imperial rule. Though within the framework of subordination to the civilian authority based in London, the military in British India was considered as the ultimate security of British rule in India and an important element in the defence of the British empire as a whole. It was for this reason the Indian legislature was not given any power regarding defence expenditure and India's defence policy; these remained a close preserve of the Viceroy and the British government.

In the post-independence period, the military was involved in the efforts to put the 'house' of the new state in order. It extended support to the civilian authorities in maintenance of law and order, humanitarian assistance to the refugees and their resettlement. The war in Kashmir placed additional responsibilities on the military at a time when it was engaged in its own re-organization. The civilian government overwhelmed by these problems felt that a strong military was needed for internal order and especially for external security. These considerations led to the tendency to allocate substantial domestic resources to defence and Pakistan joined the U.S. sponsored alliance system in order to strengthen and modernize the military.

What further added to the importance of the military was the erosion of the civilian political institutions and processes. With the death of Mohammad Ali Jinnah in September 1948 and the assassination of Liaquat Ali Khan in October 1951, Pakistan suffered from a crisis of civilian leadership. The Muslim League that led the independence movement was unable to transform itself into a national political party capable of evolving a consensus on the operational norms of the polity. Other political parties could not offer a viable alternative. The resultant fragmentation of the political forces and divisive tendencies made it difficult for the political forces to pull in one direction in a coherent manner.

With the decline of the political institutions and processes, the bureaucratic elite gained an upper hand and dominated policy-making. The military supported the ascendancy of the bureaucracy from the background. Traditionally, the state apparatus, i.e., the bureaucracy and the military, was stronger than the political institutions. This institutional imbalance accentuated after independence due to above reasons. Once the bureaucratic-military elite was entrenched, they made sure that the political forces remained divided. In fact, the process of political fragmentation and ministerial crises accelerated after Ghulam Mohammad (a former bureaucrat) became Governor General in October 1951, succeeded by another bureaucrat, Iskander Mirza, in August 1955. They had strong reservations about the parliamentary system of government and favoured a centralized polity with strong authoritarian features; prime ministers were removed, the Constituent Assembly was dissolved, and the state apparatus was used to encourage divisive tendencies in politics so that no political group could pose a challenge to their power.

The military was a junior partner to the bureaucracy in this period, supporting it from the outside and shared decision-making power on foreign and security policies and key domestic issues. However, the growing political fragmentation, ministerial crises, economic difficulties, and participatory demands accentuated ethnic and regional pressures, which further complicated political management for the tottering civilian governments installed and manipulated by the bureaucratic elite. The military felt that a chaotic political and economic situation that would threaten its professional and corporate interests was in the making. It decided to dislodge the civilian institutions and process and assumed power directly in October 1958. The change that the coup produced was the ascendancy of the military as the senior partner and supplantment of a weak and divided government that suffered from a crisis of legitimacy.

Since then, the military has either directly ruled the country under martial law or served as a protective shield for the civilianized regimes (1962–69, 1985–88) which succeeded martial law; the period between 20 December 1971 and 5 July 1977, was an exception as an elected civilian leader, Zulfikar Ali Bhutto, ruled the country and asserted the primacy of the civil over the military.[1]

The following table provides details of the various periods of the military's direct and indirect rule in Pakistan:

Type of Military Rule	Dates	Leader
1st Direct Martial Law	7 Oct. 1958–8 June 1962	Field Marshal Ayub Khan
2nd Direct Martial Law	25 Mar. 1969–20 Dec.1971 20 Dec. 1971–20 April 1972	General A. M. Yahya Khan Zulfikar Ali Bhutto, civilian CMLA
3rd Direct Martial Law	5 July 1977–30 Dec. 1985	General Zia-ul-Haq
4th Military rule (without Martial Law)	12 October 1999	General Pervez Musharraf
Indirect post-martial law	8 June 1962–25 March 1969	President Ayub Khan (under the 1962 Constitution)
Indirect post-martial law	23 June 1985–17 Aug. 1988	Muhammad Khan Junejo served as Prime Minister from March 23, 1985 to May 29, 1988 under the amended 1973 Constitution. Martial law was not withdrawn until December 30, 1985. Zia ul-Haq continued as President and Army Chief until his death on August 17, 1988.

The senior generals who assumed the command of the Army after the death of Zia ul-Haq in August 1988, allowed the constitutional and democratic processes to operate, which made it possible to hold the general elections on party basis in November and transfer of power to an elected government in December in that year. General elections were also held in October 1990, October 1993, and February 1997, and the military commanders repeatedly pledged their support to the democratic process.

Despite the changed disposition of the senior commanders between 1988–99, the military continued to be a powerful political actor which made input into foreign and security policy and key domestic issues from the sidelines. The Army Chief is a pivot in the power structure and political stability in the post-1985 political system depended on a smooth interaction between the elected civilian government and the top commanders. The military protected its professional and corporate interests which covered a vast area of policy making and allocation of resources, i.e., security and foreign policy, weapons procurement, availability of resources for modernization of the services, and the perks, privileges, and other material rewards it had amassed during its direct rule. Its role in the industrial and commercial domains greatly expanded. Furthermore, the military also guarded its autonomy and resisted interference by the civilian leaders in its internal organizational and service matters.

The military displaced the Nawaz Sharif government on 12 October 1999 because the latter attempted to undermine the professional and corporate interests of the former and violated the military's autonomy by interfering in its internal affairs. Though the senior commanders were perturbed by the civilian government's political and economic mismanagement, they would not have removed Nawaz Sharif had he not tried to dislodge the Army Chief, General Pervez Musharraf, in a bid to establish his direct control over the Army high-command. General Pervez Musharraf designated himself as the Chief Executive after assuming power. The 1973 Constitution was suspended but he neither imposed martial law nor established military courts. The Provisional Constitutional Order provided that the government would be run as close to the 1973 Constitution as possible, subject to the overriding power of the Chief Executive.

This chapter examines the military's all-pervasive influence in government and society, focusing on how it penetrated the civilian bureaucracy, government and semi-government institutions as well as the private sector, industry and commerce, business, agriculture, and education. It also examines the ethnic character and social background of the Army officers and the role of Islam in military ideology. All these aspects shape the military's profile which influences power relations in the polity and the over-all character of the society.

A. Civilian Jobs and Material Rewards

The military has become a ladder for lucrative civilian jobs after retirement in almost all states that have witnessed the rise of the military to power. Pakistan is no exception. Ayub Khan adopted this strategy during his rule and decided in 1960 to induct serving military officers permanently in the higher ranks of the civil services. This practice was discontinued in 1963. However, he appointed retired officers to top jobs in the government departments and semi-government corporations or dispatched them abroad on diplomatic assignments with good salaries and perks. Zia ul-Haq whose military regime could not overcome the crisis of legitimacy, had to rely more heavily on the military. This led him to distribute the rewards of power to the military in a more consistent and extensive manner than any previous military ruler. He institutionalized the induction of military personnel to civilian jobs in a manner that the succeeding civilian regimes could not reverse these policies. This has led to what Finer describes as the 'military colonization of other institutions' whereby 'the military acts as a reservoir or core of personnel for the sensitive institutions of the state.'[2]

In 1980, a 10 per cent minimum quota was fixed for military personnel in civilian jobs which made way for their induction into all government and semi-government jobs. Three major methods are adopted for appointment of military personnel to the civilian jobs. First, some serving officers are given prize government jobs or top assignments in semi-government corporations and agencies for a specified period after which they return to their parent service. Second, retired military officers are recommended by the service headquarters to the government for re-employment against the quota. Mostly these are renewable contract assignments. Occasionally, the civilian government on its own appoints military officers to senior jobs, a practice discouraged by the service headquarters. For the lower level jobs, various government departments and semi-government agencies are directed to make arrangements for appointment of ex-service personnel by reserving some posts for them or by giving them some credit for military service when they compete with civilians. The government seeks information from its departments and agencies from time to time if the minimum quota for ex-service personnel is being met. Third, the Ayubian practice of appointing serving officers permanently to the civil services was revived in 1980. The young officers are appointed to the elite cadres of the Central Superior Services (CSS) on the recommendation of a military selection board. They join the combined training of the CSS probationers and get the advantage of their military service in seniority. Since 1980, nine to twelve officers have joined the bureaucracy through this channel and the service cadres generally preferred by them include District Management Group (DMG), Foreign Service, and Police Service. At times, the civilian government nominated some officers to the regular cadres of the civil services. A large number of these inductees have blood relationship with the top brass or have been their ADCs; in a few cases connections with privileged political personalities have also helped. During 1980–85, 96 Army officers were inducted into the selected cadres of the CSS on a permanent basis, while 115 were employed on contracts. These practices continued after the withdrawal of military rule.

These measures have significantly increased the presence of military personnel in government and semi-government jobs. In mid-1982, eighteen out of forty-two ambassadors posted abroad came from the military. In 1992–93, half of the members of the Federal Public Service Commission were ex-Army officers and, during 1995–96, three out of four provincial governors had an army background. Two of the elite research institutes—Strategic Studies and Regional Studies—have traditionally remained under the tutelage of retired senior officers or bureaucrats. The third reputed institute—Pakistan Institute of International Affairs—was headed by a retired Major General for some time. Four universities had retired Army officers as their Vice Chancellors in the eighties and the nineties.[3] Junior positions in the universities did not attract the officers, although some brigadiers held academic appointments in Quaid-i-Azam University for some time in the 1980s; they were accommodated by changing the rules. The practice of inducting serving and retired officers to civilian intelligence agencies was strengthened during 1996–97. A plan was prepared in 1997 to appoint army officers between the ranks of captain and colonels to join the Police, Federal Investigation Agency (FIA), and the Intelligence Bureau (IB) on permanent basis.[4] This increased the Army's influence in these civilian agencies, thereby strengthening its intelligence gathering capability. It also enables the Army to provide alternate employment mainly to those captains, majors and colonels who are not likely to be promoted.

Another source of the military's increased influence in the society is the allotment of agricultural land to its personnel. This tradition goes back to the British period when the British government distributed large tracts of land as a reward for military service. This practice continued in the post-independence period. Land in the Thal desert under the colonization scheme of the Punjab government was allotted on regimental basis for settling ex-servicemen families. Similarly, land was given to service personnel in various schemes in different barrage-areas, i.e., Ghulam Mohammad, Taunsa, and Gudhu. The government gave land to the army for the ex-service personnel of the Campbellpur, Jhelum, Kohat, Rawalpindi and Hazara districts which the Army distributed among them and extended help for its reclamation and development.[5] Land was also allotted to them along the India-Pakistan border in the Punjab. The practice of land grants under various schemes to military personnel, senior bureaucrats and other well-connected people has continued in Sindh and the Punjab in the 1980s and the 1990s. The Punjab government allotted about 450,000 acres of land to 5538 military personnel during 1977–85.[6] Agricultural land was also allotted in other provinces, especially in Sindh, but the government did not release data on such allotments. Most Sindhi leaders have often objected to the allotment of land in Sindh to military personnel and bureaucrats, most of whom are non-Sindhi. Several 'progressive' groups in the Punjab which felt that the poor peasants and landless tenants were being denied land in order to accommodate the military and the bureaucracy also expressed concern.

Other material rewards offered during the Zia rule which strengthened the position of the military included assignments in the Gulf states, pieces of land for construction of houses in cantonments and urban centres, commercial plots, facilities of loans, etc. A large number of officers received more than one plot of land at cheap rates which they sold to civilians at exorbitant prices. In June 1982, the armed forces housing scheme was launched for providing houses to the retiring officers at a cost to be paid in easy installments. The first project under this scheme was completed in early 1984.

B. Industry and Business

The military controls a massive industrial and business empire which make it very important to the economy. This has also created its stake in the government's economic policies and industrial and commercial strategies. The Army's industrial and commercial interests can be divided into three major categories: those directly under the administrative control of the Army; those looked after by Defence Production Division of the Ministry of Defence but are headed by a serving officer appointed by the Army Chief; and charitable trusts set up for the welfare of ex-service personnel which operate in an autonomous manner in the private sector.[7] The first category includes the Frontier Works Organization (FWO), Special Communication Organization (SCO), and National Logistics Cell (NLC). The FWO, set up in October 1966 and staffed by the Corps of Engineers, undertook the construction of the

Karakoram Highway as its first project. Later, it took several civilian engineering projects, notably road construction in the Northern Areas and Baluchistan, and civilian works for Kot Addu power station. The SCO, manned by the Signals Corps, extends telecommunication facilities to the Northern Areas and Azad Kashmir. The NLC, set up during the Zia years, is the biggest road transport organization which moves goods for both the military and the civilian sectors, competing effectively with the railways and other transport companies.

Pakistan Ordnance Factories (POF) and heavy defence-related industry are major industrial enterprises which not only serve the military by producing weapons, equipment and a lot of other goods and services, but also make some goods available to the civilian sector; some of their products are exported. This sector is managed by the Defence Production Division but the top positions in the POF and to a large extent in heavy defence-related industry are manned by serving Army officers appointed by the Army Chief, giving him leverage on this industry. Moreover, the Army and other services are the main (in some cases sole) customers.

The Army has established two charitable foundations for the welfare of retired army personnel and their families. These are the Fauji Foundation and the Army Welfare Trust. These trusts are based on the concept that the military must look after the interests and welfare of its personnel even after their retirement, an idea inherited from the British Indian military. Originally, three main agencies were engaged in the welfare of ex-service personnel. These were the Welfare Directorate, the Post-War Reconstruction Fund, and the Armed Services Boards. These agencies were re-organized in the post-independence period and their role expanded.[8] The British established the Post-War Reconstruction Fund in April 1942, for making funds available to the provincial governments for the welfare of the war veterans. After independence, the Pakistan Army decided to invest most of this fund to generate resources on a regular basis.[9] The Fauji Foundation was established; it acquired or established industrial concerns. From a modest beginning of one or two industrial units, the Fauji Foundation has become the single biggest industrial conglomerate in Pakistan with assets of Rs 8,005.87 million in 1996.[10] It has eight fully-owned industrial projects and four share-holding projects.[11] The Fauji Foundation has also started joint ventures with foreign cooperations. A cement project has been set up in Tahsil Fateh Jang, near Taxila, with the cooperation of a Danish company. The Kabirwala power project is a joint venture with a U.S. firm. A Di-ammonia phosphate (DAP) plant is being set up at Port Qasim, Karachi, with the cooperation of a Jordanian company.

These industrial projects are important sources of employment for ex-service personnel, although civilians are also hired. The Foundation has extended welfare assistance to about eight million ex-service personnel and their families and spends approximately 70 per cent of its profits on such activities; the remaining 30 per cent is reinvested. Its advertisement in a newspaper in December 1994 described the Fauji Foundation as the 'biggest welfare/industrial group' and claimed that it offered 200,000 educational scholarships to the children of ex-service personnel and had established two colleges and fifty-eight schools in different parts of the country. There were four technical training centres and sixty vocational training centres for teaching various skills to military personnel for enabling them to settle down in their post-retirement life. The Foundation runs a 600 bed hospital at Rawalpindi, a 164 bed hospital at Peshawar and 146 bed hospital at Karachi. It also manages nine hospitals in rural areas. One more hospital is scheduled to soon start functioning in Lahore. Forty-six mobile dispensaries provide medical facilities in rural areas. A number of day-care centres are also functioning under the supervision of the Foundation.[12]

Another charitable organization is the Army Welfare Trust which is engaged in a host of commercial activities. A late entrant to the field, it is gradually shaping up as another commercial and industrial empire. Its projects include a sugar mill, a woollen mill, agro industry, cement factories, a rice mill, pharmaceutical products, power generation, an oil mill, and a shoe factory. It has also established financial institutions including the Askari Commercial Bank, a general insurance company, a leasing company, and a share register. The Army Welfare Trust has also entered small business; it is involved in running a restaurant, bakery, real estate agency, travel agency, petrol pump and a company for providing security guards and related facilities. Its most flourishing business is in real estate development, i.e., housing and commercial market schemes.[13]

The Air Force established its charitable welfare trust—the Shaheen Foundation—in 1977 for the welfare of Air Force personnel and their families. It started with initial capital of Rs 3 million which increased to Rs 1300 million by 1996. It has invested in different fields including a passenger and cargo airline, textiles, real-estate development, computers, cable television, insurance, and the advertisement business. The Shaheen Foundation owns the second national airline, Shaheen Air International, which resumed international service from Peshawar to Dubai in February 1995. The other major projects include Shaheen Airport Services (set up in 1982), Shaheen Air Cargo Service (established in 1992), Shaheen Knitwear (in operation since 1981), and Shaheen Aerotraders, which conducts import and export business, maintains a bonded warehouse of Chinese aircraft parts, and represents several foreign industrial and commercial concerns. The Shaheen Systems was set up in 1989 for providing expertise in computer technology. Other important projects include Hawk Advertising Consultants (1977), Shaheen Pay TV (first cable TV network in Pakistan, established in 1996), and an insurance company, launched in 1996. It constructed a huge commercial complex in Karachi as a real estate development project in 1984, and rented it out to business and commercial groups. Similar projects are being planned for Lahore, Rawalpindi and Quetta.[14] In May 1996, the Foundation entered into a joint venture with a Canadian firm for setting up a facility for overhauling C-130 and commercial aircraft at Chaklala.[15] The profits from these ventures are used for financing welfare activities including scholarships for students, establishment of vocational schools for women, health and medical facilities, financial support to the families of those killed on duty, construction of mosques, Haj visits to Saudi Arabia, and employment opportunities for retired personnel.

The youngest and smallest of the charitable welfare organizations is the Bahria Foundation, set up by the Navy. Its subsidiaries include Bahria Tour and Travel Company, Bahria Paints Limited, Bahria Lubricants Limited, and Bharia Complex Limited. It also launched two township schemes in Rawalpindi/ Islamabad and Lahore.[16] As it generates funds from these projects, the Bahria Foundation, like its sister Foundations, is expected to expand its operations and use part of its profits for looking after the welfare of its retired personnel and their families.

A National University of Science and Technology (NUST), set up in 1991 as a decentralized multi-campus centre of excellence, is a joint military-civil venture. It includes six military institutions: College of Engineering, Risalpur; College of Signals, Rawalpindi; College of Electrical and Mechanical Engineers (E & ME), Rawalpindi; Pakistan Navy Engineering College, Karachi; College of Aeronautical Engineering, Risalpur; and Institute of Environmental Sciences and Engineering, Rawalpindi. The President of Pakistan is its Patron-in-Chief, the Prime Minister is its Chancellor, and the Army Chief heads the Board of Governors. The Rector is a retired senior Army officer. The NUST began functioning in 1993 and offered instruction for B.Sc., M.S. and Ph.D degrees.[17] The 1998 tuition fee for M.S. and Ph.D. students was Rs 7500 per month with a one-time admission fee of Rs 5000, comparable to the tuition fee charged by new educational institutions that are being set up in the private sector.

The Navy decided, in January 2000, to establish a Bahria University on the pattern of the NUST. It comprised Pakistan Naval Academy, Pakistan Navy War College, Bahria Institutes of Management and Computer Sciences at Karachi and Islamabad, the Institute of Professional Psychology, Bahria Colleges at Islamabad and Karachi and the Faculty of Earth and Environment Sciences.

C. Ethnicity and Social Character

Pakistan officially discarded the British concept of martial races for recruitment to the Army and somewhat expanded the recruitment base. However, there has not been a significant shift in the ethnic composition of the Army. The Punjab continues to provide the bulk of the officers and personnel for other ranks, with un-official estimates as 65 and 70 per cent respectively. Since 1972, the Punjab constitutes about 56 per cent of Pakistan's population, enabling it to sustain its entrenched position in the Army. The Pakhtuns from NWFP and the tribal areas (about 16 per cent of the population) are the second largest group, constituting 22–25 per cent of officers and other ranks. Even if the Pakhtuns of Baluchistan (2–3 per cent) are taken into account, their representation compares favourably with their population. The Sindhi-speaking people and Baloch (about 12 and 3 per cent of the population respectively) are under-represented, especially in the higher echelons. The Urdu-speaking populace of Sindh, i.e., *muhajirs* (about 6–7 per cent), is fairly represented at the officer level in relation to its population but there are only a small number of *Muhajirs* at the soldiers' level. They are known to be over-represented in the Air Force and the Navy.

The traditional recruiting areas of the Punjab—the salt range region—and the adjoining districts in NWFP continue to maintain their distinction as being the heartland of the Army. However, other areas are also offering manpower such as the Northern Areas and Azad Kashmir. In addition to the districts of Jhelum, Chakwal, Attock, Gujrat, and Rawalpindi, a number of adjacent districts like Sargodha, Khushab and Mianwali are providing a considerable number of people, especially for other ranks. Now recruits both for the officers and other ranks, are also coming from urban districts like Lahore, Gujranwala, Faisalabad, and the canal colonies areas. In the NWFP, the district of Kohat, Bannu and Mardan are still the main recruiting areas, although other regions are gradually increasing their numbers. Thus, the base of recruitment within the Punjab and NWFP has expanded but the Punjabis and the Pakhtuns continue to dominate the Army as they have a decisive edge in *muhajirs*, and Sindhis.[18]

In the pre-1971 period, the under-representation of Bengalis who constituted about 55–56 per cent of Pakistan's population, caused much criticism of the recruitment policy in East Pakistan. The British treated the Bengalis as a non-martial race and their recruitment was deliberately discouraged. At the time of independence, Bengalis constituted one per cent of the total strength of Pakistan's armed forces. Their numerical strength in the Army was 155 which rose to 13,000 by 1965. An exclusive Bengali infantry regiment, the East Bengal Regiment, was set up in February 1948: by 1968, four such regiments were in place. However, their representation remained inadequate in the Army, especially from the middle to the upper levels. In 1955, only 14 out of 908 Army officers of the rank of Major or above were Bengalis. In 1963, they constituted only 5 per cent of the Army officers and the percentage at the Junior Commissioned and Other Ranks level was 7.4, which improved slightly in the post-1965 period. Their representation was much better in the Air Force and the Navy, although it was never more than one third.[19] This developed into one of the major Bengali grievances in the 1960s when the military established itself as the dominant political force.

In the post-1972 period, steps were taken to improve the representation of Sindhis and Baloch in the three services, especially in the Army. A Sindh Regiment was established and the Army began to recruit even illiterate Sindhis as soldiers.[20] The quota for Baluchistan and Sindh was raised from 5 to 15 per cent in 1991.[21] The Army increased its presence in Sindh but it faced some opposition from the nationalist elements when its first cantonment was established in interior Sindh at Pano Aqil in 1988. New cantonments were set up at Dadu, Pataro, Chore, and Sakrand which did not face opposition because the local populace realized that these created job and business opportunities. The Army also improved communication in the Katcha area during its security operation, primarily to facilitate its mobility, but the local population also benefitted from it. The Army is getting more recruits from interior Sindh now than was the case in the late 1960s or the early 1970s and its presence is accepted. However, some of the nationalists groups are unable to overcome the psychological barriers created by the allotment of agricultural land to military personnel, execution of the elder Bhutto by the military regime in 1979, and the deployment of troops in 1983 and 1986 to suppress anti-Zia agitation. In the urban areas, the Army operation (1992–94) has made its role controversial with the Urdu-speaking populace, especially the MQM.

Though the ethnic character of the Army has not changed, substantially its social composition has undergone transformation. Stephen Cohen talks of three military generations: British, American, and Pakistani. The British generation included the pre-independence officers trained at the Royal Military Academy, Sandhurst, and the Indian Military Academy, Dehra Dun (called Indian Commissioned Officers, ICOs), and those given emergency commissions during the second World War. The American generation (1950–65) refers to the period when Pakistan joined the alliance system and the military obtained American weapons and technology and the officers were exposed to American training and influences. The post-1972 officers have been described as the Pakistan generation who are quite different in their orientations from the earlier generations.[22] The British were careful in inducting Indians to the officer cadre. Those sent to Sandhurst came from the loyal, prestigious and upper strata families who joined the Army as a matter of prestige rather than to earn living. The British also sent the sons of Viceroy Commissioned Officers who did not have affluent backgrounds. The social base of recruitment slightly expanded with the start of the Dehra Dun academy in 1932 but it generally remained upper and upper-middle classes. During the War period (1939–45), regular commissions were replaced with emergency commissions and a large number of people, some of whom were purely job seekers, were inducted after limited/emergency training. Their training could not be as thorough as was the case with the first two categories but most of them obtained combat experience and their professional disposition was pretty firm.

It was the Sandhurst group and the ICOs (in addition to the British officers retained in the Army) who filled the senior slots in the Pakistan Army and set its tone, which was British in training and professional orientation. However, communal riots that accompanied the establishment of the state, dispute with India over the division of military assets and weapons, and the war in Kashmir had a profound impact on their psyche and outlook and 'Pakistanized' them in their attitude towards their counterparts in India. The American connection that developed in the mid-1950s exposed them to American military equipment, training and cultural influences which eroded some British influences, especially in the case of those who joined the British Indian Army in the 1940s or passed out from the Kakul Academy in the post-independence period. However, despite the induction of American technology, training and culture, the basic pattern of ideas and orientations of the Pakistan Army inherited from the British survived. It could not break out of the British mould in such a decisive manner that one could talk of a distinct American generation.

The major shift began to take shape as the Army expanded in the late 1960s, more so since the early 1970s, against the backdrop of the Indo-Pakistan wars in 1965 and 1971. Most of those who joined the officer corps in the 1970s and later came from modest rural backgrounds and urban lower middle and lower class backgrounds as job opportunities declined in the civilian sector. They looked upon the Army more as a career opportunity rather than a family tradition or love for the profession. Their strong career orientation was coupled with their exposure to the politicized environment of the educational institutions; some had engaged in active political activity on the campus or outside during their student days. This new element was thus more politicized and ambitious than their predecessors who came from a relatively better social background and were not directly exposed to political pressures in their pre-military days.

This new breed of officers who will occupy top staff and command positions by the end of the first decade of the twenty-first century has a different orientations towards society than did those of the past. They are quite materialist in their orientations and eagerly want to enjoy the comforts of life, i.e., a house, car, bank account, modern luxuries, and foreign trips or assignments. Some of them tasted power during the Zia years or earned money from postings in the Gulf region. They also benefitted from the extensive system of rewards, benefits and facilities developed by the military for its personnel. However, when materialism becomes a major concern, there is no limit to the appetite. These tendencies are likely to build pressure on the top brass if there is some retrenchment in the existing facilities and benefits for the military personnel or if these become inadequate due mainly to inflation and price-hikes.

A large number of officers and men of the Army and the Air Force were posted in the Middle Eastern states, especially in the Gulf region, on training and security-related assignments in the 1970s and the 1980s. This brought economic windfalls to these personnel. There was a distinct improvement in the material conditions of these personnel on return to Pakistan. The Gulf connection also strengthened religious conservatism in the armed forces. This was rather ironic: on the one hand, the returnees relished consumerism and the modern facilities of life. On the other, the tendencies towards religious conservatism were quite visible in their disposition. As the openings in the Gulf region have declined in the 1990s, the younger officers are not likely to enjoy so many opportunities to earn money through foreign assignments. They will consider themselves poorer as compared with their counterparts of a decade ago. The UN Peacekeeping assignments cannot be a substitute for the former openings in the Gulf region. Not only are the opportunities much too limited but also the assignments are much too hazardous. The non-availability of new assignments comparable to the ones that were available in the Gulf region is causing frustration at the middle and lower levels, especially because they had joined the military profession for, inter alia, improving the quality of their life. The military will therefore have to maintain a strong reward and benefit system to keep them pacified.

The tendency on the part of junior officers to make partisan political statements and their too-frequent expression of low, often contemptuous, opinion about civilians seems to have increased. Similarly, the instances of junior officers disregarding civilian laws or picking up fights with policemen or junior civilian officials, when they question such behaviour, are no longer rare.[23] The growing materialism and decline in the professional conduct have been criticized even in military circles. A retired officer commented on the changing disposition of the officers, that the motto of 'service before self' has been changed to 'self before service.'[24] Another retired officer wrote: 'Our military leadership in the past ten years has become increasingly materialistic like the rest of the society. Money, property and luxurious life styles are now the endemic part of the senior rank structures. The juniors pick on the crumbs and grow more disgruntled with time.'[25]

The military's expanded role and martial laws have seriously undermined its image as being above politics. It is viewed as one of the contending groups engaged in power politics. The civilian circles are more vocal now in criticism of the military's political role, and especially the perks and privileges the military has amassed. The Zia regime is subjected to the most bitter criticism for bringing about an all-embracing involvement of the military personnel in national affairs. However, the critical appraisals make a distinction between the senior commanders who assumed political roles and the military as a profession or an institution; the latter still commands respect. Growing materialism, incidents of junior officers not 'behaving' while off-duty, the perks and privileges of serving and retired officers, and defence purchases are targeted for censure. In 1987, a Karachi-based construction company advertised in a newspaper that it had hired a retired general as its executive director which caused much sensation. A couple of days later a satirical article appeared in a newspaper under the title 'An open application from a retired general' which enumerated the services and qualifications of the general as the break-up of the country in 1971, supervision of construction of personal houses in defence societies, management of several ranches overseas, engineering experience acquired by helping to engineer successful coups against civilian governments, and sufficient executive experience including the execution of an elected Prime Minister. The physical features were described as 'fat and flabby, overfed on power,' and for salary, the sky was the limit which was to be deposited in a Swiss bank account.[26] The entrepreneurial activities of the charitable trusts like real estate development, housing schemes, and small scale business, are also criticized. Another criticism focuses on kickbacks in defence purchases. In 1996–97, the Chiefs of the Navy and the Air Force were accused by the press of involvement in kickback scandals; the Naval Chief resigned in April 1997 but the controversy did not end.

Still another criticism addresses the organizational set up of the military. A number of writers, including some retired officers, argue that the involvement of the military in politics has undermined its professional character and that its current strategic doctrine, size, shape, and equipment need to be thoroughly revised and restructured. Some unofficial circles floated the idea of setting up a territorial force or a militia or a 'people's army' in order to reduce the strength of the professional military, although no one has fully articulated these ideas or has given some credible plan or strategy for such structural changes. The post-Cold War environment has made the civilian and military circles conscious of the need for paying greater attention to the vitality and health of the society, i.e., societal security, rather than thinking exclusively in terms of military oriented external security. This expanded concept of security calls for rationalization of the defence expenditure, adoption of political measures to defuse tension in the region and allocation of more resources to socio-economic development.[27]

The military circles are critical of the role of the political leaders and point to their poor capacity for crisis management and an absence of a sense of mutual accommodation which makes governance in a democratic context rather difficult. They hold the political leaders responsible for the military's involvement in politics. However, they recognize that the failings of the political leaders do not necessarily give them a right to rule. Some put the blame on the top commanders and absolve the institution of the criticism. In 1997, military circles complained that they were being subjected to unjustified and hostile criticism for alleged kickbacks in defence purchases and the arrest of an Air Force officer in the US on a charge of drug trafficking; many viewed this as a deliberate attempt by some elements to malign the institution.[28] In April 1997, the Army Chief warned against the 'media trial' of the armed forces. While acknowledging that the armed forces were not 'beyond the pale of accountability,' he maintained that 'a line must be drawn at some point so that the national interest is not jeopardized or compromised.'[29] Throughout the 1990s, while critical comments were appearing in the press, it also carried sympathetic articles. In fact, these outnumbered the critical ones.

D. Islam and the Military

Islam is integral to Pakistan military ideology. Islam was repeatedly invoked during the wars in 1965 and 1971 to galvanize the soldiers and the civilians for the defence of the country. When Zia ul-Haq assumed the command of the Army in March 1976, he gave the motto of 'Iman' (Faith), 'Taqwa' (Piety and abstinence), 'Jihad-fi-sibillah' (Holy war in the name of God) which reflected his strong religious inclinations. However, this was not a major departure because Islamic principles, teachings and history have always been a part of military education, training and ideology. Other commanders who preceded or have followed him highlighted Islamic ideals and teachings and have urged the officers and soldiers to imbibe Islamic values and military traditions.

Four major developments during the Zia years as the Army Chief (1976–88) had far reaching implications for the role of

Islam in the Army. First, as Zia ul-Haq was using Islam and conservative Islamic groups to legitimize his military rule, he encouraged Islamic conservatism and orthodoxy in the Army. This fitted well with the changes in the orientations of the new breed of officers who came from the middle to lower strata of the society, hailing mainly from towns and urban areas with conservative religious values. The institution of a 'regimental priest' was upgraded and strengthened and the bias in favor of Islamic conservatism also influenced the promotion policy. Second, some of the Islamic groups were allowed to make in-roads into the Army, something of an anathema in the past. Zia ul-Haq had a strong inclination towards the Tableeghi Jamaat (a purely religious organization focused on Islamic renewal which does not involve itself in politics), and he was the first head of state to attend its annual congregations at Raiwind. Encouraged by this, a good number of officers and enlisted men began to be associated openly with the Tableeghi Jamaat, attended its annual meetings, and made it a point to demonstrate their religious disposition in public. Other conservative Islamic-sectarian groups were also able to develop some connections with the personnel of the three services, especially the Army. One indicator of growing religious sentiments was the increase in the number of bearded officers in the Army and the Air Force. Some of these officers engaged in preaching Islam within and outside their service in their spare time in collaboration with the Tableeghi Jamaat and a host of other orthodox groups.

The other group that gained access to the Army and the bureaucracy was the Jamaat-i-Islami, which had a favorable disposition towards the Zia regime and was associated with the government's Afghanistan policy. The Jamaat-i-Islami with its definite Islamic political agenda, penetrated these institutions, and many officers would not hesitate to express their fascination for its ideology and the writings of its founder, Maulana Maudoodi. Religion thus became an important part of the public disposition of the in-service personnel. In the past, religious rituals and beliefs were treated as personal affairs and the in-service personnel avoided active involvement with religious groups.

Third, the Islamic Revolution in Iran (1979) had a profound impact on the civilians as well as the military circles in Pakistan. It strengthened the conservative Islamic elements and created an environment which in part facilitated Zia ul-Haq's efforts to push through his Islamization program. A number of retired and serving officers (like many civilians) talked of an Islamic Revolution in Pakistan, although none was clear as to how this would be brought about and what would be the shape of the new institutions and processes in the post-revolution period.

Fourth, the Afghanistan experience reinforced Islamic conservatism among Army personnel. A good number of them worked in collaboration with Islamic parties and Afghan resistance groups. The Inter Services Intelligence (ISI) was involved in transferring weapons to the Afghan resistance and advised them on strategy against the Soviet troops in Afghanistan. As the Muslim world in general supported the Afghan cause and Islamic militants from several Muslim countries worked closely with the Afghan resistance groups, pan-Islamic sentiments were also strengthened among them. The exit of the Soviet troops from Afghanistan in February 1989 created a sense of triumph among them and the thinking process of many Army personnel, including some senior officers, was immersed in the Afghanistan experience. A number of them believed, and often openly suggested, that the Afghanistan experience could be replicated elsewhere by the Muslims and that the Afghanistan style of military option would bring an end to non-Muslim domination of the Muslim world, especially Indian rule in Kashmir.

Changes in the U.S. policies towards Pakistan and Afghanistan after the Soviet withdrawal have also strengthened religious zealots inside and outside the military. The U.S. suspended military sales and economic assistance to Pakistan, distanced itself from the Afghan resistance movement and labelled militant Islamic groups as terrorists. These changes were bound to evoke a strong reaction in Pakistan, especially among the Islamic groups which felt that the U.S. had betrayed them. The slowing down of interaction between the militaries of Pakistan and the U.S. and especially the discontinuation of the U.S. sponsored military training programs strengthened the religious elements. Additional frustrations were caused by the stalemate in Kashmir, the U.S. directed invasion of Iraq, the Chechnya affair, and the agony of the Bosnian Muslims. The Islamic elements described the U.S. as an adversary of the Muslims and felt that the Pakistan government and the senior commanders did not adopt a forthright position against the U.S. This created a dilemma for the senior commanders who recognized the anti-American sentiments of their personnel and civilians and shared some of the their criticism, but still viewed the relationship with the U.S. as important and relevant to the modernization of the armed forces.

A number of religious zealots in the Army were arrested in September 1995 on charges of planning to establish an Islamic government after overthrowing the military and civilian leadership. The official version claimed that one Major General, one Brigadier and three Colonels, alongwith some other Army personnel and civilians, were planning to take over the Army headquarters and then replace the civilian government with an Islamic government based on strict enforcement of the Sharia.[30] Only four of them were convicted by a court martial and were sentenced to rigorous imprisonment.[31] A number of Islamic groups and parties issued statements in their favor, accusing the then government of Benazir Bhutto and the Army brass of 'witch hunting' the Islamic elements in the Army. Their efforts did not evoke any sympathy or support within or outside the Army.

As long as Islam is coupled with professionalism and service discipline, it is a source of strength. However, whenever the imperative of the military profession is subordinated to extraneous considerations, no matter what their source, the military faces internal problems. If the professional and corporate interests of the military are to be protected, no principles and ideas can be allowed to flourish independent of professional and service ethos. The post-Zia Army top brass are taking steps to rehabilitate the age-old tradition of keeping Islam and professionalism together and treating the former as a component of the latter. There is hardly any dispute as to the place of Islam in military ideology but what is being discouraged is the tendency on the part of some to pursue Islam-oriented activism at the cost of professional excellence, discipline and service ethos.

The military has thus become an all-pervasive force with expanding professional and corporate interests encompassing the government, the economy and the society. Its strength no longer depends on controlling the levers of power but it is derived from the political clout it exercises due to its organizational strength and its significant presence in the economy and the society. Its serving and retired personnel are quite conspicuous in the polity and the society. Its ethnic homogeneity contributes to internal cohesion but it becomes a source of irritation for the under-represented regions and ethnicities, especially because the military profession opens the way to a host of rewards, opportunities and prospects. However, the changing social background of the officers, erosion of the traditional value system, growing materialism and the surge of Islam-oriented activism are likely to adversely affect the military's internal character and its disposition towards politics and society. The senior commanders are taking steps to reassert the primacy of the professional and service ethos so that the military continues to operate as a cohesive and disciplined force, performing its professional responsibilities and adequately protecting and promoting its professional and corporate interests and the strategic position it occupies in the polity.

The expanded role of the military in the polity and the society makes it a key decision maker for determining politico-social and economic priorities and allocating resources for societal development. Its institutional and corporate interests make it imperative for the top brass to see to it that territorial security considerations get adequate attention in policy making and allocation of resources. This means that the policies of the government will be heavily skewed in favor of these considerations rather than towards societal development or societal security. Sectors such as health care, education, women and child development, environment, civic amenities for the common people, and participatory management of political, social and economic affairs, will continue to be neglected. However, the optimistic view is that as the military spreads out in the society, it recognizes that only a healthy, prosperous, plural, and participatory society can sustain a powerful military. There cannot be a strong military without an equally strong and vibrant society.

NOTES

1. For a detailed study of the conditions and circumstances leading to the rise of the military and an analysis of various military regimes, *see*, Lawrence Ziring, *Pakistan: The Enigma of Political Development* (Boulder: Westview Press, 1980); Ayesha Jalal, *The State of Martial Rule* (Cambridge: Cambridge University Press, 1990); Hasan-Askari Rizvi, *The Military and Politics in Pakistan* (Lahore: Progressive Publishers, 1986); Mohammad Waseem, *Politics and the State in Pakistan* (Islamabad: National Institute of Historical and Cultural Research, 1994); Omar Noman, *Pakistan: Political and Economic History Since 1947* (London: Kegan Paul International, 1990).

2. S.E. Finer, 'The Military and Politics in the Third World,' in W. Scott Thompson (ed.), *The Third World: Premises of U.S. Policy* (San Francisco: Institute of Contemporary Studies, 1978), p. 84.

3. Baluchistan University was headed by a Brigadier in the 1980s. A Major General was appointed Vice Chancellor of Peshawar University in 1993 for a brief period. A Lt.-General served as Vice Chancellor of the Punjab University, Lahore, during 1993–97. In early 1998, another Lt.-General was appointed Vice Chancellor of Lahore's University of Engineering and Technology. In September 1999, a Lt.-Gen. was again appointed Vice Chancellor of the Punjab University.

4. *Muslim*, 1 July 1997; *Dawn*, 20 May 1997.

5. Fazal Muqeem Khan, The *Story of the Pakistan Army* (Karachi: Oxford University Press, 1963), pp. 232–233.

6. Official statement of the Punjab Government, dated 17 January 1988.

7. M.A. Niazi, 'COAS as CEO: Pakistan's Military-Industrial Complex,' *Nation*, 22 June 1991.

8. Fazal Muqeem Khan, op. cit., pp. 232–236.

9. Ibid., p. 235; Raymond A. Moore, 'Military Nation Building in Pakistan and India,' *World Affairs* (Vol. 132 No. 3, December 1969), pp. 219–234.

10. *See*, the statements of the Director Finance and the Secretary of the Fauji Foundation to the press: *Dawn*, 1 May 1997.

11. The fully owned projects include three sugar mills at Tando Muhammad Khan, Khoshki, and Sangla Hill; Experimental and Seed Multiplication Farm, Nukerji; Fauji Cereals, Rawalpindi; Corn Complex, Jehangira; Polypropylene Products, Hub Chowki; and Fauji Gas, Rawalpindi. The share holding projects include Fauji Fertilizer; Oil Terminal and Distribution Company; Mari Gas Company; and Lifeline Company dealing in liquefied petroleum gas. Two projects were closed down: Fauji Metals and Fauji Autos. Another project, Fauji Electric Power Company, was dropped.

12. Fauji Foundation advertisements: *Nation*, 27 December 1994, and *Defence Journal* (Vol. 20 No. 5–6, July 1994; *see also*, *Dawn*, 1 May 1997.

13. *See*, the advertisements put out by the Army Welfare Trust in newspapers: *Jang*, 29 June 1991; *Nation*, 1 May 1994; *Dawn*, 31 October 1996 and 27 July 1997. Two housing schemes were launched in Lahore and Peshawar and plans were made in 1996–97 to launch a commercial market project in Faisalabad.

14. *See*, the officially sponsored articles: Qamar S. Kiani, 'Shaheen Foundation PAF-An Overview,' *Dawn* (Special Supplement), 12 May 1996; S. Salahuddin, 'A Landmark in the History of Shaheen Foundation,' ibid., (A Supplement on the inauguration of Shaheen Commercial Complex), 5 July 1984; see the statement of the Chief of the Air Staff, Air Chief Marshal Muhammad Anwar Shamim: *Muslim*, 7 July 1984.

15. *Dawn*, 26 May 1996.

16. Ibid., 24 January 1997.

17. For details, *see*, the admission-advertisements of the NUST: *Nawa-i-Waqt*, 14 April 1993; *Jang*, 28 September 1994; *see*, the statement of the Rector of the University, Lt.-General Syed Shujaat Hussain (Retd.) to the press: *Nation*, 27 June 1991.

18. Talat Aslam, 'The Changing Face of the Army,' *Herald*, May 1989, pp. 64–73.

19. Cited from Henry F. Goodnow, *The Civil Service of Pakistan* (New Haven: Yale University Press, 1964), p. 107; Hasan-Askari Rizvi, op. cit., pp. 135–145.

20. *See*, *Nawa-i-Waqt*, 25 February 1984; *Dawn*, 1 April 1984; *Muslim*, 25 April 1984.

21. *Jang*, 22 March 1991.

22. Stephen P. Cohen, *The Pakistan Army* (Berkeley: University of California Press, 1984), pp. 55–75.

23. The press often reported on altercations between young officers and the police. Such incidents were occasionally reported in letters to the editor. *See*, for example, a letter entitled 'Upstarts' in *Nation*, 22 July 1991. In Peshawar, the entire staff of a local girls college was taken hostage by a group of young officers after the daughter of the Corps Commander was caught by the Principal cheating in an examination. *Newsline*, June 1996, p. 83.

24. Khalid Rauf Khan, 'Officers But Gentlemen,' *Nation* (Friday Review), 7 May 1993.

25. Muhammad Yahya Effendi, 'Pakistan Army Officer Corps: Values in Transition or the Erosion of a Value System?' *Pakistan Army Journal* (Vol. 34 No. 1, March 1993), pp. 45–58.

26. *Star* (Karachi), 1 October 1987. *See*, two letters to the editor entitled 'Perks for Generals,' *Dawn*, 7 and 27 April 1996.

27. For comments and views, *see*, Zafar A. Chaudhry, 'National Defence: Aims, Strategy and Cost,' *Dawn*, 19 February 1988; by the same author, 'Our Defence Chimera and Reality,' ibid., 29 September 1996; 'The Army is Bluffing,' an interview by Nur Khan: *Nation* (Friday Review), 26 August 1994. Both Zafar Chaudhry and Nur Khan are former Air Force Chiefs. *See also*, Afzal Mahmood, 'Security at Lower Costs,' *Dawn*, 19 August 1997.

28. A retired Air Force officer maintained that the officer arrested in the U.S. for drug trafficking was lured into this by a staff member of the American Drug Enforcement Agency based in Islamabad as a part of a CIA–DEA 'conspiracy' to undermine the reputation of the Pakistan Air Force and to neutralize Pakistan's efforts to have the Pressler law rescinded. Ayaz Ahmad Khan (Air Marshal Retd.), 'PAF-Target of the Sting Operation,' *Muslim*, 26 August 1997.

29. *Muslim*, 26 April 1997.

30. *See*, the statement of the Defence Minister: *Nation*, 15 November 1995; *Dawn*, 12 November 1995; *New York Times*, 12 April 1996.

31. *Dawn*, 31 October 1996.

PART FOUR

New Contenders and Issues in Power Negotiations

9

POWER CONFIGURATIONS IN PUBLIC AND PRIVATE ARENAS:
THE WOMEN'S MOVEMENT'S RESPONSE

Farzana Bari and Saba Gul Khattak

This chapter analyzes the women's movement as a stakeholder within civil society that continuously negotiates women's interests with the state and society. We maintain that it constantly engages with the state to negotiate increased space and rights for women in the public and private arena through affirmative actions but not through direct political activism via party politics. The chapter confines itself to assess and analyze the response of the women's movement to power configurations at three different levels: (i) the family (ii) the community and (iii) the state. In all three arenas, the movement has displayed certain strengths and achievements while being constrained by its own composition along the lines of class, urban bias and the structures within which it must work. Our emphasis is on the collective aspect of the movement and not on individual initiatives, which often help to forge the movement for rights forward. We thus limit our attention to women's individual negotiations and voices within the family, with their community/ communities and with the state in their individual capacity insofar as these help to transform the movement and vice versa. In this context, the chapter also examines the issue of NGO-ization of the women's movement so as to underscore the constraints and advantages of funded activism.

A. Definition of the Women's Movement[1]

What is the nature of the women's movement in Pakistan and what constitutes it? Can we chart a history of the women's movement by documenting the emergence of women's organizations? Can urban-based organizations represent women of the entire country and constitute a movement? Are class differences relevant? Does the construction of knowledge, and individual and collective consciousness result from class and the site/geographical area that people occupy? Answers to these questions are crucial for theoretical clarity and analysis.

Many feminist activists like to make a distinction between the women's rights movement and the feminist movement in South Asia. They contend that although there is an overlap between the two, yet the underlying stances that inform the two types of movements are different. One champions equal rights within a liberal-democratic framework while the other has an active feminist agenda which challenges the very legitimacy of the system within which it operates. Thus, while the two overlap, they also diverge due to the difference in the underlying principles that inform their different stances. Somewhat similar distinctions have been made by Peterson (1993) and Hayes (1997) who take Molyneux's (1985) concept of practical and strategic interests as the basis for distinguishing among women's movements.[2] We regard both types of movements as two distinct streams within the larger context of working toward women's emancipation from oppression. If we consider them to be a result of oppositional consciousness,[3] we would be able to view the movement in its entirety rather than as a splintered phenomenon. Such an approach will also help to integrate the concerns of many of the women who generally consider themselves excluded and are, therefore, compelled to position themselves outside the mainstream movement. However, we exclude women's wings of fundamentalist parties including the far right religious parties as the objectives of these organizations or parties are different. They primarily support intolerant agendas, not women's emancipation.

Many women maintain that the women's movement is not new at all; that, in fact, it is quite old because women's perception of their oppression has existed for centuries. They base these claims on women's writings and oral traditions. Thus, for many the movement is very old.[4] On the other hand, others maintain that resistance and subversion among women do not necessarily translate into a movement:

> ...in a sense, without a history, forced to rediscover the past anew, forging again and again the consciousness of their sex. Given this perpetual disruption and also the self-hatred that has alienated women writers from a sense of collective identity, it does not seem possible to speak of a 'movement.' (Elain Showalter 1977, 11–12)

Many feminists consider both individual and collective consciousness to be integral parts of the women's movement while they maintain the distinction. In the latter case, a whole collectivity responds to particular signals and sees/reacts collectively to particular kinds of oppression. The former type of consciousness finds self-expression in literature, art, poetry or rebellion/resistance in one's own life. This kind of self-expression may not necessarily reflect the attitude of a collectivity. In the women's movement context, it is difficult to assert that the first forms a part of the movement because there is an element of collectivity, while individual forms of protest or expression of a particular consciousness are not part of the movement because they represent the individual and, therefore, do not extend to a larger community. Individuals do not live in a vacuum; often their ideas are derived from or in reaction to lived social experience. A large majority of feminists emphasize the collective and organized aspect:

> The movement does not refer to isolated and sporadic actions or any one group or forum. A movement has a coherent ideological base which is involved in guiding all its actions and underlies its positions. When defining strategies are formulated, based on a well thought-out ideological stand, it becomes a movement. It has political as well as social, personal, and cultural elements and must also take into account

international issues which have an impact on national and local issues. (Anis Haroon, 1995)

Political consciousness and a well-thought out ideological stand will also result in a movement because there will be a clear sense of self-righteousness and justice. Movements are usually born from a self-perception of oppression and seek social (rather than state) power through social mobilization. (Frank & Fuentes, 1988). In the context of the women's movement in Pakistan, while it displays the aspects of self-righteousness, it has seldom been able to achieve street power and mass mobilization. However, what is important to note is that it has been able to constantly construct itself as a player in civil society vis a vis other contenders of power as well as sometimes vis-à-vis the state itself.

We conclude that the women's movement is made up of individual and collective expression. Unlike other civil society institutions, it does not have any formal organizational, institutionalized structure. It is both concrete and fluid, made up of NGOs, feminist and women's rights groups, literature, and the media when it supports women's causes. Furthermore, often third world women's movements are interconnected with and sometimes merge with human rights movements (Chai, 1997: 169). Thus, it is an intricate grid of relationships that collectively constitute the women's movement in the context of being a contender in civil society.

B. The Women's Movement and Civil Society

What constitutes civil society? The concept of civil society, long debated within social and political theory,[5] is seen here to be the formal expression of mediation and interpenetration between the state on the one hand and the individual on the other. The existence of civil society helps to attain collective action through institutionalized, organized forms of interaction between the state and the individual. In a sense then, it provides a zone of engagement between the state and the individual. According to Neera Chandhoke (1995:9), states invariably seek to control and limit the political practices of society by constructing the boundaries of the political. The state attempts, in other words, to substitute the political discourse. However, politics as articulatory practices which mediate between the experiential and the expressive are not only about controls and the laying down of boundaries. They are about transgressions of these boundaries and about the reconstitution of the political. The site at which these mediations and contestations take place, *the site at which society enters into a relationship with the state can be defined as civil society.'* [emphasis ours].

Clarifying the concept, this definition expands the boundaries of civil society from its popular usage. Currently the terms in which civil society is popularly understood relate to associations with formal legalistic structures such as trade unions, chambers of commerce, lawyers and doctors associations, teachers' associations, religion-based associations etc. Cohen and Arato (1994: ix) help identify the spheres of civil society which for them 'consists of the intimate sphere (especially the family), the sphere of associations (especially voluntary associations), social movements and forms of public communication'. This definition works best for our purposes since it accounts for an expanded terrain of civil society.

The concept of civil society is intrinsically tied up with masculinist interpretations of the state. It follows, then, that civil society is also restricted by similar qualifying factors that limit the state. The relationship between the women's movement and civil society in Pakistan is necessarily problematic, especially for feminists. This is so because the concept of civil society, within which the women's movement is taken to be embedded, is itself a concept steeped in constructs emanating from patriarchal arrangements, in particular, the state. Feminist critiques of the state have recently gained some degree of acceptance with a small but growing set of feminists writing about the different aspects (see for example, Pateman, Elshtain, Enloe, Peterson, Kandiyoti, Jayawardena, Yuval-Davis).

Feminists argue that state theories (Marxist, statist, pluralist, liberal etc.) display shortcomings also because these are gender blind while trying to explain a fundamentally gendered phenomenon. Wendy Brown (1992: 14) explains, 'the multiple dimensions of socially constructed masculinity have historically shaped the state–this is what it means to talk about masculinist power rather than the power of men.' Furthermore, the state privileges men over women through the manner in which it constructs citizenship.

We should understand that the very terms of citizenship are tilted against women. In the past, citizenship was granted to men who owned property. This right was extended slowly in the West to women and slaves. The abstract citizen is always addressed by liberal political and legal codes as masculine, not only because for centuries the political has been the domain of man, but also because he is considered to be morally oriented toward autonomy, autarky and individual power. Often, many marginalized women live in a state as if they are not citizens at all (Grant 1991, 12; Harrington 1992, 70–71). This is possible due to the alienation that they face in the absence of strong civil society institutions that will provide them the site at which they can enter into a relationship with the state.

C. The Women's Movement's Response to Power Configurations in Pakistani Society

In this section, we look at the women's movement as it negotiates for power in three contexts: the family, the community and the state. This analysis is limited in that it focuses upon the women's movement in civil society and does not directly account for the unequal terms of citizenship (both conceptual and actual issues) at the individual level. (For further discussion of this dimension, refer to Weiss in Chapter 4 of this volume.) The caveats identified in the section above with regard to masculinist ideologies informing the construction of the state, civil society and its institutions are carried over into the analyses.

C. i. Women and the Family

The family is the primary institution of civil society upon which the state depends for many of its ideological functions. It is also the first site where contestation and negotiation between women and patriarchal power structures takes place. According to Robina Saigol (1997a, 11), the 'analysis of the family and community are ... important for an understanding of statist processes, in particular the process of the gendering of national and personal identity.' She adds, 'The family, as a pillar of the state, consciously and unconsciously, colludes with the state in the upholding of patriarchal norms and values. This institution is, therefore, as integral to the state as an army and an overarching ideology.'

While the family is identified as a site of oppression, Patricia Jeffery explains why it is so difficult for feminists to challenge it. She writes (1998: 229–230), 'Globalization processes have spread universalistic frameworks that tend to devalue or oust local ones. In South Asia, critics of feminism generally see it as an instance of such processes. When feminists critique the family (and also the religious community) as a key site of women's subordination, their assaults on local values and identities generate a backlash that decentres their universalistic claims by pointing to their ethnocentrism, that asserts the equal (or even superior) validity of locally produced frameworks, and that insists on the contextual specificity of morality.

Women's rights and space within the family vis-à-vis male members is defined according to religion and the specificity of local culture and is manifested in customary practices and statutory law. The disparities in the rights between male and female members of the family range from the value attached to sexual differences, access to family resources, opportunities, control over their sexuality, and the right to make choices. The impact of disparity and discrimination is reflected in gender differentials in almost all indicators of human development.

Malnutrition and anemia is higher among females than males; in poor households women bear the burden of poverty more than men. As far as ownership of property or land is concerned, according to a 1995 survey of a thousand households in rural areas of Punjab, only thirty-six women owned land in their own names while less than 2 per cent women representatives sit in the national parliament. The legal status of women is also unequal to that of men.

The low entitlement of women due to the ideology of the sexual division of labor becomes the basis for male power over women. However, we do not argue that all women have low entitlement; our assertion is that in all social relationships men have power over women due to their superior material and ideological status. This is the reality of women's lives, which cuts across class, region, ethnicity, and rural/urban divides. Nevertheless, these divisions do impact and determine the nature of power in gender relationships. Power configurations within the family also constantly change with women's life cycle while maintaining essential male control and power over women's sexuality.

Thus the family becomes an arena where women at the individual level are constantly negotiating and pushing the margin of familial boundaries and men try to maintain the status quo, at times through coercive means. Women's position within the gender hierarchy of the family depends upon a complex combination of factors. These pertain to class, age, marital status, education, level of consciousness, as well as the cultural contexts and the rural/urban settings in which they live. Although these factors contribute to their relative power (or powerlessness) to negotiate for increased space, rights and power within the family, they are fundamentally negotiating from a position of subordination and weakness. They thus attempt to carve spaces for themselves in a setting that is pitted against them.

Women's negotiations to make their own decisions at the family level are viewed as personal and private and do not enter the public arena. It is only when there is a complete breakdown in this negotiating process that we witness a manifestation of the negotiating process in its entirety. This breakdown is signaled when women leave their home or are made victims of violence by their own family members. The growing number of women entering *dar-ul-amans* (refuges) and police stations are one such indication. Male power manifests itself in high incidents of domestic violence. According to Amnesty International's 1998 Report, 70 per cent of women are subjected to violence in their homes. Only in cases of particular cruelty does the women's movement respond. A systematic analysis of gender relations and awareness raising about gender disparities in rights within the family has not been central to the women's movement. The movement's response has been mostly reactive to the situation where gross violations of women/human rights takes place. The issue is then usually raised in the public arena with the media, the judiciary and the state at a discourse level as the women's movement has an extremely limited capacity to provide support services to the survivors of violence. On a day-to-day basis, many rebellions by women of disadvantaged sections of society are contained and receive no attention. Although their existence necessitates that the women's movement needs to question and highlight the oppressive aspect of the family and advocate restructuring of controls within the family, the movement has largely been silent. Such situations structurally limit the movement's ability to demand and pursue social change.

Therefore, the ability of the women's movement to articulate negotiations by individual women has remained weak. However, in extreme cases of violation of rights, it has mobilized support for women, often with support from other civil society organizations. There have been cases of gross violations of women's human rights, compelling human and women's rights activists (in some cases the same persons in Pakistan, for example, Asma Jehangir and Hina Jilani) to support individual women facing unusual usurpation of their rights. For example, in 1993, Zainab Noor was sexually/genitally mutilated by her husband on charges of 'disobedience.' The case received the attention of Prime Minister Benazir Bhutto as well as other top women government functionaries. Zainab Noor was sent abroad for medical treatment at state expense and to this day a woman's organization looks after her. This case opened up a sympathetic space for women in the media with regard to marital rape and sexual violence. Since the government swiftly came forward to help her and took action against her husband, women's groups did not have to play a critical role in trying to obtain justice for her.

However, in the Saima Waheed case, women's organizations played a major role in fighting for justice for her. Saima married a man of her choice against her parents' wishes. Despite her legal right to marry a person of her choice, Saima was denied this right by her father, who used violence and blackmail against her to make her obey his wishes. He later charged her and her husband under *Hudood* laws for *zina* (extramarital sexual relations) and tried to forcefully take her home from the refuge where she was provided protection. In this case, opinion—even among the judges who gave the final verdict was divided as people were torn between upholding parental and familial (as well as patriarchal) authority and upholding an individual's right to marry out of choice and not compulsion (Neelam Hussain 1997:237). Riffat Afridi and Humaira, who left their homes to marry men of their own choice, followed this case. Women's groups demonstrated in support of these women's decisions to exercise their religious and constitutional right to marry and offered them protection against the wrath of their families. In another case, Samia Imran was murdered in the office of AGHS in Lahore because she wanted a divorce from her violent husband and took refuge in Dastak (a shelter run by AGHS). This incident invoked the most sustained protest from women's groups.

It is important to note that all cases where the women's movement showed militancy in protesting against the violation of women's rights by the family happened to be of those women who belonged to influential upper-middle class families. Incidents of violence committed against women from low-income groups reported in daily newspapers, especially in the vernacular press, hardly triggered the same response from the movement. Even gruesome incidents such as chopping off a wife's nose or bride-burning and death due to the bursting of cooking stoves in kitchens barely provoked a concerted response. The class background of women leaders in the movement is one explanation for the varying degree of militancy in the women's movement's response to violations of women's rights in different class settings. These women feel directly touched or threatened when another woman from a similar class background is violated.

Although the women's movement has been advocating for women's rights and, within a liberal framework, has advocated for reforms that will ensure basic justice, the women's movement has been weak on questioning the family as a construct. Issues of marital rape, abortion, unequal gender rights in family laws in case of termination of marriage, minimum age at marriage, natural guardianship of children, polygamy, inheritance, and restrictions on women's mobility are ones that merit to be raised on a more systematic and regular basis. However, they are only mentioned in relation to extreme cases of violation of women's rights within the family. The reasons range from the need for support from men who are powerful within state structures, to many women's own refusal to see the oppressive aspects of the family. According to Robina Saigol (1997b: 161), because 'the family is not analyzed as a system of knowledge and source of identity, it is not the focus of women's activism.' She also asserts that the middle class character of the women's movement prevents it from attacking the institution of the family, outright.

The women's movement is largely dictated by the need to gain social legitimacy. If its demands pose a threat to the basic structure that helps the edifice of the state to exist, it will alienate all those who are in power. Unable to risk such an eventuality as well as dictated by personal investments in relationships within the family, women in the movement have kept clear of the family in general. Many women of privileged classes 'collaborate, consciously or unconsciously, with patriarchy and collude with powerful men against rural women who do not have material luxuries under the double and triple burdens imposed by their class, position and patriarchy. Rural women are killed and regularly battered by their husbands with the result that they have no idealized or romantic visions of "the happy family".' (Saigol 1997b: 164). Therefore, the women's movement response to power hierarchies within the family has been limited in terms of its expression and scope.

On the other hand, the urban bias in the Pakistani women's movement has been pointed out by many. However, Alavi (1991) discusses the presence of the lower middle class in the vanguard of the movement since the 1980s. The battle for women's rights is certainly being fought in the cities, he asserts.

Furthermore, Fareeda Shaheed (1998: 143) asserts that 'the ability of the women's movement to bridge women's distinct identities of class, ethnicity, and urban–rural locations has so far been analyzed in terms of the class background of activists and whether the feminist discourse was secular or not'. Class— though significant—is not enough to explain the current women's movement inability to cut across other identities.' The reasons may have less to do with the language of feminist discourse than with the public political nature of the women's movement: the marked tendency to focus on national-level legal rights almost excludes women's personal lives, where definitions of gender and attendant control mechanisms are experienced on a daily basis.

We conclude that the women's movement has carefully turned a blind eye to women's issues within the family. While such a stance might bestow some social legitimacy, and is probably also circumscribed by the masculinist nature of the state and civil society, in the final analysis it serves to highlight the weakness of the movement vis-à-vis the larger structures within which it operates.

C. ii. The Women's Movement vis-à-vis the Community

The concept of community is quite fluid in urban settings and fairly concrete in rural areas in Pakistan. In rural and tribal areas, people live in geographically small localities where they frequently interact with each other on a daily basis. Living together for centuries in a geographical space with shared cultural and religious values and common interests helped to form a collective sense of a community. Historically, decision-making structures have also evolved in such communities. In urban areas especially in big cities, the concept of community is more problematic. Because of urbanization and migration, the concept of community exists at multiple levels in people's perception, even when there are no concrete community structures in terms of decision-making. The community/communities construct a set of values and ideal images especially for women, and then exert pressure on individual members to conform in order to protect and guard the collective identity of the community. As Moghadam maintains,

> ...Women are seen as the transmitters of group values and traditions and as agents of socialization of the young. When group identity becomes intensified, women are elevated to the status of symbols of the community and are compelled to assume the burden of the reproduction of the group (1994:18).

Since the ideal of womanhood is at the heart of the community identity, it seeks to control women and ensures conformity by prescribing socially sanctioned punishments ranging from dispossessing them from entitlement of their share of community resources to death.

When people violate women's bodies and their rights in the name of protecting family honour, their act of violence becomes possible due to its wide acceptance at the community level. According to the HRCP report (1998), out of 888 murders of women in Punjab, 286 were by relatives on suspicion of immorality on the part of the victim. In tribal/feudal areas of Sindh and Baluchistan, men and women suspected of illicit sexual relations are denounced as *karo* and *kari* and killed by the family in the name of *ghairat* (honour of the family). Since tribal honour rests primarily in women's bodies, in cases of illicit sexual relations, women are more likely to be killed by the family and community than are men. According to the Amnesty International Report (1998), in Larkana, a district of Sindh, of eighty-six reported honour killings in 1997, fifty-three were female victims. The community socially and morally sanctions such killings. The patriarchal state also helps shape community identities by not taking action against them. Honour killings rarely lead to criminal prosecution or convictions due to the lack of witnesses willing to come forward due to community pressures.

Male–dominated community structures, including tribal *jirgas* and village councils, unlawfully impose punishments on those who assert their individual rights against the prescribed norms of the tribe or the community. In Hyderabad, a tribal council of the Manzai tribe imposed a death sentence on a newly married couple guilty of unlawful sexual relations. They were shot dead in Hyderabad in September 1997. Similarly, a couple was convicted of adultery and given death sentences by a tribal Islamic council and were executed in the presence of some 15,000 people in Bara in the Khyber Agency (Amnesty International, 1998:11). A village council near Mithankot in Punjab ordered a wife of a man convicted of rape to be raped by the victim's husband. The eight elders then watched the sentence being carried out (Amnesty Report, 1995:16).

Other forms of violence against women by non-family members include systems of retribution whereby women are exchanged or killed to settle the scores between two warring factions. Women are also humiliated by being stripped naked in public. While a total of fifty-four such cases were reported in the Lahore press, there were hardly any cases registered or investigated by the police due to the involvement of influential people in such cases (HRCP Report, 1998: 221).

How does the women's movement mediate for women's rights at this level? We have already mentioned the cultural manifestation of the control of women's bodies, carried out through cultural practices and sanctioned and endorsed by community members. This includes controlling women's movement and mobility, rights and property in the name of honour, using women as an object of exchange for purposes of marriage or for appeasing an enemy, or controlling their sexuality through *karo kari* or other honour killings.

The women's movement has seldom posed any direct threat to cultural constructs. However, there are small welfare-oriented or community-based organizations that work within a liberal framework and demand certain reforms so women may escape outright injustice. Such organizations have limited goals and their initiatives are localized. It is difficult for the women's movement to consolidate the everyday forms of resistance and small gains achieved against biased traditions in rural settings that are divided by geography, culture, language, and lack of communication with one another. No information sharing takes place. Thus while at the local level the overarching goals of the women's movement are being realized and promoted, they seldom fall within the purview of macro level initiatives.

There are several other reasons why the response of the women's movement to practices that objectify and treat women as property has been weak. Firstly, the focus of the women's movement on the state and legal structures has contained its attention so that many cultural practices (e.g., *karo kari, watta satta, wulwar,* and *swarah)* have escaped critical attention. Additionally, for many women it is easier to challenge an abstract state and its legal structures (which are seen as the locus of the problem and therefore its solution) than to challenge cultural practices which come under the rubric of 'our customs', 'our indigenous traditions' and 'our values.' (Saigol 1997b: 164). Secondly, the middle class origin of the mainstream women's movement, best represented by the Women's Action Forum, inhibits it because middle class women are not directly affected by these practices. Thirdly, the urban bias in the women's movement works against rural settings where many of these practices are effected. It is not rooted within the social context of rural communities and thus has few links with women there. Fourthly, at a broad level, information pertaining to the implementation of such cultural practices is sporadic, disjointed and geographically spread out. Therefore, the women's movement's response is often not timely or immediate, taking it away from any effective role in negotiations at the community level. The women's movement turns out to be a weak mediator at the community level. Only when other civil society groups (usually with male backing) take initiatives against discriminatory cultural practices is anything substantive achieved.

Furthermore, while the reports on violence against women have risen, indicating a qualitative and quantitative shift in civil society, we also need to understand that this is indicative of a mixed phenomenon. Shahnaz Rouse explains (1998: 61), 'Given the increased violence against women, we see, on the one hand, the establishment of innumerable groups agitating, educating and providing women with services hitherto unavailable to them. On the other hand, we also see a privileging of the previous state of affairs, wherein women were supposedly accorded *izzat* (honour) in the public domain. Women were always, and continue to be, verbally harassed in public. However, prior to the current transformation such public behaviour was at best rhetorically considered unacceptable. It is primarily in this sense and with the increase in public assaults on women, that there is a breakdown of the public/private split regarding women. The breakdown in regard to the mistreatment of women lends itself to a call for a reprivatization of the issue and a return of *izzat* lost to women.'

C. iii. The Women's Movement and the State

The relationship of the women's movement with the state has been full of contradictions. Here, we look at two issues: the ability of the women's movement to negotiate on behalf of women with the state vis-à-vis the formal political-legal structures of the state, and its ambivalent relationship with the state as a patriarchal construct. The latter limits the women's movement's effectiveness as it has to forge a relationship with an entity which it at once identifies as the problem as well as the authority capable of providing a solution.

Mainstream political party politics and the national government have been defined and reproduced as a predominantly male arena. Therefore, very few women have been able to enter this arena with the main purpose of improving women's position within this sphere or any other sphere discussed so far. Any moves by the few who have entered the political arena have, so far, been extremely circumscribed. This is so because political party structures are male dominated. Women in political parties cannot reach decision-making levels easily and are often not fielded as candidates by their parties during elections. Several reasons account for this, e.g., women's main role is defined in the family context only and politics remains outside their culturally defined legitimate role. This marginalization has not only resulted in social, political and economic discrimination but has also robbed women of developing formidable political skills. Furthermore, the nature of political parties, the criminalization of politics and the culture of corruption that permeates public life, effectively block women's participation in government structures in all three (legislative, executive and judicial) contexts.

Women's rights organizations (especially NGOs) have been concerned about the deteriorating status of women and have campaigned for increased women's representation in political affairs and in political decision-making. They maintain that it is imperative for women to gain political representation for any substantive change to occur in women's lives. Furthermore, they have been campaigning for increased representation of women in government departments and organizations at all levels.

The constant break-down in the democratic process whereby democracy becomes a facade as well as the failure of government structures to deliver adequate social services to women has led to rethinking among women activists. Many are convinced that women must influence politics in their own favour. They are debating their position and status in mainstream politics to determine whether they should distance themselves from, or join mainstream politics. The question is whether to influence politics from outside, or whether to attempt to influence it directly by joining political parties. For now, women are pushing the state and political parties to create political space for them through affirmative action. This can be seen in their demand for an amendment in the Political Parties Act and the People's Representation Act in favor of women;[6] their demand for 33 per cent women's representation at the local, provincial and federal government levels as well as within political parties. Women have also demanded that 33 per cent of seats be reserved for women through direct election.

In all these negotiations, the women's movement has been in the forefront. Although they have not succeeded in attaining their objectives, they have been able to influence thinking and rhetoric about women's political representation. One way of ascertaining this is by looking at political party manifestos. All political parties have raised the issue of women's representation, including the conservative Jamaat-e-Islami. Similarly, even the Jamaat condemns the Taliban government in Afghanistan for its denial of fundamental rights to women[7]. Similarly, the recent Shariat Bill (Fifteenth Amendment) had been openly opposed by several leading women's organizations for being anti-women.

The area of law has been questioned and problematized effectively by women's and human rights organizations. The women's movement through women's organized campaigns was responsible for some women friendly legislation such as the 1961 Family Laws Ordinance.[8] However, it has been criticized, even from within,[9] for its inability to get the government to repeal the discriminatory laws passed in the 1980s. In defence of the movement, one may assert that the campaign against these laws has been continuous; however, the lack of political will in the government has prevented these laws from being repealed.[10] Similarly, there are initiatives with regard to personal law that NGOs have taken (e.g., Shirkat Gah's Women, Law and Status Programme) which attempt to bring legal literacy to empower women in both rural and urban areas. Such programmes often attempt to question discriminatory cultural norms by demonstrating that these are transgressions of religiously sanctioned laws of Pakistan. The women's movement is now beginning to problematize traditions and cultural practices by demonstrating that they are fundamentally unjust. It has successfully raised the issue of legal reforms but has been unable to make significant headway.

Violation of women's rights by the state in maintaining and recreating socio-economic and cultural environments that continue to oppress and exploit women has not been raised in a holistic manner on a regular or systematic basis by women's groups. The movement appears very selective in its resistance to the violation of women's rights by the state. There has been relatively little focus by the movement on issues such as custodial rape by male police and denial of justice to women by the male dominated judiciary. Torture and rape of women by the police is widespread but vastly under-reported due to obvious reasons of criminal involvement of police, in such cases, as perpetrators. For example, only forty-one cases of violence against women in police custody were reported in Punjab during 1998, a figure which certainly under-represents the intensity and prevalence of the problem. Similarly, the legal system does not encourage women victims to use it for the redress of the violation of their rights. High cost and delays in obtaining justice further discourage women victims/survivors to use law for the protection of their rights.

This is not to say that there is no awareness of these issues in the women's movement. This point has been raised, however, to highlight that as compared to the pervasiveness of such cases that consist of gross violation of women rights, the women's movement's response has been inadequate.

The direct relationship of the women's movement with the state has been one of ambivalence. It has looked up to the state as the ultimate initiator, manager and arbiter of positive social change. In this context, ironically enough, it has related to the state as the patriarch/father. It has constantly made demands upon the state for reforms and social change and in turn has acted within socially acceptable parameters. These demands are based on a widely-shared view that the state can ensure and implement meaningful change in women's lives. Simultaneously, the women's movement perceives the state as the perpetrator of discrimination, maintaining policies that are detrimental to women.

A common view within the movement is that the state is not neutral and that it maintains and reproduces discrimination, which results in complex identity politics. This is so because the movement has been able to develop and sustain its identity due to the presence of the state as the Other. This Other is easily constructed as the enemy when it exhibits patriarchal characteristics, reified in discriminatory practices (such as those discussed earlier).

Overall, however, the women's movement's relationship with the state has been one of mutual cooperation and complementarity. A study of the historical changes in the character and nature of the state and of the women's movement in Pakistan demonstrates that only during the 1977–88 period was there a direct conflict between the two (Khattak, 1995).[11] This does not imply that the periods of cooperation were marked by total harmony; of course, a certain amount of friction and tension were intrinsic to the relationship. However, these did not take away from the overall relationship of cooperation.[12]

On the one hand the women's movement has succeeded in placing its agenda for women on the table. It has raised issues centred on women's political and legal status. On the other hand, because it is operating within the boundaries of the state (there are some spill-overs), it is constrained from within and outside in what it can achieve. Furthermore, its own relationship with the state is problematic since it regards the state as the patriarch and accords it appropriate respect as well as deriving its own sense of identity in counter-positioning itself against it.

D. The NGO-ization of the Women's Movement

While the history of volunteerism and community based organization is fairly old and indigenous, the NGO sector in its present form is hardly a two-decade-old phenomenon in Pakistan. It primarily took off during the late 1970s and mid-1980s when MNAs and MPAs who came into power through non-political party based elections encouraged the growth, of NGOs to absorb development funds for their constituencies. Coincidentally, in the 1980s there was a shift in international donor priorities as well as greater availability of donor funding. This time period coincided with a shift in the development approach toward women so that more resources became available to women's organizations.

Various leading women activists from the movement went to the NGO sector and established their own NGOs. Applied Socio-Economic Research (ASR), Shirkat Gah, Aurat Foundation, Bedari, Simorgh, and AGHS are cases in point. Women in these NGOs were disenchanted with the mainstream space provided through employment with the state or semi-state entities (universities) and the limitation of working with political parties and voluntary women's bodies. These women decided to create an alternative space where they could work, debate and dialogue issues that were foremost for them. They were addressing (masculinist) power issues in the public arena. The issues of patriarchy that were shaping society in a very masculinist framework were taken up and challenged in different ways such as through challenging discriminatory laws, through street demonstrations, through writing, and through social activism. In the early 1980s when the state used its power in a most naked manner by enacting anti-women policies and legislation (e.g., *Hudood* Ordinance), most women came out into the public arena to protest. This protest took on an organized character in the shape of the Women's Action Forum (WAF). WAF established chapters in all major cities and introduced work on a non-hierarchical basis in the public arena. It refused to accept contributions from any foreign donors and continues to be a purely voluntary organization. WAF's overall stances have been informed by a secular and feminist agenda.

On the changing nature (i.e., the NGO-ization) of the women's movement, some compelling questions have emerged about the role and impact of donor money on the women's movement. Can the women's movement maintain its autonomy and militancy while being financially dependent on international donor agencies? Could the women's movement remain value driven while taking money from international agencies? Would donor funding not push them into service delivery?

Some people argue that the women's movement in Pakistan is being coopted by international donor agencies. The advocacy component of the community work by women's organization is fairly weak. Lobbying with policymakers, parliamentarians and those in positions of power has been given preference over advocacy work at the grass-root level. Women leaders frequently use developmentalist jargon, far removed from the ordinary women who they profess to serve. Others assert that donor funding has enabled women's groups to raise gender issues systematically and more consistently which has resulted in placing women's issues in the centre of public policy and debate.

Our analysis of the situation does not validate either of the positions mentioned above. NGO-ization of the women's movement is marked with contradictory patterns. There are advantages as well as disadvantages of funded activism. Collective awareness of some aspects of women's oppression— which comprise NGO projects and programmes such as women's political empowerment, reproductive rights of women, and violence against women—has been created by the NGO arm of the women's movement through well planned interventions at the individual, community and state levels. However, women's ability to protest spontaneously against violations of women's rights reported in the press has been greatly undermined due to pressure and demand of NGOs' time and energies working on their projects. For example, in the latest case of Samia Imran's murder, women's groups organized several demonstrations, rallies, protest marches, and press conferences. They also lobbied to pass a resolution on the issue in the Senate. However, no concrete results were achieved by such efforts which demanded a stronger and continuous pressure on the state to respond. The women's movement had limited capacity to sustain the momentum as most of its activists had to go back to their jobs to continue with their work. Since the nature of work within NGOs and in the movement is of similar nature, there is hardly any awareness among women's rights activists that the movement's inability to protest forcefully in public against violations of women's rights will pose challenges to their activism through NGO work. A discredited women's movement will not be able to protect or proclaim the potency of its other outlets of expression.

Therefore, while there have been critiques of funded activism (largely centered on the issue of dilution of the movement) it is asserted that many women activists (e.g., those associated with WAF) have now become NGO professionals. They are often over-stretched for time, consequently they can no longer allocate time to WAF in an effective manner. WAF has thus suffered. While funded activism and advocacy have grown, voluntary activism has not. Generally, no major initiative can be launched without funding, which restricts the kind of advocacy campaigns that can be initiated.

Another important emerging feature of the NGO-ization of the women's movement is its shifting priorities linked with donor agendas and their funds. Some women activists had started NGOs to focus on those aspects of women's oppression towards which they felt committed as individuals. However, the NGOs' focus would change with the availability of funds in different areas of women's rights. Today, some women's NGOs are working simultaneously in four or five different areas of women's rights (health, education, political empowerment, etc.) without really having the intellectual and/or developmental capacity to perform and deliver.

The women's movement is diluted because women's energies are directed toward fairly non-threatening issues within the development context (e.g., women's health, education, micro enterprise and micro-credit). They are often not funded for projects that take gender as an independent category of oppression; in fact, no project claims that it is about the re-organization of gender relations or power relations. Most donors claim that they are not here for 'social engineering.' Funding agencies feel comfortable with an approach that promotes women's education and health, with the assumption that once their status in these areas improves, gender relations will automatically improve. While it is true that gender relations will likely improve, the point of contestation is to what degree might this occur? Additionally, there is no automatic linkage, similar to the lack of an automatic linkage in the past when the political left used to maintain that when social indicators change, class relations will automatically change. Similarly, school enrollment rates will not necessarily change gender relations in the family or the public sphere unless curricula and attitudes change as well.

A certain amount of depoliticization of the movement has also been instituted through the creation of NGOs. They have generally demanded concessions and reforms from the state, not any radical restructuring. They argue that policy and social change are necessarily slow and non-threatening. They prefer to work within the parameters defined for them by the state so as to continue to accrue advantages and continue to be able to have a voice in state policies. This situation is further complicated when funding for women's development is provided for contradictory aims. For example, funding for women's rights is provided at the same time as funding for protecting and strengthening families (Saigol 1997b: 166). In accepting such funding, NGOs and indirectly the women's movement have had to forego the option of developing a critical voice in the longer term.

Furthermore, NGOs are perceived to be financially opaque. Many NGOs suffer because some NGOs have been launched as money-making enterprises without any demonstrable convictions and commitments. Therefore, there is a fundamental suspicion of NGOs and their advocacy among people at large. This has made it difficult for women's NGOs (whose mandates do not always meet local and social approval) to be effective. They have to work twice as hard to make themselves acceptable besides couching their programmes and aims in the most non-threatening conformist language possible.

The personalized character of NGOs in Pakistan is both blamed for the relatively small success of the phenomenon as well as heralded by those who consider them to be successful. Many NGOs' 'ownership' is individual, i.e., they revolve around a personality or family who are usually the founders. The causes for which they fight have also, in a sense, become exclusive patents of particular NGO leaders and their organizations. There is thus a sense of territoriality. This prevents people from joining NGO campaigns in large numbers. In addition, people's likes and dislikes of those who have founded and are running NGOs are extended to the organizations themselves. The mainstream power relations and structures are thus reproduced in people's relationship with NGOs and their leaders.

As personalities dominate and define their NGOs, no alternative ways of relating to each other on any other non-hierarchical basis have been developed. Funding requirements make NGOs more bureaucratized as they reproduce hierarchical structures. Often, women's NGOs critique such hierarchies for being male centered and patriarchal. There is thus an existing dualism that women's NGOs are faced with. They have developed alternative power structures to the state and negotiate with the state from their alternative power position. However, there are permanent power hierarchies within these alternative power structures as they become the centres in the margins. Because of the reproduction of this pattern of social relations, women have not been able to develop an alternative culture and the movement in that sense is weak. The chances of strengthening an indigenous feminist viewpoint have thus been greatly reduced.

Class, as one of the most important explanatory variables of the women's movement's selective response to power configurations in society and within the state, has been set aside in the analysis of NGOs' dominated or headed by women. Selection of geographical areas for operation and focus on issues of women's rights reflects the continuity of class bias in the NGO sector as well. The majority of NGOs run by women activists are concentrated in urban areas. The nature of their work is primarily researched-based: documentation, printing and publication for a (predominantly illiterate) civil society. The priority to work in urban areas through research and lobbying with policymakers serves to reproduce women's status and class in the NGO sector. Such organizations also have more access to financial resources available from international NGOs, multilateral and bilateral agencies due to their familiarity with the language and culture of the donors.

Some NGOs have developed links with CBOs (community based organizations) and claim, therefore, to be operational at the grass-roots level. Most CBOs, however, have a social welfare approach and reproduce class and male hierarchies in their organizations. Most community development work in rural areas is carried out through government-sponsored Rural Support Programmes (RSPs). NGOs are in no position to challenge their style of work even when they themselves have an entirely different style or vision of development work.

E. Conclusion

This analysis is by no means comprehensive; some of the questions and explorations need to be investigated further. Situational analysis and empirical data are required from different studies to extrapolate upon these issues.

In Pakistan, the women's movement has generally worked within social parameters in order to continue to have social legitimacy of sorts. It became dominated by a feminist agenda during the Zia period when it became more radical and vocal in the face of an extreme threat of oppression. WAF came to symbolize the ethos of the women's movement during that era. However, it stayed aloof from issues that revolved around cultural constructs or addressing issues considered to belong to the private sphere, such as the family, marital rape or domestic violence. Over the last decade, it has lost its vibrancy as it has become institutionalized, largely through the NGO phenomenon. As a mediator for women's interests within civil society and through civil society with the state, the women's movement cannot claim substantial success, especially when it comes to family and the community. However, with regard to formal apparatuses of the state, it has been able to establish itself as an effective spokesperson for women's rights and political representation.

A potentially strong role for the women's movement is constrained due to the patriarchal structures within which it must function. To work within the framework of a masculinist culture necessarily impedes its options. Additionally, the extent to which it is able to negotiate for women's voice at the individual, family, community, and state levels is dependent upon its relationship with other stakeholders within civil society (including fundamentalist groups). Furthermore, the position of the women's movement within civil society is marginal vis-à-vis other contenders for power. It negotiates from a position of relative powerlessness. Therefore, its chances of achieving a voice for women consistently across contexts are not very high at present. Its response to a large number of women's needs is constrained because of its limited development at the grassroots level, its NGO-ization, as well as its class position. It would be able to be more forceful if it were able to address its own limitations. This process can begin when the women's movement begins to popularize itself, which will imply a move toward self-empowerment at all levels.

References

Alavi, Hamza. 1991. 'Pakistani Women in a Changing Society' in Hastings Donnan and Pnina Werbener (eds.) *Economy and Culture in Pakistan.* London.

Amnesty International. 1995. *Women in Pakistan: Disadvantaged and Denied their Rights.* New York.

Brown, Wendy. 1992. 'Finding the man in the state' in *Feminist Studies.* Vol. 18, No. 1 Spring.

Chai, Alice Yun. 1997. 'Integrative Feminist Politics in the Republic of Korea' in Lois A. West (eds.) *Feminist Nationalism.* New York, London: Routledge.

Chandoke, Neera. 1995. *State and Civil Society: Explorations in Political Theory.* New Delhi: Sage Publications; London: Thousands Oaks.

Cohen, Jean L. and Andrew Arato. 1994. *Civil Society and Political Theory.* Cambridge Massachusetts, and London: MIT Press.

Elshtain, Jean Bethke. 1991. *Public Man, Private Woman: Women in Social and Political Thought.* Princeton: Princeton University Press.

Enloe, Cynthia H. 2000. *Maneuvers: the International Politics of Militarizing Women's Lives.* Berkeley: University of California Press.

Grant, Rebecca, 'The sources of gender bias in international relations theory' in Rebecca Grant and Kathleen Newland (eds.), *Gender and International Relations.* Indiana University Press. 1991.

Haroon, Anis. 1995. *Unveiling the Issues.* Lahore: ASR.

Harrington, Mona. 1992. 'What exactly is wrong within the liberal state as an agent: of change' in V. Spike Peterson (eds.), *Gendered States: Feminist (Re) Visions of International Relations Theory.* Boulder and London: Lynne Rienner Publishers.

Human Rights Commission of Pakistan (HRCP). 1998. *State of Human Rights in 1997.* Lahore.

Hussain, Neelum. 1997. 'Narrative Appropriations of Saima: Coercion and Consent in Muslim Pakistan', in Neelum Hussain, Samiya Mumtaz, and Rubina Saigol (eds.), *Engendering the National State.* Lahore, Pakistan: Simorgh Women's Resource and Publication Center.

Jalal, Ayesha. 1991. 'The Convenience of Subservience: Women and the State of Pakistan' in Deniz Kandiyoti (ed.), *Women, Islam and the State.* Macmillan Press.

Jayawardena, Kumari. 1986. *Feminism and Nationalism in the Third World.* London: Zed Books.

Jeffery, Particia and Amrita Basu (eds.) 1998. *Appropriating Gender: Women's Activism and Politicized Religion in South Asia.* New York: Routledge.

Jeffery, Patricia. 1998. 'Agency, Activism and Agendas' in Patricia Jeffery and Amrita Basu (eds.) *Appropriating Gender: Women's Activisim and Politicized Religion in South Asia.* New York: Routledge.

Kandiyoti, Deniz. 1991. *Women, Islam and the State*. McMillan.

Malik, H. Iftikhar. 1997. *State and Civil Society in Pakistan: Politics of authority, ideology and ethnicity*. London: Macmillan Press Ltd.

Moghadam, Valentine M. 1994. *Identity Politics and Women: Cultural Reassertions and Feminisms in International Perspective*. Boulder: Westview Press.

Mumtaz Khawar and Farida Shaheed. 1987. *Pakistani Women: One Step Forward, Two Steps Back?* London: Zed Press.

Pateman, Carole and Mary Lyndon Shanley. 1991. *Feminist Interpretations and Political Theory*. Cambridge, UK Polity Press in association with Basil Blackwell, Oxford, UK.

Peterson, Janice and Douglas M. Brown. 1994. *The Economic Status of Women under Capitalism: Institutional Economics and Feminist Theory*. Aldershot, Hants, England; Brookfield, VT, USA: Edward Elgar.

Rouse, Shahnaz. 1998. 'The Outsider(s) Within: Sovereignty and Citizenship in Pakistan', in Patricia Jeffery and Amrita Basu (eds.) *Appropriating Gender: Women's Activisim and Politicized Religion in South Asia*. New York: Routledge.

Saigol, Robina. 1997a. 'Introduction' in Neelum Hussain, Samiya Mumtaz and Robina Saigol (eds.), *Engendering the Nation State*. Vol. 1. Lahore: Simorgh Women's Resource and Publication Center.

_____. 1997b. 'Family and the Women's Movement', in Nighat Saeed Khan and Afiya Shehrbano Zia (eds.) *Unveiling the Issues in Pakistani Women's Perspectives on Social, Political and Ideological Issues*. Lahore: ASR Publication.

Sandoval, Chela. 1991. 'Us Third World Feminism: The Theory and Method of Oppositional Consciousness in the Postmodern World'. *Genders* No. 10, Spring, pp. 1-24.

Shaheed, Farida. 1998. 'The other side of the discourse: Women's experience of identity, religion and activism in Pakistan', in Patricia Jeffery and Amrita Basu (eds.) *Appropriating Gender: Women's Activisim and Politicized Religion in South Asia*. New York: Routledge.

Tharu, Susie J. and Ke Lalita. 1993. *Women Writing in India: 600 B.C. to the Early Twentieth Century*. Vol. I. Delhi: Oxford University Press.

Weiss, Anita M. 1998. 'The Slow Yet Steady Path to Women's Empowerment in Pakistan' in Yvonne Yazbeck Haddad and John Esposito (eds.) *Islam, Gender and Social Change*. Oxford University Press, pp. 124-143.

Yuval-Davis, Nira. 1993. *Women, Ethnicity and Empowerment*. The Hague, Netherlands: Publications Office, Institute of Social Studies.

NOTES

1. This section relies heavily upon Saba Khattak's earlier article entitled, 'The women's movement and the state in Pakistan', SDPI working paper series, 1996. This is not to suggest that the two authors have not reached consensus upon the position they take regarding defining the women's movement but only to state that they agreed upon much of what had previously been written by Saba Khattak.

2. Practical gender interests are concerned with immediate economic gains while strategic gender interests are concerned with empowering women so they may change their subordinate status.

3. We take this term from Chela Sandoval's article 'Us Third World Feminisim: The Theory and Method of Oppositional Consciousness in the Postmodern World' in *Genders*, No. 10, Spring 1991, pp. 1–24.

4. *See*, for instance, the discussion in Susie Tharu and K. Latifta's Introduction in *Women Writing in India*, Vol. 1, and Frank and Fuentes in *idfa dossier*, 63, P-27, January/February 1988.

5. Historically, the concept of civil society has been debated in classical and medieval western political thought (Keane, 1988, pp. 32–33; for a detailed analysis, *see*, Cohen and Arato, 1994). During the seventeenth and nineteenth centuries, it came to be viewed with regard to individual rights vis-à-vis the state and society. Different theses about the relationship between the civil, political and economic are developed by philosophers like Locke, Rousseau, Hegal, Marx, Adam Smith, J.S. Mill, Gramsci and Habermas. For further elaboration of conceptualizing civil society in Pakistan, *see*, Mustafa Pasha's discussion in chapter two of this volume.

6. Zia ul-Haq appointed the Pakistan Commission on the Status of Women in 1983. It began work in 1984 and submitted its report in 1985. The Commission Report recommended the continuation of reserved seats for women at all levels including local government. Furthermore, it urged political parties to seek maximum enrolment of women members and recommended that 'a political party which does not have at least 20% women membership should not be allowed to contest elections'. (quoted in Iftikhar H. Malik, 1997:157),

7. Personal interview with Qazi Husain Ahmed, leader of Jamaat-e-Islami.

8. The Family Law Ordinance resulted from an APWA (All Pakistan Women's Association) campaign launched in 1955 against polygamy. The immediate catalyst had been Prime Minister Mohammad Ali Bogra's second marriage, which went against his first wife who, as the patron of APWA, enjoyed extensive support. Many have criticized this move as class based, i.e., inspired by class loyalties. A Family Laws Commission was established which prepared the Family Law Ordinance, approved by General Ayub Khan in 1961. This made second marriage conditional upon consent of the first wife and the local union council. Similarly,

divorce could only be final after three months and not simply upon pronunciation three times. All marriages were to be registered after a standardized *nikahnama* (marriage contract) was signed. It raised marriagable age for girls to 16 from 14 and for boys to 21 from 18 (Iftikhar H. Malik, 1997:145)

9. For a detailed and fair asessment, *see*, Mumtaz and Shaheed, *Pakistani Women: One Step Forward, Two Steps Back?* London and Lahore. Zed Books, 1987.

10. For a longer discussion of this subject, *see*, Mumtaz and Shaheed 1987, Jilani 1998, and Weiss 1998.

11. Ayesha Jalal propounds a similar thesis. *See*, 'The Convenience of Subservience: Women and the State in Pakistan' in Deniz, Kandiyoti (ed.), *Women, Islam and the State.* 1991.

12. Hamza Alavi makes this distinction in the context of the state and the ruling classes. He asserts that one needs to distinguish between cooperation and conflict. Conflict denotes open opposition while cooperation may include elements of tension and friction.

10

MICROFINANCE IN PAKISTAN: PERPETUATION OF POWER OR A VIABLE AVENUE FOR EMPOWERMENT?[1]

Lynn Renken

Microfinance or microcredit programs have gained popularity throughout the world because they are seen as viable and sustainable strategies for combating poverty. Microfinance institutions such as the Grameen Bank in Bangladesh or the Accion International affiliates in Latin America represent microlending facilities as financially viable institutions that tailor products for the poor. Microlending institutions target women, in particular, as they are regarded as excellent investments and good credit risks; credit programs with primarily female borrowers boast sustained repayment rates of 90 per cent and higher. Moreover, women often feel a moral obligation to repay their loans as well as, in the long term, expend profits from their enterprises back into improving their families' well being.

This chapter addresses how power issues influence the establishment, access and maintenance of microlending institutions and their microfinance delivery systems. I argue that although there has been a rise of microfinance institutions in the Punjab, which in theory strive to reach the Punjab's poorer and rural sectors, many of the facilities primarily serve middle-to-upper class urban women. Many of the microlending institutions have developed alternatives to asset-based collateral requirements. In theory, these flexible collateral requirements should help women, particularly low-income women, obtain loans. In practice, the lending facilities rarely advertise or promote these alternative loan schemes to clients. Therefore, these credit-lending facilities fail to operationalize alternative credit delivery mechanisms they have created, and therefore they generally have not been successful in reaching the Punjab's lower-income women. Because credit-lending facilities offer subsidized interest rates and many have not been successful in mobilizing their clients' savings, few will be self-sustaining without additional cash inputs from the government or international donors like the World Bank.

Studies of microenterprise and microcredit-lending facilities in Pakistan are few compared to those conducted in other parts of South Asia such as Bangladesh and India. Research conducted in Pakistan focuses on the credit activities of specific, successful Non-governmental Organizations (NGOs) such as the Aga Khan Rural Support Program (AKRSP) in the Northern Areas and the Orangi Pilot Project (OPP) in Karachi. However, little information has been collected on the availability and access of microfinance services through non-NGO facilities at a province-wide level.

In 1994–95, I examined women's access to credit and the microlending facilities that target women in the Punjab province. I investigated three different types of credit-lending facilities: the First Women's Bank Limited (FWBL), the Agricultural Development Bank of Pakistan (ADBP) and eight NGOs so as to gain a broad, province-wide understanding of the availability of microcredit at Punjab's newly emerging microfinance institutions.

In this chapter, I present highlights of findings gathered through talking with representatives of credit-lending organizations and with a sample of women who have received loans from these facilities. Over a course of nine months, I interviewed eighty-seven women who had received credit from facilities in ten of the Punjab's twenty-seven districts. I talked with these women about their perceptions of the facility through which they had secured a loan and how they had utilized it. I documented their thoughts on the locations of credit-lending facilities, who financed these institutions, to what model each investigated facility adheres, and their target clientele. I also explored each institution's loan procedures, the type of individuals benefitting from each facility's loans, and the effectiveness of each institution in meeting its organizational objectives and responding to client needs. This chapter, therefore, is organized by type of credit-lending facility, and concludes with my assessment of the extent to which the institutionalization of microcredit in Punjab is transforming prevailing power relations in Punjab's emergent civil society, or is instead serving to maintain them.

A. The First Women's Bank Limited

The First Women's Bank Limited (FWBL) is one of the primary credit-lending facilities in the Punjab. Over one-quarter of the women I interviewed had received small loans from this facility. It was established in December 1989 under the first government of former Prime Minister Benazir Bhutto. It is currently the only formal banking institution designed exclusively to serve Pakistani women. According to FWBL president Akram Khatoon, the bank has seven key objectives: 1) to provide a variety of banking services to women in a 'congenial atmosphere'; 2) to offer easily accessible credit at low interest rates to middle-and-low-income women; 3) to capture the savings of women; 4) to provide advisory and consultative services to female entrepreneurs to ensure that their income-generating activities are profitable; 5) to upgrade the technical and managerial skills of its clients by creating a training center; 6) to help its female clients identify national and international markets; and 7) to decrease unemployment by providing loans designed to enhance self-employment opportunities for women (Khatoon 1990).

The FWBL extends microloans to eligible clients involved in small-scale, income-generating activities. Women engaged in such enterprises as producing ready-made garments, manufacturing, fast food restaurants, private schools, hospitals, beauty parlors and boutiques, poultry farms, cattle breeding and dairy farming are eligible for loans from Rs 1,000 to Rs 25,000 ($20–$500).[2] Small loans are extended for a maximum of two years at a ten per cent flat, annual interest rate. Larger loans exceeding Rs 25,000 are disbursed at an 18 per cent annual interest rate. Women repay their loans in monthly installments. As of 1994, the FWBL boasted of an excellent overall repayment rate of 97.5 per cent, and the recovery rate for its small loan scheme was over 90 per cent. Since Pakistan's inflation rate in 1995 was 10 per cent and exceeded 10 per cent in 1998, the FWBL's portfolio is losing value in real terms, even if it reaches a 100 per cent recovery rate.

Five years after its founding, the FWBL had twenty-nine branches throughout Pakistan with plans to establish an additional twenty-one the following year (Ali 1994: 114). As of March, 1995, the FWBL had disbursed 3,803 loans throughout Pakistan since its creation, totaling Rs 98.926 million (approximately $3.297 million).

In conjunction with its branch offices, the FWBL's outreach program employed mobile credit officers (MCOs) whose goal was to reach female entrepreneurs in rural areas. In 1994, the bank had eight MCOs, but all of them were working in Sindh province, and none in the Punjab. Obviously, the FWBL had not prioritized lending to rural women in the Punjab, the most populous province in the country. The FWBL claimed that it intended to increase its involvement in rural areas by adding fifty more MCOs and by intensifying its involvement with rural commercial banks, cooperatives and NGOs. However, as of August, 1998, no MCOs were yet working in the Punjab and little progress had been made in rural areas. Similarly, although the FWBL had put forth a strategy of working with NGOs and rural commercial banks, no action plan or time-line had been identified nor had the FWBL's Punjab branches begun discussions with NGOs about how such a collaboration would work. Although a few NGOs (such as the Aurat Foundation) have solidified a partnership with the FWBL, it is largely due to the initiatives taken by NGO representatives who often do not have the capital to provide loans to their constituents. Several NGO representatives have shared with me their frustrations and disillusionment with the FWBL, as the majority of its branches are established in affluent neighborhoods such as Defence, Cantonments, Blue Areas, and Mall Roads—areas generally not accessible to women the FWBL claims to target.

The Ministry for Women's Development, researchers, NGOs, and other relevant personnel were not consulted regarding the determination of FWBL's branch locations. Instead, those who held high places of power within the federal government such as the Prime Minister and the Finance Minister were responsible for creating the FWBL. This is despite that it is professionals within relevant ministries who have the knowledge and information as to which areas are most accessible to middle-and low-income women and who, presumably, could facilitate the bank's goals of reaching low-income entrepreneurs. Some critics have argued that the creation of the FWBL seemed more like a 'political gesture' rather than a facility created with well-defined policies and objectives. The then Finance Minister stated, in November, 1989, 'We have set it [the FWBL] up for women and they would know how to handle it' (Bilquees 1991: 746–747). As a result, the bank's locations and staff cause it to attract wealthier clients and in many cities, particularly Lahore, make it inaccessible to lower-income individuals. When I left Pakistan in 1995, the FWBL was making progress in reaching broader socioeconomic classes as it was about to open its Lahore branch on the Mall. Compared to its other two Lahore locations—Main Road in Gulberg, and in the Cantonment—its newest branch is indeed more accessible to lower and working class women than the others, though it remains somewhat inaccessible to the poor. Had parties serving middle-to-low-income women been included in the planning stages, the bank's objectives and target population may have been better defined and they would have created policies that require the FWBL to serve low-income women. As it stands, the FWBL's objectives and mission differ widely depending on who is questioned.

The FWBL offers a range of services that detracts from its seven-fold mission that emphasizes access to credit, savings, training, and technical services for middle- and low-income entrepreneurs. Faiz Bilquees, a Senior Research Economist at the Pakistan Institute of Development Economics in Islamabad, argues that the 'bank is a mix of a [sic] development finance institution, a commercial bank and a social welfare organization' (Bilquees 1991: 746). With the FWBL's objectives so vague and widespread, the FWBL could be any one of the above mentioned facilities. I argue that those in the GOP and the well educated, upper class female staff who constructed the FWBL's policies, purposefully made the FWBL's policies vague and all encompassing, as they had no intention in making a conscious effort to serve low-income women and financially empowering them. Therefore, the FWBL can maintain the guise that the bank serves low-income women, as it is stated in its objectives. However, when looking closely at how the bank has reached the poor, one will find that only a few low-income women benefit from the bank. I conclude that the FWBL primarily serves middle-to-upper class, well-educated women, many of whom have some personal connection to the FWBL.

It remains contradictory and unclear why the FWBL offers banking services other than loans to men while trying to maintain a 'congenial atmosphere' for women in a gender-divided society. The FWBL argues that men are allowed to save at the FWBL only because it does not want to discriminate against them. However, I contend that the FWBL needs to mobilize savings to increase its liquidity, an essential component of a financially viable bank. The FWBL's reliance on male savings indicates the FWBL leadership does not believe that Pakistani women, in and of themselves, possess the necessary capital to create and maintain a viable bank. As a result of the FWBL's reliance on male savings, the FWBL does not actively encourage women to save at its facilities. Instead, a larger overall portion of my respondents, 33 per cent, stated that they utilized the informal, rotating savings and credit associations (ROSCAs), which in Pakistan are termed 'committees' or the 'BC' system, to save funds. ROSCAs are neighborhood savings schemes in which individuals monthly deposit a fixed, determined amount of money or goods such as rice. Each member of the group receives the total sum of the pooled funds in turn. Despite the serious limitation of this savings instrument, such as only being able to receive the deposited funds at fixed, often infrequent intervals, this system is widely utilized in Pakistan, particularly among women (Ayub 1994). I argue that few women trust the Pakistani banking system and for many, it is safer, easier and more convenient to save in these informal groups. Facilities such as the FWBL need to reassess their savings policies, learn how they can mimic ROSCAs and possibly use women's savings as partial collateral for loans.

In spite of it being widely assumed that Pakistani women are consumers, not producers, my research indicates that women are active economic contributors who are able to and do save large sums of money. Savings are important for women, as they allow individuals to be protected from borrowing from exploitative sources like moneylenders during times of emergencies and hardship. Undoubtedly, savings assist women to take more economic control of their lives. Lending facilities such as the FWBL need to capture women's savings to create a viable financial institution. Although the FWBL requires all of its borrowers to open and maintain a savings account of at least Rs 100 ($3), women seldom reported depositing additional capital in their savings accounts. If the FWBL wants to encourage borrowers to save, the staff should explain to clients why they feel compelled to instate this requirement. Education, not extensive but basic education regarding the importance of savings, needs to be incorporated into the FWBL's loan procedures. Women also need to be encouraged to save, especially if they are not accustomed to saving within the formal banking environment. Facilities also should offer incentives that encourage women to save at commercial facilities rather than in informal ROSCAs.

The FWBL offers services that stray away from serving its target clientele such as the provision of low-interest loans to female students who wish to study abroad. The FWBL also offers financial incentives to clients who shop at designated stores and supermarkets owned by FWBL clients. Although all of the above mentioned services are important ones, they do not contribute to the FWBL reaching its target group and fulfilling its organizational objectives. Perhaps the bank is trying to be everything to all people. Clearly its mission and focus on serving women entrepreneurs, particularly middle-to-low-income women, is greatly diffused.

If the FWBL is committed to reaching a middle-to-low income, female clientele, it must define its target group and clarify what constitutes the middle-to-low income sector. Without targeting a specific population, measuring progress in serving this population is very difficult. For instance, the Grameen Bank in Bangladesh identifies a target group of individuals who own less than one-half an acre of irrigated land, or 'assets with a value equivalent to less than one acre of medium-quality land' (Hossain 1993: 12). Only people who meet this criteria are eligible for a loan. The FWBL needs to narrowly define its target group just as the Grameen Bank and other successful microlending facilities have. Otherwise, it will become, and perhaps has already become, a facility that meets several kinds of peoples' interests, especially middle-income and elite women's needs.

Although the FWBL is mandated to reach middle-and-low income women, their lending criteria is vague enough so that famous Pakistani actresses and other wealthy women can benefit from the FWBL's small loan scheme. Because the FWBL offers low interest rates, they invite fraud and corruption, and those who benefit most from these 'special programs' are those individuals who have connections and power. This phenomenon has been documented in many other developing countries where subsidized loans are provided. Therefore, subsidized credit programs, intended to serve vulnerable individuals, are rarely accessible to those individuals the program was intended to serve. Since upper class women can provide the bank with stronger collateral than a low-income woman can, the wealthy woman or others who may be able to obtain credit elsewhere, such as men, tend to secure the majority of the FWBL's loans, in spite of the bank's mandate to serve middle-to-low income women. For instance, one in every four clients I interviewed had misused their loans. Misused loans are those used for a purpose not specified in the borrower's loan application, such as to pay for a daughter's dowry or to benefit another individual's (often a male family member's) business. The only way the FWBL will be able to reach more middle-to-low income women is for the FWBL to make a conscious effort to target them by setting more defined lending criteria, adhering to it and increasing their interest rate to match or exceed commercial rates charged in Pakistan, thereby decreasing fraud and corruption.

In Pakistan, it is widely assumed that charging commercial rates of interest on higher to low-income individuals is taking advantage of people who are perceived as unable to pay such rates. Research shows that individuals can and will pay a little more for accessible and permanent lines of credit (Otero 1994). Credit-lending facilities in Pakistan are providing a disservice to entrepreneurs when they supply them with subsidized credit that they never may be able to have access to again due to depleted loan funds and therefore defunct institutions.

However, convincing some of Pakistan's elite that low-income entrepreneurs need access to reasonable lines of credit, not to be treated with 'special programs' or as welfare recipients, is a tough battle to win. In Pakistan, *riba* (usury), also termed interest, particularly at market rates or higher, is perceived as unfair especially when charged to those thought to be less fortunate. As a result, credit-lending facilities try to keep their rates low, particularly lower than commercial rates and sometimes below the inflation rate. A compromise must be reached among credit-lending facilities, as those that charge subsidized interest rates, such as the FWBL, invite clients outside the facility's target population, thereby excluding those who were intended to and should benefit from the facility. Because of the high transaction costs associated with disbursing small loans, global best practices standards recommend that microlending facilities charge higher-than-market rates, yet rates far below those of informal moneylenders. If facilities such as the FWBL were to charge one rate, equivalent to the commercial rate or slightly higher, many facilities will have a better chance of surviving longer, thereby better serving the female entrepreneurs who need access to permanent lines of credit the most.

The FWBL makes their credit programs inaccessible to low-income female microentrepreneurs not only through the location of its branches and not having a well-defined strategy to include low-income women, but also through complicated and excessive loan requirements. In order to receive a loan from the FWBL in 1995, a potential client must first locate an account holder within the FWBL or at another Pakistani bank such as the Habib Bank. The account holder must be willing to introduce her (act as a reference) to the FWBL. After locating a suitable reference and furnishing the bank with the reference's name, signature and bank account number, the client must open a savings account and maintain a minimum balance of Rs 100 ($3). She is then required to complete a one-page application form. Applications are available in both Urdu and English, but given Pakistan's high illiteracy rate (only 23 per cent of Pakistani women are literate), three-fourths of women will need assistance to complete the application (UNDP 1996). Therefore, this application method is an inappropriate way to encourage low-income and often illiterate women to apply for loans.

If a woman advances to the application stage, the potential female borrower must show that she possesses personal assets exceeding Rs 25,000 ($833), or alternatively, physically bring into the bank two personal guarantors with documents proving that they each have assets exceeding Rs 25,000. Although I did not find evidence of it in any of the FWBL's literature, I was told by several sources that unofficially the FWBL requires at least one of each applicant's guarantors to be a government servant of the 18th grade or higher. Several interviewees confirmed that this is a prerequisite to obtain a loan from the FWBL, and I also witnessed several female loan applicants becoming dismayed with the FWBL and the loan procedure after hearing of this unwritten requirement. One potential FWBL client responded to the government servant requirement with, 'If we knew people of that rank, we would not need a loan'.

The FWBL's one-page loan application seems relatively easy to complete, provided that the applicant can get assistance if she is unable to read it. However, what is more difficult and frustrating is the bureaucracy and red tape these women encounter when applying for a loan. Many low-income women do not know individuals who have bank accounts at the FWBL or elsewhere, nor do they know a government servant of the 18th grade or above, willing to vouch for their loans. Therefore, in addition to further defining its target group, the FWBL needs to simplify its loan application procedure. Prerequisites that guarantors be government servants are cumbersome, unnecessary and indicate to the borrowers that they are not worthy of loans without the approval of a government servant who wields some power and influence.

Utilization of a group-guaranteed lending model can circumvent applicants' reliance on cosigners. The group-guaranteed lending model is internationally proven as an effective way to reach large numbers of novice, low-income and female entrepreneurs who lack collateral and assets. Because members of each group are collectively responsible for loan repayment, they choose individuals whom they regard as trustworthy and likely to repay their loans. Group lending provides group members with a comparative advantage over the traditional borrower-lender relationship in that all members are required to choose all individuals in their group. But the FWBL refuses to utilize this methodology except in rare cases in the Punjab due to the fact that the elite management of the bank does not seem willing to entrust low-income women with more control of the credit process. Bank management is unwilling to believe that low-income women are willing and capable to repay loans, nor are they interested in granting the poor an opportunity to better their socioeconomic status. Why else would a bank supposedly committed to the empowerment of lower income women not promote or utilize the group lending model, proven to be effective in combating poverty worldwide?

Throughout my research, I located and tracked the progress of one of the first female groups to receive a group loan from one FWBL branch in Lahore. Although this type of loan has been available to clients since 1991, neither the FWBL nor its staff members properly advertise this scheme to clients who lack assets or guarantees needed to apply for an individual loan. When I first met this group in 1994 they were in the process of applying for a loan that would be secured against the group.

All women involved in the group were active with a local NGO branch in a neighborhood in Lahore's outskirts. An NGO representative introduced the group members to the FWBL and the services it provides. In the NGOs training classes, the instructor urged the women to sell the goods they were making with their newly acquired skills. Before I met the group, the NGO had given the two women associated with the NGO a joint loan of Rs 4,000 ($80) for their candle-making business. After the two women repaid their loan in-full, they expressed interest in receiving another, larger loan. Since this NGO had a limited loan fund, the NGO staff member referred the ladies to the FWBL. The NGO staff member further explained to the women that they must have assets of Rs 25,000 ($500) to offer the FWBL as collateral or provide the bank with two consigners that meet the FWBL's criteria for each applicant. Accompanied to the FWBL by an NGO representative, they began to investigate other options. The group lending model surfaced as a viable strategy for the women to pursue, since they were relatively poor and lacked collateral. The only constraint the women faced was that the FWBL's group loans require five members. With the help of an NGO representative, the women recruited three other female microentrepreneurs from their neighborhood. The FWBL eventually changed the make-up and leadership of the initial group because they did not believe some group members had viable businesses and stated that two related members could not be in the same group. The FWBL should have previously told the group members about their lending and group criteria. Although the FWBL's criteria of not allowing two immediate relatives to be involved in the same group is a standard criteria worldwide, I found that the FWBL did not enforce or adhere to this criteria in all circumstances. I question why the FWBL became involved with the group formation and leadership issues. The group guarantee model must remain a decentralized one in order to be cost effective for the credit-lending facility and an empowering process for the group. The essence of this credit methodology relies on group members' adopting trustworthy members that have viable businesses. Therefore it is questionable if it was the FWBL's responsibility to pick and choose who could and could not be in the group and appoint group leadership. This is another situation in which the FWBL has exerted their power to control the fate of its lower-income clients.

The fact that the FWBL took five months to process the first group members' loan, and that the group went back and forth to the bank over twenty-five times to check on the progress of their loans is inexcusable. This was an extreme inconvenience for the women and gave them the impression that the FWBL believed they had time to spare. I am concerned about how the women interested in obtaining loans would have been treated and received at the FWBL without the support and presence of a prominent NGO representative. I believe they would have been turned away and may not have even been told about the group guaranteed lending option, without a NGO representative's ability to exert pressure on FWBL management. This again proves that it takes someone connected, as the NGO representative was, to help low-income women secure loans from the FWBL.

B. The Agriculture Development Bank of Pakistan

The Agriculture Development Bank of Pakistan (ADBP), Pakistan's primary lending institution for agricultural and rural cottage industries, introduced its Agricultural Credit Program (ACP) in 1992. The primary objective of the ACP is to increase rural women's access to institutional credit. In 1995, the ACP had five components: small scheme enterprises, lending to women, group lending, lending in coordination with NGOs, and lending against the pledge of gold ornaments. The ADBP program targets female micro-entrepreneurs who are interested in receiving loans to expand their small businesses. Unlike the FWBL, the ADBP strives to serve women who previously have been uninvolved in income-generating activities, but who would like to start one. The ADBP has formulated a list of approved activities for which women can obtain a loan, the most popular of which were sewing-related dairy production and chicken rearing.

Of my total respondents, 54 per cent received loans from the ADBP. As of 1994, the ADBP, with the guidance of the World Bank and the International Fund for Agricultural Development, selected twenty-nine of its branches throughout Pakistan to initiate a credit delivery program for women. Of the twenty-nine branches identified in 1994, nineteen were located in the Punjab, four in Sind, four in NWFP, and two in Baluchistan. I interviewed women who had received loans from eleven of the Punjab's nineteen branches.

The number of loans each branch disburses varies depending upon a number of factors. A key component that affects how active an ADBP facility is rests on the persistence of its female mobile credit officers (MCOFs). The ADBP uses MCOFs and village assistants as their primary vehicle for loan outreach and provision of credit to female borrowers. As of 1995, there were thirty MCOFs and twenty-seven village assistants employed at various ADBP branches. MCOFs are responsible for processing and appraising loan applications, loan recovery and mobilizing savings deposits. They explain loan possibilities to potential clients at their homes. The provision of 'doorstep credit' is a different approach from that of the FWBL, which requires its clients to come to its facilities. Because MCOFs and their assistants market ADBP's credit services to women at their homes, they are directly exposed to clients' businesses and therefore understand a part of their clients' lives and their living conditions. FWBL staff are not privy to understanding their clients' businesses or their living conditions, as they rarely go to women's homes to market loans or monitor repayments. As a result, I found that the type of staff at the ADBP and the FWBL differ widely. The ADBP loan officers and support staff often are from the areas in which they work and therefore have formed affinities with the communities in which they work. They tend to be more from working class, backgrounds and many of them have studied agriculture at the university level. The FWBL staff are often well educated, upper class women who often dressed for the office, not to visit low-income women in villages.

Some of the most successful ADBP branches are established in Bahawalpur, one of the Punjab's more conservative districts though one renowned for textile handicrafts. Since the inception of the credit delivery program, Bahawalpur MCOFs disbursed close to a thousand loans to women, and they have been able to maintain an 85 per cent recovery rate. Alternatively, some branches have performed poorly, particularly where the MCOFs were less aggressive or dedicated. For instance, by March of 1995, the Gujranwala branches maintained a cumulative recovery rate of 52 per cent, in spite of a small clientele of 111 women. In short, the success of the ADBP's credit delivery system depends a great deal upon the outreach capabilities of the MCOFs and their support teams as well as their dedication to their work.

Two types of loans are available to women under the Agricultural Credit Program. Short-term loans of Rs 20,000 ($666) or less are available for a maximum of eighteen months to individual borrowers who do not possess any land or other types of surety. Borrowers secure loans through one guarantor, who possesses assets sufficient to secure the client's loans. The ADBP's repayment schedule revolves around harvest seasons in order to ensure that their clients have funds available for repayment. Clients make three payments every six months, in January and June of each year. Loans of Rs 50,000 ($1,666) or less are also available for a maximum of five years, to clients who own land or other types of immovable assets. All borrowers are charged a 13 and one-half per cent interest rate. ADBP's practice of standardizing interest rates is advantageous over the FWBL's system of charging two different interest rates. Although ADBP charges higher interest rates than the FWBL, both rates are still too low to create permanent, sustainable microfinance institutions. As a result, facilities like the FWBL and the ADBP that charge subsidized rates will invite fraud and bribes, as subsidized interest rates are attractive to individuals outside a facility's target clientele. Banks such as the ADBP and the FWBL need to charge commercial rates at least of 18 per cent or higher in order to begin covering their operating costs.

Although the ADBP requires collateral from all borrowers, its prerequisites are less stringent than the FWBL's, as it only requires potential clients to secure loans with one guarantor instead of two. The ADBP also extends loans to women against the pledge of gold ornaments from sixteen ADBP branches. However, I did not meet any women who received a loan through this method and I am under the impression that few women have. This is an innovative strategy that has been successful in India and other areas of South Asia. Lending against gold ornaments needs to be promoted further by the ADBP and integrated into the facility's permanent banking environment, as gold is often the only asset a woman may possess.

Coupled with its strategy of lending against the pledge of gold items, the ADBP initiated a strategy to extend loans in collaboration with NGOs. Similar to lending against gold, the ADBP identified specific branches in which to initiate this model. Although I visited some of these designated branches, I did not interview any women who received loans through this method. As with the lending against gold strategy, few women have received loans through NGOs, as the ADBP does not promote this method nor does it encourage women and NGOs to participate. It is also unclear if the ADBP has developed a viable plan regarding how it will collaborate with NGOs and what role the NGOs will play if one of their members have the approval to obtain a loan through the ADBP.

The ADBP also advertises a female group-lending scheme. Five to fifteen women are required to form a cluster. A maximum of Rs 20,000 ($666) is available to each female group member. However, unlike the prerequisites for group lending under the FWBL, at least one of the ADBP cluster members needs to be a landowner with a minimum of 6.25 irrigated acres or 12.5 acres of unirrigated land. Although the ADBP introduced this lending model in selected branches, yet again I never met any woman who obtained a loan by this method. This, too, is a lending model that the ADBP needs to promote if they truly are committed to reaching low-income women. Group lending could be extremely effective in mobilizing novice borrowers in Pakistan, while simultaneously rapidly increasing the ADBP's scale. However, the ADBP must revamp its group lending criteria so that no group members need collateral to obtain a loan—the group guaranteed lending scheme must rely upon the peer pressure within the group to ensure repayment. This way it will not displace women who need credit, but who do not know someone with collateral necessary to secure a group loan. The group guarantee lending methodology was created to break down power structures like the requirement of collateral. Therefore, the ADBP's group lending model cannot rely on one group member to possess land and thereby all the power over the other group members.

Between the inception of the ADBP's Agricultural Credit Program in 1992 until March of 1995, the bank disbursed 3,803 loans totaling Rs 98.926 million ($3.29 million) to Pakistani women. The majority of these loans were extended to women who reside in the Punjab because the majority of ADBP's branches are located there. Its ACP recovery rate in June of 1994 was 92 per cent and the bank anticipated a slightly higher rate in 1995. While the ADBP has not been successful in utilizing alternative methodologies of collateral, the ADBP has been successful in mobilizing rural women and extending loans to them through the assistance of the MCOFs and their village assistants. I argue that the ADBP is one of the few avenues in the Punjab through which rural women could obtain credit, provided that they could locate a guarantor with assets sufficient to secure the loan. Certainly, the ADBP branch facilities through which the Agricultural Credit Program is available to women are located in much more rural locations that the FWBL facilities, which are generally located in district capitals such as Multan, Faisalabad and Sialkot. The ADBP provides credit to women in more rural locations such as Chakwal, Shakargarh and Ahmedpur East.

In spite of reaching rural women in the Punjab, the ADBP was not successful in mobilizing client savings. More FWBL respondents reported utilizing their FWBL account to keep savings than reported by ADBP borrowers. However, on the whole, respondents prefer to utilize informal savings methods such as ROSCAs. Like the FWBL, the ADBP needs to devise a way to encourage and educate women to save at their facility. The ADBP also should actively promote all lending models, including group lending, lending against the pledge of gold ornaments and coordinating with NGOs. I argue that the ADBP offer alternatives to asset-based collateral such as lending against gold, because it was mandated to do so in order to secure funds from its donors like the World Bank. Clearly ADBP management is not committed to utilizing these alternative surety mechanisms in the Punjab, or it would have completed a concrete strategy to do so. Similar to the FWBL, if the ADBP were committed to consciously targeting low-income women who cannot provide guarantors or collateral, it would actively market ways in which potential clients can secure loans against an alternative to asset-based collateral such as through group-guaranteed lending.

C. Non-governmental Organizations

In addition to interviewing women who received loans from the FWBL and the ADBP, 20 per cent of my interviewees received loans from various Pakistani NGOs. The institutions from which respondents obtained loans include: the All Pakistan Women's Association (APWA), the Association for Business, Professional and Agricultural Women (ABP&AW), Community Development Concern (CDC), the National Rural Support Program (NRSP) and the Family Planning Association of Pakistan (FPAP). While some of the organizations solely have women-related objectives, others have multisectoral concerns with a strong women's component.

In comparison to the FWBL and the ADBP, investigated NGOs are often small, offer more flexible loan terms and possess limited financial resources that comprise their loan portfolios, such as Rs 100,000–200,000 ($3,333–$6,666). While loan policies and procedures for different NGOs vary, the investigated NGOs generally disburse loans to a few individuals and at low interest rates, such as ten percent or lower (the inflation rate in Pakistan in 1995). Credit-lending NGOs often receive their funding from donors such as UNICEF or the UNDP. NGOs that offer heavily subsidized credit are detrimental both to the organization and to their clients, as the facilities that offer such rates become heavily dependent upon outside funders and, therefore, its credit program and subsequently women's access to credit may become short-lived. Women need permanent lines of credit, and research indicates that borrowers are willing to pay higher interest rates to secure long-term credit services.

Although the majority of credit-lending NGOs that I investigated operate small, subsidized credit programs, a few stand out as committed to global microfinance standards of creating sustainable credit institutions. An example of an organization in the Punjab that is committed to creating sustainable credit-lending institutions is the National Rural Support Program (NRSP). The NRSP extends loans at commercial interest rates, and interest income allows the organization to begin covering its operating expenses. The NRSP has become more self-reliant, as it has discontinued its funding from the Government of Pakistan. Another important element of the NRSP's operation is that it requires all borrowers to save at least one-fourth of the amount of their loan prior to loan disbursal. Mobilizing borrowers' savings is an important component in striving toward sustainability and empowering women. The NRSP is also successful in tailoring its loans to the actual financial needs of the borrowers, whereas the FWBL and the ADBP tend to consistently disburse the maximum loan amounts available through the small loan scheme available at their facilities. Research (Otero, 1994) shows that the smaller the loan, the more likely it is that a facility is reaching the clients in greatest need. As of March, 1995, the NRSP disbursed a total of Rs 1,954,060 ($65,135). I conclude that the NRSP is an example of a more sophisticated and successful NGO that operates credit programs in the Punjab.

Investigated NGOs were successful in maintaining very high repayment rates. Recovery rates of 100 per cent were not uncommon but few organizations were worried about on-time repayment. Unfortunately, many organizations achieve such high repayment rates because they only have a handful of borrowers, or a few hundred at most. A limited number of borrowers allows client follow-up to remain quite easy for the organizations, especially given that the investigated NGOs either prioritize disbursing loans to their members, or extend loans only to their constituents. Therefore, if an individual is not a part of the organization's activities, she would have an extremely difficult time securing a loan from an NGO, which thereby limits the availability of loans to women and limits NGOs' outreach.

While some organizations disburse loans directly from their facilities, others work in conjunction with a bank, such as the FWBL, to disburse loans. For instance, the Association for Business, Professional and Agricultural Women (ABP&AW) in Rawalpindi acts as an intermediary with the FWBL, in order to secure credit for some of its members. In Pakistan, many women's organizations and NGOs have formed affiliations with local commercial banks, largely because of the efforts of the NGOs. For instance, six of Pakistan's NGOs that address women's issues—the Aurat Foundation; HAWWA Associates; the All Pakistan Women's Association; the Business and

Professional Women's Organization; Association for Business and Professional and Agricultural Women; and Family Planning Association of Pakistan have established linkages with the FWBL. Some women's organizations have formulated an unofficial 'referral system' with the FWBL, in which the women's organization can send a woman to the FWBL with a referral slip. Referral slips may state that the potential client is an active member of a specific organization, the type of work in which she is involved and a statement from the organization stating why the candidate is deserving of a loan. This referral service is helpful for both the clients and the banks, as the bank is notified that the loan candidate is affiliated with an NGO that may offer her helpful employment skills such as information about marketing or advanced skill training, thereby increasing the viability of a woman's business and the likelihood that she will be able to repay her loan. The referral system is also a useful tool for the FWBL; they can then contact the specific NGO from which the loan candidate is referred and receive additional information about her and her business.

The role and responsibilities of the banks and the NGOs needs to be further clarified so that each party understands their role when an individual attached to an NGO obtains a loan from a credit-lending facility like the FWBL. Some NGOs I met with argued that the FWBL asked the NGO with whom a woman was affiliated to guarantee her loan. This again confirms that the FWBL does not believe that female entrepreneurs will repay their loans. As a result, the FWBL fails to relinquish control of the lending process to clients. It prefers to keep the NGO, or an individual attached to the NGO, personally accountable for the repayment of a woman's loan, instead of utilizing its non-traditional group-guarantee lending methodology. Therefore, alternatives to asset-based collateral, a proven way to mobilize female entrepreneurs who do not have the ability to provide collateral or a guarantor, are rarely prioritized or used by the FWBL. Some of the investigated NGOs feel that providing guarantees for FWBL clients, whether or not an individual is affiliated with an NGO, is not their role. One NGO representative stated that if they wanted to be involved with the banking industry they would lend funds themselves. Women's NGOs also allege that many of the commercial banks with which they have forged alliances tend to rely upon the organization if they are having problems with a borrower affiliated with an NGO, such as a client making late payments to the bank. Instead of the bank directing its staff to the problem, they often phone the intermediary women's organization to which the client is associated and demand that the NGO locate the member and require her to make payments promptly or correct whatever she was doing incorrectly. Suddenly, the client becomes the responsibility of the women's organization and not the bank, in spite of her having taken a loan from their facility. This implies that the management staff of the lending facility perceive lending to female NGO constituents as granting the borrower and/or the NGO a favor, as opposed to an activity that helps to meet the facility's objectives or mandate. It also indicates that without being affiliated to an NGO, the client would probably not have received a loan, as she would have had a difficult time proving her credit worthiness and providing the bank with adequate guarantors.

Despite the confusion regarding which party—the bank or the NGO—is responsible for securing a client's timely repayment, Pakistani NGOs play a critical role in securing women's access to credit in the Punjab. Although many NGOs are currently forging relationships with the FWBL, which thereby assists NGO constituents to obtain loans, little progress has been made with the ADBP in this arena. Since only a few NGOs have the resources to extend loans to their clients and only limited loan capital, many organizations must work with commercial banks to obtain loans, especially larger loans, for their constituents. The linkages being created between NGOs and commercial banks are important ones that should be expanded. NGOs assist the bank in assessing an applicant's credit worthiness and help them increase the volume of borrowers they can reach, with little effort exerted by the banks. NGOs also help to secure funds for those entrepreneurs who need it most, which is a different clientele than the one that is comfortable approaching a commercial facility like the FWBL or the ADBP. NGOs also facilitate their constituents' ability to gain access to formal sources of credit, thereby enabling them to build a credit history the first time for many of them. Once a borrower has established a credit history with a facility like the FWBL, she is more likely to be able to have access to larger amounts of capital in the future without the assistance of the NGO, provided that she repays her loan on-time.

The roles and responsibilities of the banks and NGOs need to be further clarified if their relationship is to remain an amicable one. NGOs will continue to play an increasingly significant role in increasing the lending scale of banks, and their efforts and dedication to securing women's access to credit will directly affect the number of women who obtain access to credit in Pakistan.

D. Strategies to Improve the Effectiveness of Micrilending in the Punjab

Despite an increasing number of credit-lending facilities that extend loans to Pakistani women, they continue to have difficulties securing small loans in the Punjab. Although this chapter has focused on facilities that disburse credit and women who managed to acquire it, the majority of women in Pakistan cannot get credit from either NGOs or credit-lending facilities such as the First Women's Bank and the Agricultural Development Bank of Pakistan. In 1994–1995 when I conducted my research, I did not visit some districts within the Punjab as I could not locate any credit-lending facilities in places such as Mianwali, Bhakkar, Rajanpur, and Muzzafargarh. Therefore, women's access to credit in the Punjab greatly depends upon the district in which they live, their proximity to a lending facility and the institution's lending requirements. Those women who live in district capitals or larger towns within the Punjab such as Multan or Faisalabad have better chances of securing credit in comparison to women who live in remote areas located far away from a district capital or major town. Although only a small percentage of women have access to credit facilities in the Punjab, credit services for women are even more limited in other provinces such as Baluchistan.

The credit-lending facilities I investigated primarily not only offer loans to individual entrepreneurs but also extend loans that are secured against groups or through working in conjunction with NGOs. Although many facilities such as the FWBL and ADBP have systems which theoretically entitle eligible women to obtain a loan without asset-based collateral, such as through group-guaranteed lending, their facilities do not promote these alternative surety mechanisms and, therefore, they are rarely used. As a result, only women who can provide the required collateral or guarantors can have access to credit.

Those women who generally benefit from credit in the Punjab are middle-to-upper class, urban women, with few rural or low-income women being served by the investigated facilities. The management staff of the credit-lending facilities that offer alternatives to asset-based collateral such as loans secured against the pledge of gold items, do so for the sake of appeasing ministries and donors. Bank management hold no stake or organizational commitment in these programs, nor do they generally employ staff at their facilities who are committed to empowering low-income entrepreneurs. Equally true is that bank management regard the provision of alternatives to asset-based collateral as 'extra' or 'special programs,' which are outside of their organizational mission, and therefore, they are not incorporated as part of an institution's general microfinance strategy. Hence, the investigated credit-lending facilities did not offer alternatives to asset-based collateral in all of their facilities, but instead only in a select few. Donors like the World Bank along with other national ministries have pressured these microfinance facilities to adopt these alternative strategies, because of the success that worldwide lending programs have achieved in reaching the poor and combating poverty when they utilize such strategies. Attractive systems are in place that appease donors and convince outside audiences that Pakistan has begun to target low-income entrepreneurs and practice the true principles of microfinance. However, much of the value of these programs has not been realized by their intended clients. International donors and national ministries need to monitor how these programs impact their intended clients or those who possess no assets or collateral. Otherwise, these programs will only exist in name.

It is only on a rare occasion that female interviewees received a loan without collateral. Many women also would not have received loans if influential organizations or individuals had not pressured the credit-lending facilities to process their loans, or in some cases acted as their guarantor. Within the facilities I investigated, for the most part, obtaining a small loan has been linked to supplying the bank with individuals who possess power and clout—guarantors who have the funds to cover a woman's loan in case of default. In other South Asian countries, institutions successfully operate microlending programs without requiring asset-based collateral, yet maintain extremely high repayment rates. In contrast, top management at investigated Pakistani microlending institutions have failed to relinquish their power and require groups of borrowers to collectively be responsible for assessing each group member's business and credit worthiness. Instead of Pakistani institutions promoting decentralized credit schemes that empower the poor, they require applicants to seek approval from those who have traditionally held power and been responsible for decision-making in the society. If cosigners who possess adequate assets are not willing to provide low-income individuals with guarantees, then low-income entrepreneurs are prohibited from obtaining credit.

, In spite of the problems associated with the facilities I investigated, it is important to note that there are other organizations in Pakistan that currently operate successful credit programs. For instance, in 1998 I was please to find newly emerging organizations such as the Kashf Foundation in Lahore, which offers group-guaranteed loans to women in rural areas of the Lahore district. Kashf, a Pakistani NGO established in 1996, is exclusively involved in microfinance and credit support services such as training. Committed to global microfinance standards, Kashf charges above market rates of interest for short-term loans for women and encourages them to save. Organizations such as Kashf show that women entrepreneurs need small loans such as Rs 4,000 to expand their businesses. Not all women need or demand Rs 20,000 or Rs 25,000, as facilities I interviewed assumed. On the contrary, approximately 60 percent of the women I interviewed received loans under Rs 20,000 ($666 or less) and five had secured loans of Rs 1,000 ($33) or less. This is testament to the fact that women can use amounts of capital less than Rs 25,000 ($833). The average loan amount that a facility extends is commonly used as a proxy for the type of women and businesses benefitting from the loans, as 'small loans tend to reach the smaller businesses' (Otero, 1994: 98). Thus, organizations such as the Kashf Foundation, are reaching smaller businesses and those women in greater need of capital. Such organizations, which are committed to providing sustainable credit and support services, provide hope for the microfinance field in Pakistan. It is also refreshing that lessons learned by other prominent credit-lending facilities such as AKRSP and OPP have been shared with Kashf staff, and Pakistani credit-lending facilities are coordinating with each other to maximize results and impact.

Although microfinance services are not the sole elements that can transform Pakistan's financial and social sectors, they do play a critical role in providing financial services to microentrepreneurs who have historically been excluded from services offered by Pakistan's formal financial institutions. As a result, credit-lending facilities have the capacity to enhance Pakistan's civil society, as they facilitate the provision of alternative credit services and the ability for women, who were previously excluded from Pakistan's financial sector, to obtain microfinance products for the first time. Without a doubt, the investigated facilities have contributed towards the socioeconomic advancement of women in Pakistan. There are clear ways in which the investigated facilities can better serve the individuals they are mandated to assist, as outlined in their program objectives. Providing women with access to credit is an important and effective technique to integrate women into Pakistan's economy, and to have women recognized as important economic actors within society.

References

Ali, Nayare. 1994. 'A Landmark Achievement: The First Women's Bank.' *She* September, p. 114.

Ayub, Nasreen. 1994. *The Self-Employed Women in Pakistan.* Karachi: First Association for Women's Studies.

Bilquees, Faiz. 1991. 'The First Women's Bank—Why and for Whom?'. *The Pakistan Development Review.* Vol. 30, Winter, pp. 745–753.

Khatoon, Akram. 1990. 'First Women Bank Ltd.—An Investment to Induct Women in Mainstream for Economic Development: New Directions for Policy.' Islamabad: Ministry of Women's Development, April. Unpublished.

Hossain, Mahabub. 1993. 'The Grameen Bank: It's Origins, Organization and Management Style' in *The Grameen Bank: Poverty Relief in Bangladesh* edited by Abu N. M. Wahid. Boulder, Colorado: Westview Press, pp. 9–21.

Otero, Maria. 1994. 'The Evolution of Nongovernmental Organizations Toward Financial Intermediation.' in The *New World of Microenterprise Finance* edited by Maria Otero and Elisabeth Rhyne. West Hartford: Kumarian Press, pp. 94–104.

UNDP. 1996. *Human Development Report 1996.* New York: Oxford University Press.

NOTES

1. I am grateful to the Fulbright Program for funding this research in Pakistan, 1994–95.
2. Here and elsewhere, the conversion from rupees to US dollars being used is at 1995 rates. As the rupee has lost value against the dollar, the amount available for loans has increased.

11

CRITICAL ENGAGEMENTS: NGOS AND THE STATE

Omar Asghar Khan

This chapter traces the history of advocacy Non-governmental Organizations (NGOs) in the context of state and society in Pakistan. There is a particular focus on efforts by the state to restrict the transformative role of NGOs. It is in this context that there is a discussion of the tensions in NGO-state relations. An attempt will be made to draw out the different approaches that are being adopted by NGOs to bring about policy and institutional changes in Pakistan. The chapter then examines the impact of the mobilisational and advocacy work of NGOs over the last few years in Pakistan. Towards the end, there is a discussion of some of the challenges facing NGOs and the responses that are being articulated.

A. Advocacy and the Development Role of NGOs in Pakistan: A Historical Perspective

The past few years have seen a rapid increase in the number of NGOs in Pakistan. There are, however, various types of NGOs, distinguishable by the factors that have led to their genesis, their organizational objectives and their linkages with other civil society organizations.

Charitable self-help groups, small and large, inspired by religious faith or humanitarian concerns, have been in existence for a long time in the Indo-Pakistan subcontinent. Housing societies, cooperatives and other kinds of membership organizations have also proliferated. It was during the Afghan War in the 1980s that there was a rapid increase in foreign-funded NGOs involved in cross-border relief operations. The proliferation of NGOs also extended to religious *madrassas* (schools) in the 1980s when funding to religious educational institutions increased substantially from both the Pakistan state and from foreign sources, mainly from the Arab states and Iran.

As compared to charitable NGOs involved in politically neutral activities, NGOs working in the field of development and advocacy are a more recent phenomenon in Pakistan. Their genesis can be traced to the latter half of the 1980s when a combination of a number of factors led to the emergence of the social mobilisational approach with a focus on advocacy amongst NGOs in the country. The failure of a top-down, centralized approach to the planning and implementation of programs in Pakistan was an important determinant in catalyzing the formation of a number of groups which initiated a bottom-up and people-centred approach to development. Besides these experiments in participatory development at the grass-roots level, a number of groups came into existence to protect the rights of vulnerable and marginalized groups, be they minorities, child workers, industrial workers, women, etc.

Ironically, it was during the military regime of General Zia ul-Haq when political repression and human rights violations were on the rise and the country was witnessing a rising trend of intolerance especially towards women and minorities following the passage of discriminatory laws. A number of individuals came together to form groups or associations to work to protect the interests of the vulnerable and marginalized sections of society. State control over the media, art and culture as well as the purge of universities led many socially committed activists to seek expression by forming or joining advocacy-based 'civil society' or non-governmental organizations.[1] Individuals working in these organizations played an important role in supporting the Movement for the Restoration of Democracy, an alliance of political parties opposing military rule in the 1980s.[2] Besides playing this political role, these groups were also actively involved in putting certain issues of rights and entitlements concerning vulnerable sections, such as women, children, minorities, and migrants living in urban slums, on the 'developmental' agenda in Pakistan.

The general elections in 1988, immediately after the death of the military ruler, General Zia ul-Haq, raised the hopes of the vast majority of Pakistanis. With the end of the military government and a 'return to democracy', many thought that a new era of democratization and socio-economic reforms was going to be instituted.

However, the dismissal of the government of Benazir Bhutto in 1990 on charges of corruption and incompetence, under Article 58(2)B of the Constitution, only eighteen months after it had been elected to office, saw the beginning of a process of disillusionment with the mainstream political system. This dismissal of the Peoples Party government was followed by a succession of 'elections' and dismissals of elected governments by Presidents who derived their power from a constitutional amendment introduced by the now late General Zia ul-Haq. Each election has seen lower and lower turnout by voters. Accusations of rigging of elections have been a common occurrence. These charges of election rigging were also corroborated by foreign observers in the case of at least the 1990 elections.[3]

In a case before the Supreme Court of Pakistan filed by a former Air Chief of the Pakistan Air Force, the Inter Services Intelligence Agency has been accused of manipulating the electoral success of the Islami Jamhoori Itehad (IJI) of which the Pakistan Muslim League, led by Mian Nawaz Sharif, was a coalition partner in 1990. An affidavit of the former head of the ISI is part of the petition where he has acknowledged giving state funds to selected candidates of the IJI.[4]

B. State and Civil Society

The post-colonial state in Pakistan has been characterized by a heterogeneous population divided into diverse ethnic, religious and cultural groups. These divisions have been further compounded, and in some cases accentuated, by rising socio-economic disparities. This has fuelled ethnic and religious conflict. In the absence of a major restructuring of the system of governance aimed at arresting the widening gulf between the different regions and social groups that make up the Pakistani polity, the state has been catalyzed into searching for transcending and homogenizing symbols to overcome the pressures being exerted by a heterogeneous population that is increasingly experiencing social fragmentation.

When ideology fails to homogenize populations, the state resorts to co-option and manipulation. When this fails, it resorts to the use of force. This is what we see happening in Pakistan. In an attempt to control the lives of an increasingly ungovernable polity, the state—while losing legitimacy—has become more oppressive. Both military and civilian rulers have resorted to patronage and authoritarian measures to perpetuate their rule over a people whose basic needs have largely been unfulfilled.

It is important to distinguish between the state and governments. Governments in Pakistan have been weak, intermittent and fragile. The state on the other hand has always been authoritarian and resilient and has succeeded in holding political governments hostage. Political governments have not been able to fulfil their responsibility to the people. Whether it is the provision of essential social services such as health, education, water, sanitation, or security of life and property or the functioning of the justice system, successive governments have failed to deliver.[5] As has been pointed out, 'the state is powerful not through the provision of goods and services and security; it becomes powerful against its own people for its own preservation.'[6] However, the past five decades have seen significant changes in the socio-economic structure with implications for power relations. The emergence of a significant middle class, the commercialization of the economy, and the rise of associations and groups has created a mosaic of civil society groupings. While the grip of the traditional elite may be weakening, civil society had not been able to fill this void. Its emergence is characterized by conflict with the more traditional social forces.

Never before in the history of the country has a government tried to concentrate powers in its hand as had the government of Prime Minister Nawaz Sharif since it came into office in February 1997. Having been elected to office with a two-third majority, it soon embarked on the task of bringing about far reaching changes in the Constitution. By abolishing Article 58(2)B of the Constitution and then electing Mohammad Rafiq Tarar as the President, the Prime Minister thought he had eliminated any possibility of his rule being cut short. The passage of the Fourteenth amendment eliminated the possibility of dissent within the ruling parliamentary party. Then an attack on the higher judiciary by the ruling party seriously impaired the independence of the judiciary. The removal of the Chief Justice of the Supreme Court and the subsequent changes in the superior judiciary brought about a qualitative change in the role of the higher judiciary. By this time the media had started pointing out the increasingly dictatorial style of governance of the ruling Muslim League. It was around this time that India and then Pakistan first tested their ballistic missiles and nuclear devices. The government of Mian Nawaz Sharif declared an emergency and suspended all fundamental rights immediately after Pakistan had tested its nuclear devices. With sanctions imposed by Western countries and Japan following the nuclear test blasts, the already difficult economic conditions further deteriorated. It was not before long that the euphoria of the nuclear tests started wearing off and people were confronted with the harsh socio-economic realities of rising prices, growing unemployment and lawlessness. Hence, some sections of civil society started questioning the government's decision to go nuclear. For the first time protest rallies were organized to denounce the government's failure to contain the deteriorating socio-economic situation as well as its militaristic policies. These developments led to the emergence of the Pakistan Peace Movement which by the end of 1998 had assumed an organizational form in the shape of the Pakistan Peace Coalition, a confederation of different citizens groups working against the nuclearisation of South Asia in the cities of Karachi, Lahore, Rawalpindi, and Peshawar.

C. Shrinking Spaces for Civil Society

As a part of its response to sanctions, the Nawaz Sharif government announced its policy of self reliance. In addition to a number of other measures, it announced the controversial decision to construct the Kalabagh dam. This announcement galvanized a divided opposition in a campaign which drew widespread support in the three smaller provinces of the North West Frontier, Baluchistan and Sindh; the strongest opposition came from Sindh and the North West Frontier Province. Besides large public protests against the project, a media campaign with the involvement of civil society and environmental groups was launched. In order to deal with the growing resistance from the political opposition, the media and sections of civil society, the government moved the Fifteenth Constitutional amendment, commonly known as the Shariat Bill, which if passed would give sweeping powers to the Prime Minister and the executive arm of government. It would increase the powers of the federal government vis-à-vis the federating units, thus weakening an already fragile union. Thus by centralizing powers in the executive, the system of parliamentary accountability would be dealt a serious blow. In order to get the proposed bill through parliament, the government conveniently used Islam. Anyone opposing this undemocratic amendment was threatened with dire consequences by the Prime Minister himself. For example, the Muslim Students Federation, the student wing of Nawaz Sharif's Pakistan Muslim League, sent letters to the opposition Senators threatening them of dire consequences if they opposed the Shariat Bill.[7]

Despite such threats, civil society organizations, the media and the political parties organized protests. It is no wonder that both the media and advocacy NGOs had become the target of attacks by the Muslim League government since they had become the most consistent in their critique of the proposed amendment. The *Jang* group of papers (the largest newspaper group in the country), the monthly *Newsline, The Frontier Post* and a number of senior journalists became the target of the government's campaign aimed at silencing the independent press. Another target of attack of the Muslim League government had been the trade unions and professional associations such as independent organizations of doctors and teachers. With the suspension of trade union activities in WAPDA, the Pakistan Hydroelectric Labour Union, one of the largest unions in the country, has for all practical purposes been banned. Large-scale downsizing of the public sector, the closure of thousands of manufacturing units because of recession and the extension of the Essential Services Act to the power sector, are developments that do not auger well for the trade union movement in the country.[8]

The last target of the Nawaz Sharif government's attack on independent and autonomous organizations were advocacy NGOs. About 2,500 NGOs were dissolved by the Punjab, NWFP and Sindh governments without following legal procedures.[9] The government felt very uncomfortable with particularly those groups which had played an active role in questioning its administration on a number of fronts: economic management, nuclear policy, the Fifteenth amendment, and the Kalabagh dam.[10] This attack on NGOs had, in particular, been articulated by the Minister for Social Welfare of the Government of Punjab in response to the campaign of advocacy NGOs against the passage of the Fifteenth Amendment by Parliament. He went to the extent of calling NGOs anti-Islam and anti-state.[11] The NGOs reacted strongly to these utterances of the Provincial Minister and asked the Government to clarify its policy and stand on the role of NGOs in social development.[12] Earlier, the Planning Commission, in a paper on the government's Poverty Alleviation Strategy for the *Ninth Five-Year Plan*, had proposed that NGOs should receive funding from foreign donors only after the government had given approval to them (as was in force during the Zia ul-Haq years). This appears to have been a move to control an increasingly independent and vocal NGO sector and not to be motivated by considerations of accountability since provisions in existing laws allow for this.[13]

It is within this context that some NGOs which are trying to intervene on behalf of the marginalized and the disadvantaged are faced with serious challenges. State institutions at the local, regional and the national level have not been able to meet the needs and demands of the disadvantaged and the marginalized. By and large, these institutions are being used by powerful vested interests to further their own agendas and interests at the cost of the ordinary people. The struggle for control over resources as well as access to services and to centres of decision making can be witnessed in both the urban and rural areas of Pakistan. These struggles are at times peaceful but in the absence of credible justice systems frequently assume violent forms.[14] There have been instances when concerted efforts by citizens' groups in urban areas and communities at the local level in rural areas have been successful in creating the space for the voices of the poor and the marginalized to be heard. To what extent has this been translated into actions that point towards policy and institutional change is, however, another matter.

The state is more comfortable with NGOs which restrict themselves to traditional activities such as welfare, relief or service provision. It is not entirely comfortable when NGO work is aimed at democratizing the state. Similarly, NGOs have faced difficulties in working with state institutions on issues such as peace, dams, minorities, and women rights, to list a few. The state is compatible with NGOs as long as they do not challenge the basic power equation. But a number of NGOs have moved beyond the traditional service provision/charity mode of functioning into an advocacy role. Through their advocacy and development work they are broadening the concept of governance from the traditional one of government and administration to include fundamental questions such as the nature of democracy, citizenship, access to services, control over resources, and access to centres of decision making.

D. New Contenders for Sharing Power

The failure of the mainstream political parties to respond to peoples' aspirations for socio-economic change has led to a general disillusionment with traditional forms of politics as a means for political change. The domination of the mainstream political parties and the legislatures by feudal and big business interests, the lack of community perspectives in discussions in the legislatures on issues of distributive justice, poverty, economic policy, minorities and women rights, and ecological degradation has meant that these issues are increasingly being taken up by peoples' organizations and advocacy NGOs. Consequently, people have started responding by organizing for themselves the provision of such services and the protection of rights. NGOs, however, cannot substitute for the state. The state owes a responsibility to its citizens for the provision of essential services. Nevertheless NGOs can, by creating innovative models, present examples for the state and society to adopt.

With the end of the cold war and the withdrawal of Soviet troops from Afghanistan, there has been a growing interest on the part of donor agencies to work with advocacy-oriented NGOs. Advocacy is no longer considered to be 'subversive.' The failure of the donor supported top-down development approach common in the past few decades has led to a rethinking on the part of the international development community. Development cooperation is now being extended to include advocacy-oriented, non-governmental actors as well. However, there are differing perceptions on the part of the NGO community as well as the donors regarding what is meant by this 'cooperation'. Some NGOs in Pakistan view donor funds as a means to complement the state's and the private sector's role in the provision of productive and social services; others view the process of 'globalisation' as economically unjust, socially and culturally alienating and ecologically damaging. There is still a third strand amongst the NGOs in Pakistan which question local structures and policies that perpetuate oppression and exploitation without establishing the linkages between international financial and political structures and the underdevelopment of Pakistan's economy and society.

E. Autonomy of the NGO Sector

At a time when there appears to be increasing donor support for NGOs, the state and some donors, in their support of Government Organized NGOs, may be influencing the nature of the NGO sector in Pakistan. To influence the NGO 'movement,' the state is engaged in setting up and sponsoring 'NGOs' which should more appropriately be called parastatal organizations. A significant share of donor and government funding is being given to these government organized NGOs. Efforts are afoot to legitimize this approach, based on the experience of one Rural Support Programme in the Northern Areas of the country, by extending it to other regions of Pakistan. It must, however, be mentioned that the successful replication of this approach in other parts of the country has yet to be proven. Despite this, there appears to be a concerted effort by official quarters to affix the stamp of legitimacy on this model. A case in point is the report of the Task Force on Poverty Alleviation set up by the Nawaz Sharif government in 1997 soon after being elected to office.[15]

The Task Force has only considered the officially sponsored Rural Support Organizations to be viable institutions for poverty eradication. It has not recognized the work of advocacy oriented groups which have undertaken innovative work in addressing issues of deprivation, ecological degradation, gender discrimination, and human rights violations by following an approach which combines community development work with advocacy. It is in recognition of this work that some of these organizations have received both national and international recognition. It should be noted that some of the Rural Support Organizations have been facing institutional challenges because of a desire to scale up rapidly, government interference, political pressures, and weak linkages with other NGOs and civil society organizations. In order to replicate and scale up the Rural Support Programme approach, the Task Force has recommended the setting up of 100 District Support Organizations.

A number of issues emerge from the findings and recommendations of the Task Force. The fundamental problem with this approach is the limited and narrow interpretation of poverty.[16] This has obvious implications for the strategy recommended by the Task Force for poverty alleviation. Poverty is defined in terms of a lack of access to markets, credit and essential services. Such a definition does not see poverty in terms of the socio-economic and political structures which combine together at the local, national and international level causing deprivation, powerlessness and oppression.[17] These factors in turn determine the space available for the deprived and the powerless to move out of their state of deprivation and oppression.

The Task Force, although having as its members a few NGO leaders, did not consult the larger NGO community. Even the NGO members of the Task Force were not consulted at the stage of finalization of the recommendations. It is for this reason that not only did the report evoke a sharp critique from the NGO community but its publication led to at least three members from the NGO community disassociating themselves from it. In a similar development, another NGO member of the Working Group on Poverty Alleviation for the *Ninth Five-Year Plan* withdrew from the Task Force when his recommendations which articulated the point of view of the advocacy oriented NGOs were not incorporated into the final report.

Despite the controversy surrounding the Task Force Report on Poverty Eradication, the Muslim League government decided to go ahead with the idea of setting up Rural Support Organizations, the latest being the establishment of the Punjab Rural Support Programme. This is happening at a time when more and more citizens groups and NGOs are coming to realize that the present structure of a centralized system of governance will only perpetuate an inequitable and oppressive social system causing political instability.

F. Tensions in State–NGO Relations

The exclusion of local communities from the processes of governance and the benefits of development is resulting in local initiatives by the people to organize themselves with the aim to make state institutions more responsive and accountable to the people. The pluralism and diversity that is inherent in the response of such groups could strengthen civil society in a situation where centralization of power and authority are dominating trends in the realm of politics and socio-economic development. The main function of groups involved in advocacy-based community development work is to create conditions so that the weakest sections of society have a voice in the decision-making processes at all levels. However, this is only possible if far reaching structural changes are brought about in the socio-economic and political structures of the country. Given the nature of the state in Pakistan, this process of bringing about changes in institutional structures inevitably leads to tensions in NGO–State relations at various levels. There have been many instances where tensions have arisen between the state and the NGOs. Probably one of the first instances of these tensions arose in the late 1980s when the government, after having experienced the role of NGO activism during the anti-martial law movement of the 1980s, was not entirely comfortable with an increasingly vocal NGO sector. The government was quick to support the idea of establishing a central funding mechanism to channel funds to NGOs. USAID and other donors were approached to support the idea. Except for USAID, other donors did not respond favourably, partly because of concerns expressed by a nascent NGO sector which viewed this move as an attempt to control NGOs.

At this stage, the first attempts at NGO coalition building at a national level with an advocacy focus were initiated when the NGO Dialogue was formed.[18] The NGO Dialogue was a forum where NGO leaders from all the four provinces came together to discuss issues of mutual interest and concern. Successive governments continued to think of ways and means of regulating NGOs, ostensibly from the point of view of promoting accountability. However, advocacy NGOs have viewed these moves as aimed at restricting their advocacy and mobilisational role. It was, however, not until 1994 that the government's intentions of imposing controls and restrictions on NGOs became obvious when a press campaign was unleashed against them. This was followed by a proposed bill to regulate their functioning.[19] This led to a concerted and somewhat coordinated NGO response largely spearheaded by a few advocacy NGOs.

This also led to a process of reflection within the NGO community about the need for greater transparency as well as discussions on the role of NGOs in terms of advocacy and the risks associated with such work. The Advocacy Development Network, a coalition of nine NGOs, organized a national workshop on Accountability and Legitimacy of NGOs which concluded with a statement enunciating principles of accountability for NGOs, donors and the government.[20] The relationship of NGOs with the state and with civil society (including the media) also came under discussion. After dialoguing amongst themselves, the NGOs and the government started talking to each other through newly formed regional and national coalitions. Thus, it was the NGO bill that catalyzed the NGO movement into coming together into coalitions to oppose the government's moves to impose restrictions.[21]

The coalitions that came into existence at the time of the NGO Bill exist at regional levels with varying degrees of success. However, this process of coalition building began a process of developing a collective identity within the NGO sector. Moreover, it brought together smaller community-based organizations and larger NGOs and, more importantly, legitimized the advocacy role of NGOs. It was not until this response by the NGOs to the government's attempts to control and regulate them that NGO advocacy was considered to be risky and politically motivated. This suspicion was reinforced by the fact that a few of the NGO leaders in the fore-front of the movement against the NGO bill were either affiliated with oppositional political parties or had been active in party politics. Given that the organizations that they were heading were still developing their institutional identities, it was their personalities that in many cases were overshadowing their organizations. This in many cases led to suspicion and mistrust amongst NGOs, between the government and the NGOs, and between donors and the NGOs. It took a while for each of these groups to adjust to the changing realities and new roles.

While the NGO bill created tensions between the government and the NGOs, it opened doors for dialogue between the government, parliamentarians, the media, and civil society on the role of NGOs in development. This was not the only occasion for NGO–Government contact. There had been other instances of such collaboration, notably around the formulation of Pakistan's Environmental Action Plan which resulted in the *National Conservation Strategy*. During that process, the Government and select NGOs worked together to formulate a strategy to use natural resources sustainably and protect the environment from degradation. This process has had a positive impact on mobilizing public opinion in support of environment-friendly policies and practices. It also reduced some of the mistrust and tensions between the government and the NGOs and in some cases even led to collaborative efforts for natural resource management. But in some other cases, mobilization around issues of control over and access to natural resources has led to increasing tensions between advocacy-based environmental groups working on issues such as community based forest management or a cleaner urban environment and strongly entrenched mafias who enjoy the patronage of the state.

Another significant move in the context of NGO–Government collaboration was the NGO–Government interaction in the context of the pre- and post-Beijing United Nations Women's Conference process. It was during this collaboration that the Women's Enquiry Commission brought out its report on the status of women. It, to a large extent, reflected the views of the women-based advocacy NGOs. However, the government did not take its recommendations seriously. In the context of the post-Beijing process, a National Plan of Action was prepared jointly by the Government and the NGOs. However, despite this collaboration, the government has yet to agree to repeal discriminatory laws against women. While the government expressed its willingness to be a signatory to CEDAW, discriminatory laws enacted during the martial law days of General Zia ul-Haq remain on the statute-books.

With the resignation in October 1998 of NGOs from government committees related to women and legal reforms, NGO–Government relations took a new turn. This decision by the NGOs followed attempts by the government to get the Shariat Bill in the form of the Fifteenth Constitutional Amendment passed by Parliament. The 1973 Constitution already guarantees that no laws repugnant to Islam can be enacted. This move by the Nawaz Sharif government was creating an environment in which women were feeling threatened by zealots who were demanding that restrictions should be imposed on them. A case in point is the enforcement of the Nizam-i-Adl regulations in Malakand and an Ordinance in Kohistan district by the NWFP government. Taking advantage of the environment created by the enforcement of the Shariah in parts of the NWFP, so-called 'Islamists' have demanded the same in other parts of the NWFP. In Battagram district, bordering Kohistan district, they have organized protests against a woman Assistant Commissioner and have also been calling for the suspension of all women-related social development programs being implemented by NGOs in the district. The Battagram district administration, under the pressure of religious zealots, imposed Section 144 banning a 'Kissan Conference' which was to be held in a village of the district under the auspices of an advocacy NGO and its partner community men and women organizations.[22]

G. Legitimizing NGO Advocacy

NGO advocacy is the logical outcome of the present socio-economic and political crisis. In such a situation the challenge for NGOs is to work with the disadvantaged and marginalized to remove barriers in the way of their access to resources and centres of decision making. In other words the overall objective of NGO advocacy is to democratize unequal power relations. It is the recognition and legitimacy of this role amongst NGOs and the state that can neutralize the tensions which exist between the development and advocacy work of NGOs.[23]

In this approach the development and advocacy work of NGOs are essentially two sides of the same coin because even the smallest development interventions affect unequal power relations. However, it should be noted that for advocacy to be effective in terms of mobilization it must be rooted in the community. It has often been observed that NGOs involved in global or 'big' campaigns lose touch with the reality of local conditions and get drawn away from their 'constituency'. Moreover, it is important that the local communities on whose behalf, in many cases, NGOs undertake advocacy campaigns are actively involved in the agenda setting process. This is not easy in a situation where the NGOs have a 'modernist' worldview as compared to their more 'tradition'-oriented constituency. It must also be noted that NGOs involved in advocacy campaigns face risks of a political and physical nature. This is because NGOs involved in grassroots advocacy work challenge the status quo; advocacy brings forth the truth which is not always appreciated by vested interests. This is why sharing of risks within coalitions and organization and with partners is an integral part of such work.

Recurring retaliation is faced by Public Interest Organizations (PIOs) from a range of vested interests. In mid-1997, the land mafia attacked the NGO Shehri as the organization worked to highlight and remove irregularities in land use in Karachi. This included an attempt to murder Shehri's President. SUNGI has dealt with recurring malicious campaigns led by the local power elite against its rights-based work, particularly its advocacy against deforestation that exposes the role of the timber mafia.[24] Personal attacks on the staff of the organization, particularly its female staff, are regularly made by the local power elite through press statements and other methods. The retaliation is not restricted to a few organizations; also victimized have been members of ASR, the Aurat Foundation, HRCP, Dastak, Ajoka, and Shirkat Gah, all highly reputable national advocacy and women's rights NGOs. RISE and Aurat Association, two CBOs actively working in NWFP to promote the rights of women and children, are some other PIOs that regularly deal with hostility from vested interests.

The escalation in the retaliation to rights-based work is coupled with increased intensity in its hostility. *Fatwas* (religious pronouncements) and threats of violence and physical attacks are often part of the campaigns to malign and intimidate rights-based organizations. Death threats have publicly been made against well-known human rights campaigners Asma Jehangir and Hina Jilani following the murder of Samia Imran in their offices in April 1999. Religious extremists attempted to assault a peaceful procession organized by the Joint Action Committee in Peshawar on 13 April 1999 to protest honour killings. State inaction and inability to check this escalation in hostility is also a cause for concern. Thousands of religious extremists were able to assemble in Peshawar at a public meeting where they brazenly threatened those working for human rights and women's rights. Reportedly they pledged to break the limbs and gorge the eyes of activists. The state appears to have capitulated to these gun-wielding extremist groups which are threatening to undermine the efforts of PIOs aimed at organizing the marginalized and disadvantaged sections of society.[25]

In order to bring about change in policies and institutions in a country like Pakistan, where state institutions have not been very responsive, there is a need to combine local level social mobilization with lobbying at the regional and national levels. How does one distinguish between lobbying and mobilisational work as far as NGO advocacy is concerned? Moreover, what is the relationship between the two? Lobbying is a tool used to influence relatively open institutions—getting them to accept changes in laws, policies, institutional arrangements, and procedures. An example of this is the lobbying efforts of a group of NGOs through the NGO Standing Committee of the Ghazi-Barotha Hydro Power Project which is being funded by the World Bank and the Water and Power Development Authority (WAPDA). Much of the lobbying has been directed at the World Bank and WAPDA, and to some extent at other NGOs in order to elicit their support. It has been seen that influencing decisions regarding land compensation, resettlement or adherence to environmental protocols could benefit thousands of project-affected people. The effect of such decisions would outweigh the benefits of more tangible development interventions such as disbursement of loans or implementation of Productive Village Investments. Moreover, precedents are set; policies, laws and procedures can be changed.

Besides lobbying, social mobilization at the local level is necessary for creating the conditions for the poor and the disadvantaged to have access to resources and centres of decision-making. This is particularly imperative in a situation where these resources are controlled by a small elite who, at the local level, derive their strength and legitimacy from the existing political, legal and institutional structures. It is through facilitating a process of individual and collective self awareness that the disadvantaged and powerless are activated into organizing themselves so as to be able to take decisions about changing their lives for the better.

H. The Impact of NGO Advocacy

In reality, however, lobbying and mobilisation are best used together. Lobbying becomes more effective when mobilisation has already taken place to ensure that commitments made are honoured, and laws and policies framed are enforced. A case in point of effective mobilisation is the campaign of NGOs and activists for the abolition of bonded labour. Anti-bonded labour legislation was enacted in response to the campaign. However, the enactment of legislation is not enough to eliminate bonded labour, a system deeply rooted in the prevailing social and economic systems. The work of a group of NGOs and community based groups in the North West Frontier Province on the issue of forest management through the NGO Forestry Working Group has seen a combination of both these approaches.[26] The mobilisational work had two dimensions. The first step was to enter into a dialogue with the community to understand the political economy of a very complex issue. Action research, public consultations and rallies were the means adopted for this at the regional level. Secondly, a process of local level analysis and bottom-up village development planning using participatory rural appraisal methods was initiated. These were combined with dialogues with the forest department, forest users, owners, non-owners, and representatives of grazing communities. This is resulting in drawing in the professionals, the forestry officials, to look at things from the point of view of the users, the non-right holders, the small forest owners, and the nomadic grazers. These discussions have not only been confined to the technical aspects of natural resource management but have focused on issues such as the top-down attitude of the forest department, uncontrolled grazing by the community itself, violation of forest laws by influentials, unclear property rights, etc. Having identified the key issues and planned steps for overcoming constraints and for mobilizing resources equitably and sustainably, the villagers themselves are taking concrete actions. These are aimed at the development of their village and community on the one hand, and lobbying with the large forest owners and the forest bureaucracy, on the other, for changes in the system of governance and management of the forests. Fundamental questions of ownership, control, power sharing, and conflict management have come up during these engagements. The mobilisational impact of such a process of local village level analysis, dialogue, lobbying and action planning is fast being realized. When this is combined with the process of coalition building at the regional, national and international levels, the possibilities for influencing institutions, policies, laws, and practices increase manifold.

For advocacy to be successful in bringing about changes in power structures, it is essential to work at three levels through a combination of mobilization and lobbying. The first is at the level of the community, following a process of reflection and mobilisation with local people being the analysts and the strategists. The second level is sectoral, be it forestry or any other issue where there is a need for strategically-focused lobbying by the community and other partner organizations in both the NGO sector and civil society. The third is at the macro level, the level at which there is a need to intervene, where NGOs are working to create an enabling environment for the deprived and powerless. A number of NGOs have been involved in trying to prevent the state from encroaching on the space for NGOs to exist and function as autonomous civil society groups. An example of this work is the joint campaign by NGOs on the NGO Bill. Advocacy thus is not only about being reactive but should be proactive in that alternatives can be developed keeping in view the realities of the marginalized and dispossessed.

It is such engagements that are leading to the development of alternative institutional arrangements and practices. For example, a process of reflection and analysis with the villagers of Kurli in district Abbottabad, NWFP, revealed how the local people have managed to protect their communal forest from indiscriminate cutting when they decided to form a forest protection committee in 1992. A walk through this forest eight years later is a pleasant experience. It now has a thick growth of different kinds of plant species not to mention wildlife. The community has collectively hired a guard to look after the forest. A fine is imposed on offenders and is enforced by the community. This and contributions by the community pay for the salary of the Community Forest Guard. It is obvious that it was a process of collective reflection and community mobilisation that led to this dramatic change in the forest cover around Kurli. In another village not far from Kurli, the demonstration effect of the Kurli experience is now quite visible. In Payan, the women were instrumental in preventing women from Khora, the adjoining village, from chopping trees for fuel wood consumption. Women from both these villages, after many a conflict between the two villages, arrived at an agreement in 1994 not to use the other village's forest for fuel wood purposes. At the time of the agreement the Forest department's range officer was also invited. This has led to a change in the attitude of the forest department towards the local people in the area. There is a slow but growing realization amongst some of the officials that people are concerned about the degradation of natural resources and they can protect these resources from being degraded. These experiences are now becoming examples for others in the area.[27]

Combining work on advocacy and development is not very common amongst the larger rural development NGOs in Pakistan. It has been considered a somewhat risky business within the socio-political milieu of the country. But the environment is fast changing. As socio-economic and ecological problems multiply, civil society and the government are having to respond. In such a situation, the work of NGOs becomes extremely challenging. Unless issues of equity and justice are addressed at the level of the village, elites will continue to monopolize resources at the level of the region, the nation-state and globally, to the exclusion of the poor, causing ecological degradation, social dislocation and political turmoil.

Issues of access, ownership and control over resources are therefore central to the development of strategies to eradicate human deprivation and suffering. Marginalized and disadvantaged groups are developing the confidence and capacities to constructively engage local elites and government officials in discussions on policy and institutional change. There are no standardized intervention packages for community mobilisation. The strategies adopted by communities for mobilisation (and which are empowering) are diverse—each community responding to a particular situation and in the process following a dynamic of its own.

I. Civil Society's Response

As the political, social and economic crisis deepens, and the state and its institutions largely remain unresponsive to citizens' demands, the pressure on civil society groups to fill the ever-growing political vacuum increases. But citizens find their efforts to organize for civic ends frustrated by the state, at times actively repressed and on other occasions just ignored. Increasingly aggressive forms of civic associations emerge and more and more ordinary citizens are compelled to engage either in militancy against the state or devolve into 'self-protected apathy'. Never before in its history has Pakistan been so close to social upheaval. The incidence of self-immolation by frustrated young people has increased alarmingly, indicating the gravity of the situation. Despite the conditions being ripe for the mobilisation of people for political change, there is no credible platform to lead the people out of the present crisis. The system of governance as practised in Pakistan's feudal socio-cultural milieu has failed to give a voice to the disadvantaged and marginalized in the affairs of the state. However, as far as the response to the present crisis by civil society groups is concerned, one can discern a few distinct trends. In the wake of the nuclearisation of Pakistan, individuals and groups working for peace have come together in various cities to form peace committees. In another move, in response to the Fifteenth Amendment, Joint Action Committees have been formed or activated in major cities. Another development underway for some time is the emergence of issue-based coalitions with an advocacy orientation. Some of the issues that these groups are focusing on are child labour, violence against women, dams and displacement, forestry, and alternative agriculture. Thus besides issues concerning constitutional rights, issues focusing on livelihood rights of marginalized communities are increasingly being taken up by advocacy groups. Some of these groups are also supporting the peace initiatives and the struggle of civil society and political organizations against the Fifteenth Constitutional Amendment.

While these developments are scattered, there is the potential to bring them together on common platforms in response to the growing crisis of state, economy, ecology, and society. However, if this response is to be effective in mobilizing the powerless and marginalized, it has to be rooted in their day to day struggles. The struggles for social, economic, ecological, and cultural rights needs to inform and should be integrated into the struggle for constitutional and political rights. While one can discern this connection in certain responses, there is a need to articulate the connection between peoples' struggles for access and control over resources and the campaigns of advocacy NGOs for political and constitutional rights. This connectedness should inform, in practical terms, the strategies of both community groups involved in coping with livelihood concerns at the local level and the national level campaigns of civil society organizations.

J. Conclusions

NGOs have come to play an important role in the process of socio-political change in the country. It is this role that is creating tensions with a state which has lost its autonomy. The state is increasingly coming under the influence and control of traditionalist forces and vested interests. This is not to say that only NGOs are playing a role in the process of social and political change. The media, professional associations and political groups are all-important actors on Pakistan's political landscape as well. It is the emergence of these new contenders for political power—civil society organizations—that is creating the space and an opportunity to democratize a state that has seen its writ being challenged by increasingly dissatisfied sections of society

The process of creating spaces for social change will require careful political management on the part of civil society organizations. Until deprived and marginalized groups are engaged through people's organizations, the momentum for democratization and socio-political change will not be generated. On the other hand, unless policy makers, opinion leaders, legislators and political parties are engaged neither will a pro-poor enabling environment be created nor will people-centred institutional and policy change be brought about.

In such a situation NGOs are faced with a number of challenges ranging from attacks on them by local power elites, the institutional constraints that their relationship with donors and the government entails, to the ambivalent relationship between them and the mainstream political parties. As the crisis of the state and society deepens, NGOs are going to be pushed increasingly into an advocacy role. It is in such a situation that they have to be clear about the strategies to be adopted. If they opt for a greater mobilisational role they will have to be rooted in the local community while at the same time be part of a solidarity network at the national and international levels. Vested interests will not view such a role with favour. Therefore it will be important to create effective linkages with groups such as the media, academia, professional associations, and peoples' organizations and movements with a view to generating the momentum for social, political and economic change.

NOTES

1. Groups such as Women's Action Forum (WAF), War Against Rape (WAR), Pakistan Institute of Labour Education and Research (PILER), Applied Social Economic Research (ASR), Society for Advancement of Higher Education (SAHE), and a number of alternative theatre groups

including Ajoka, Lok Rehas, Dastak, and Lok Tamasha were set up during the military regime of General Zia ul-Haq.

2. The Movement for the Restoration of Democracy (MRD) initially included parties such as the Pakistan People's Party (PPP), Tehrik-i-Istiqlal, Jamiat Ulema-e-Islam (JUI/Fazlur Rehman Group), National Democratic Party (NDP), Pakistan Democratic Party, Pakistan Muslim League (PML/Malik Qasim Group), Mazdoor Kissan Party (MKP), and Qaumi Mahaz-e-Azadi.

3. *See*, 'How an Election was Stolen,' the Pakistan Democratic Alliance (PDA) White Paper on the Pakistan elections held in 1990. It was published and distributed by the weekly *MID ASIA*, Islamabad, 1991.

4. *The Nation* Islamabad, 28 May 1998.

5. *See*, The Human Development Centre's Annual Report *Human Development in South Asia—1998* Karachi: Oxford University Press, 1998.

6. 'The Advocacy Role of NGOs' Workshop Report. SUNGI Development Foundation, Islamabad, 1995.

7. *The Nation* Islamabad, 17 December 1998.

8. *See*, Karamat Ali 'Privatization and Labour Rights' *Dawn* Karachi, 2 January 1999.

9. *See*, Omar Asghar Khan 'The Anti-NGO Campaign' *Dawn* Karachi, 3 June 1999.

10. *See*, Omar Asghar Khan 'State and Public Interest Organizations' *The News* Islamabad, 22 May 1999.

11. *Dawn* Karachi, 19 March 1999.

12. The Joint Action Committee, formed by thirty-six organizations, at a news conference at Lahore, condemned the statement of the Punjab Social Welfare Minister. *See*, *Dawn* Lahore, 31 January 1999.

13. See, chapter on Poverty Alleviation *Ninth Five-Year Plan: 1998-2003* (Planning Commission, Government of Pakistan, Islamabad, 1997).

14. *See*, Mushtaq Gadi 'Malakand Saga: Fundamentalist Insurrection is a Logical Outcome of Impotent State and Sterile Politics' *The News On Sunday* 28 March 1999. *See also*, Robert Nichols 'Challenging the State: 1990s Religious Movements in the Northwest Frontier Province' in *Pakistan: 1997* (edited by Craig Baxter and Charles H. Kennedy, Westview Press, 1998).

15. 'Alternative Perspectives on Poverty Eradication: A Critique of the Task Force Reports on Poverty Eradication' Advocacy and Development Network, Islamabad, 1999.

16. Haris Gazdar *Review of Pakistan Poverty Data* Sustainable Development Policy Institute (SDPI), Islamabad, 1999.

17. 'Alternative Perspectives on Poverty Eradication: A Critique of the Task Force Reports on Poverty Eradication' Advocacy and Development Network, Islamabad, 1999.

18. The NGO Dialogue, a coalition of national NGOs, was formed in early 1989 largely in response to the government's attempts to control and regulate NGOs.

19. Draft of the *Voluntary Social Welfare Agencies Registration and Regulation (Amendment) Act, 1995* Government of Pakistan, Social Welfare and Special Education Division, Islamabad, 1995.

20. *See*, Advocacy and Development Network 'Accountability and Legitimacy of NGOs' The Network, 1999.

21. It was in 1995 that the Pakistan NGO Forum, a coalition of NGOs, was formed. The Pakistan NGO Forum consists of the Punjab NGO Coordination Council (PNCC), Sindh NGO Federation (SINGOF), Baluchistan NGO Federation (BNGOF), Sarhad NGOs Ittehad (SNI), and the Coalition of Rawalpindi/Islamabad NGOs (CORIN).

22. Mazhar Arif 'Hounded out by the Forces of the Status Quo' *The News on Sunday* Islamabad, 9 May 1999.

23. *See*, Peter Van Tujil 'Giving Meaning to Globalization: An Outline of NGO Advocacy' *The Advocacy Role of NGOs: Workshop Report* SUNGI Development Foundation, 1995.

24. 'Limits of Activism' *Herald* Karachi, August 1997. *Also see*, Zafaryab Ahmad 'Coping with Local Power Structures and Conflict: The case of Jared in Kaghan Valley' SUNGI Development Foundation, 1999.

25. Omar Asghar Khan 'Civil Society under Attack' *The News on Sunday* Islamabad, 4 July 1999.

26. The Forestry Working Group consists of SUNGI Development Foundation, Sustainable Development Policy Institute, Environmental Protection Society (Malakand), Carvan (Malakand), Kurram Rural Support Organization, and Hayat Welfare Association.

27. *See*, *SUNGI Newsletter* SUNGI Development Foundation April–June 1997.

INDEX

A

Abbasy, Khakan: 131
Abbottabad: 294
Accion International: 248
Accountability: 3, 110–111, 117–118, 280, 282, 286–287; accountability cell: 131; accountability and legitimacy of NGOs: 287
Adler, A.: 52
Adorno, T. W.: 52
Afghanistan: 11, 171, 174, 176, 182, 186, 207–208, 234, 283; Afghan War: 170–171, 174–175, 208, 276
Africa: 181
Afridi, Riffat: 226
Aga Khan Rural Support Program (AKRSP): 249, 273
AGHS: 226, 237
Agra (city in India): 96
Agricultural Development Bank of Pakistan: 249, 260–267, 269–271; Agricultural Credit Programs: 261–262, 264–265; mobile credit officers: 261–262, 264
Ahmed, Imtiaz: 138
Ahmedpur East (district in Punjab): 265
Air Force: 137, 197, 199–200, 203, 205–207, 213(n28), 277; Airforce Chief: 137, 205–206; Hawk advertising consultants: 197; Shaheen organizations: 197
Ajoka Theatre: 291, 299(n1)
Alavi, Hamza: 35–36, 38, 228, 247(n12)
Ali, Karamat (general): 86

All Pakistan Women's Association (APWA): 246(n8), 266, 267
Amin, Samir: 42(n7), 43(n19)
Amnesty International: 225, 230
Arab States: 276 (also see Saudi Arabia)
Arato, Andrew: 221
Argentina: 153
Aristotle: 23
Army: 78, 123, 125, 128, 131–141, 164, 177, 191-210 (also see Military); Army Chief: 131, 134–135, 137–138, 143, 177, 190, 194–195, 198; Army Welfare Trust (AWT): 195–197, 212(n13); Fauji Foundation: 195–196, 212(n11, 12); Post-War Reconstruction Fund: 195; Welfare Directorate: 195
Asia: 171, 176
ASR: 237, 291, 298(n1)
Association of Agricultural, Business and Professional Women (ABPAW): 266–267
Attock (district in Punjab; previously called Campbellpur): 193, 199 (also see Campbellpur)
Aurat Association: 291
Aurat Foundation: 237, 251, 267, 291
Authority: 94, 97, 99, 102–104, 114, 118, 127, 134–135, 138, 141, 154, 159, 178–179, 226, 233, 286; authoritarian: 49, 52, 142, 188, 278; authoritarianism: 35; formal authority: 5; historical relations of authority: 5; legitimate authority: 26; real authority: 5; traditional centers of authority: 3

B

Baluchistan University: 211(n3)
Baluchistan: 8–9, 126, 160, 195, 199–200, 229, 261, 270, 280; Baluch: 183, 199, 200
Baluchistan NGO Federation: 300(n21)
Bangladesh: 112, 136, 165(n1), 166(n7), 248–249, 255 *(also see Pakistan [East Pakistan])*
Bannu (district in NWFP): 199
Basic Democracy: 9
Battagram (district in NWFP): 289
Bedari: 237
Beg, Aslam: 138
Beijing Conference: *See Fourth World Conference on Women*
Beijing Platform for Action: 67, 77
Beijing: 161
Bengali(s): 8, 124, 136, 200, Mukti Bahini (movement): 136
Bhakkar (town in Punjab): 270
Bhutto, Benazir: 3, 62, 78, 117, 130, 138, 144, 146, 154, 159, 209, 225, 250, 277
Bhutto, Zulfikar Ali: 9–11, 17(n7), 59, 61–62, 113–115, 128–130, 133, 136–137, 140, 143–144, 154–155, 159, 166(n10), 189, 201
Bilquees, Faiz: 253
Bogra, Mohammad Ali: 246(n8)
Bosnian: 209
Brazil: 150
Bretton Woods institutions: 168, 184
Britain: 80, 98–99, 103, 142; British: 6–7, 59, 77, 98, 100–107, 151, 187, 193, 195, 199–202; British bureaucracy: 6; British Empire: 187; British India: 187, 195; British Indian Army: 104, 195. 202; British policy: 6, 8, 33; British rule: 96, 187; British Unionist Party: 7 *(also see United Kingdom)*
Brown, Wendy: 222

Burkina Faso: 4, 16(n2)
Burqa (veil): 84

C

Calcutta: 109
Campbellpur: 193 *(also see Attock)*
Canadian: 160, 197
Capitalism: 13, 21, 24, 26, 31, 94, 98, 101, 103, 105, 118; capitalists: 119, capitalist democracy: 31; capitalist economy: 94, 99–100; capitalist order: 24–25, 29; capitalist society: 25–26, 98; capitalist transition: 27; crony capitalism: 32; global capitalism: 32; savage capitalism: 20–21, 39–40, 42(n7)
Carvan: 300(n26) *(also see Malakand)*
Cassette revolution: 34
Central Superior Services (CSS): 192
Chaklala (town in Punjab): 197
Chakwal (district in Punjab): 199, 265
Chandoke, Neera: 221
Chechnya: 209
Chief Executive Officer: ix, 190
Chief Martial Law Administrator (CMLA): ix
China: 94; Chinese: 94, 197
Chiniot (city in Punjab): 109
Chore (town in Sindh): 200
Choti (village in Punjab): 134
Christians: 183
Cicero: 23
Civil society: viii, 6, 8, 10–15, 18–31, 66, 81, 86, 156, 167, 175, 178–185, 217, 220–225, 228, 232, 242–243, 250, 273, 275, 278–281, 285–288, 294–298; as 'associational life': 24; in Pakistan: 31–41; literature on: 43(n15, 19, 22), 246(n5)
Clinton, Bill: 141
Coalition of Rawalpindi/Islamabad NGOs: 300(n21)
Cohen, Stephen: 201, 221
Cold War: 9, 135, 205, 282
Colombo: 131–132, 139

Commission of Inquiry for Women (1994): 81, 289; Report (1997): 81–82, 289
Commonwealth: 142
Community Based Organizations (CBOs): 231, 237, 242, 291
Community Forest Group: 295
Constitution: 123–124, 126, 133–134, 141, 144, 147; constitution of 1956: 8; constitution of 1962: 8, 17(n7), 189; constitution of 1973: 184, 189, 289; constituent assembly: 188; constitutional: 82, 164, 189, 226, 277, 280–281, 289, 296–297; 8th Amendment: 134, 138; 13th Amendment: 134; 14th Amendment: 279; 15th Amendment (Shariat Bill): 85, 86, 88(n2), 234, 280–281, 289, 296–297
Convention on the Elimination of all forms of Discrimination Against Women (CEDAW): 67, 82, 289
Corruption: 3–4, 83, 85, 103, 110–111, 114, 117, 133, 142, 147, 159, 169, 179, 233, 255–256, 277
Criminal Law Amendment Act: 82

D

Dadu (town in Sindh): 200
Danish: 196
Darling, Malcolm: 151
Dastak: 226, 291, 299(n1)
Daultana, Mumtaz: 107
Davis, Kingsley: 151
Dawn (newspaper): 156
de Charms, R.: 52
de Tocqueville, A.: 21, 24–25
Delhi: 96
District Management Group (DMG): 192
Diyat (blood money): 82
Dubai (U.A.E.): 197
Durban (South Africa): 142

E

East Asia: 163, 171, 174; East Asian: 116
Eastern Europe: 24
Economy: viii, 3–5, 12–15, 18–20, 27–28, 31–32, 35, 65, 67–68, 70, 76, 81, 83–84, 93–120, 123–164, 167–185, 186–188, 203, 208, 210–211, 233, 235, 251, 254, 273, 279, 281, 284, 293, 297; economic changes: 9, 283, 298; economic conditions: 188, 279–280; economic crisis: 4, 117, 147, 169–170, 174, 290, 296–297; economic disparities: 278; economic globalization: 29; economic group(s): 10; economic growth/ development: 18–20, 29, 93, 97, 130, 151, 156, 167, 177, 180, 273, 286; economic management: 169, 180; economic performance: 167, 173; economic policy: 14, 22, 167, 172–174, 177, 194, 283; economic problems: 188, 295; economic reforms: 128, 146, 149, 163, 173, 277; economic role: 37, 111; economic status: 67, 259; economic structures: 12, 94, 148, 278, 285–286; global cultural economy: 34; global political economy: 28, 30, 33; global/world economy: 32, 94; inflation: 4, 73, 171, 203, 251, 256, 266; liberalization: 30–31; political economies: 20–21, 24–25, 94, 97, 107, 112, 167, 293; socialist economies: 93
Education: 16(n2), 75-76, 78, 83–85, 129, 155–158, 172–173, 180–181, 190, 206, 254; drop-out rates: 76; education of women: 76, 78, 80, 86, 156, 158; English-medium: 11; enrollment rates: 75, 89(n10); higher: 79; perpetuation of gendered power relations: 75–80; primary: 75,

156, 158, 161, 180–181; secondary: 75–77, 159; tertiary: 75, 77, 158

Elections: 112, 123, 126, 156, 161, 189; 1937 elections: 7; 1970 elections: 113, 128; 1977 elections: 128, 138, 150; 1988 elections: 277; 1990 elections: 178, 277; 1993 elections: 78; 1997 elections: 279

English: 11, 14, 59, 89(n6), 156, 257

Enlightenment: 21, 23–24

Environmental Protection Society: 300(n26) (*also see Malakand*)

Essential Services Act: 281

Ethnic groups: 10, 109

Europe: 99; European: 97, 99, 101; European discourse on civil society: 23

Evidence Law: 82

F

Faisalabad (city in Punjab): 69, 88(n4), 199, 212(n13), 265, 270

Family: vii, viii, 11, 13–14, 24, 54, 65–86, 99, 109–110, 112–113, 116, 118–119, 144, 193, 195-198, 201–202, 217, 221–230, 233, 240–243, 256

Family Laws Commission: 246(n8)

Family Law Ordinance: *See Muslim Family Law Ordinance*

Family Planning Association of Pakistan (FPAP): 266–267

Fateh Jang (town in NWFP): 196

Fauji Foundation: *See Army*

Federal Intelligence Agency (FIA): 193

Federal Public Service Commission: 192

Federal Shariat Court: 82; Shariat Courts: 178–179; Shariah Law: 178

Ferguson, Adam: 23

Financial Times (newspaper): 145

First Women Bank Limited (FWBL): 249–271; mobile credit officers: 251

Five Year Plans: Seventh: 76; Eighth: 76; Ninth: 77, 85, 282, 285

Foley, James: 143

Forestry Working Group: 293, 300(n26)

Fourth World Conference on Women (FWCW): 81, 88(n3), 289; follow-up: 289; Pakistan National Report (NATREP): 81

Freud, Sigmund: 51

Frontier Post (newspaper): 281

G

Galbraith, John K.: 63

Gandhi, M.K. 106

Gellner, Ernest: 17(n8)

Germany: 99; German: 100

Ghazi-Barotha HydroPower Project: 292

Ghulam Muhammad Barrage: 193

Global economy: 32, 94; cultural economy: 34; political economy: 28, 30, 33

Globalization: 22, 28, 30–31, 223, 284

Governance: 129–130, 142, 145, 167, 169, 171, 173, 180, 184

Grameen Bank: 248, 255

Gramsci, Antonio: 44(n37)

Gross Domestic Product (GDP): 4, 16(n2), 75, 148, 157, 163, 172

Gross National Product (GNP): 75, 172–173

Gudhu Barrage (dam): 193

Gujranwala (district in Punjab): 199

Gujrat (district of Punjab): 199; Gujrati: 109

Gulf States: 34, 194, 203 (*also see U.A.E. and Dubai*)

H

Hassan, Gul: 137, 166(n8)
HAWWA Associates: 267
Hayat Welfare Association: 300(n26)
Hayat, Shaukat: 107
Hayat, Sikandar: 106–107
Hazara (district in NWFP): 193
Hegel: 21, 24, 26
Highly Indebted Poor Countries (HIPC): 180
Hindu(s): 100, 105–106, 109, 124, 151, 183; hegemony: 59
Hono(u)r Killings [Karo Kari]: 72, 83, 229–231, 291; prosecution of: 89(n15)
Horney, Karen: 52
Hudood laws: 82, 226, 237; Zina (extramarital sex): 72–73, 82, 226
Humaira: 226
Human Development: 151, 155, 163, 172, 179–180, 299(n5); Human Development Index (HDI): 4, 16(n2)
Human Rights Commission of Pakistan (HRCP): 229, 291
Human rights: 82, 181, 185, 225; movement: 220; organizations: 234; violations: 276, 284
Hussain, Mushahid: 131
Hussain, Qazi: 246(n7)
Hyderabad: 230

I

Imran, Saima: 226, 291
India: 7, 9, 105–111, 117, 123–128, 131–132, 135, 140, 142, 151, 154–157, 163, 177, 183, 186–187, 193, 202, 208, 249, 263, 279; Indian legislature: 187; Indian military: 136–137, 140, 175, 201; Indian Muslims: 7, Indian National Congress: 106–107
Indo-Pakistan subcontinent: 275

Industrialization: 93, 100, 102, 111, 127; industrialized nations: 93; pre-industrial: 96, 98, 101
Institute of Information Technology (IIT): 156
Intelligence Bureau (IB): 193
Inter Services Intelligence Agency (ISI): 132, 139, 208, 277
International division of labor: 66
International Fund for Agricultural Development (IFAD): 261
International Monetary Fund (IMF): 168, 169, 181
Iqbal, Allama M.: 106
Iran: 179, 208, 276 (also see Middle Eastern States)
Iraq: 209 (also see Middle Eastern States)
Islam: 7, 10–15, 81–82, 85, 109, 130, 191, 206–210, 230, 280, 289; anti-Islam: 281; Islamists: 81, 85–86, 289; Islamization: 17(n7), 37, 67, 72, 76, 130, 208; Sharia(h): 81, 178, 209
Islamic: economic system: 179; ideology: 37; socialism: 17(n7); studies: 79
Islamabad (national capital): 88(n4), 131–134, 143, 160, 182, 198, 253
Islami Jamhoori Ittehad (IJI): 277

J

Jeffery, Patricia: 223
Jamaat-i-Islami (JI): 207, 234, 246(n7)
Jamiat Ulema-e-Islam (JUI): 299(n2)
Jang (newspaper): 281
Japan: 279
Jatoi, Ghulam Mustafa: 137
Jehangir, Asma: 291
Jehangira: 212(n11)
Jhang (district of Punjab): 109
Jhelum (city in Punjab): 71
Jhelum (district of Punjab): 193, 199
Jihad (striving; holy war): 206

Jilani, Hina: 291
Jinnah, Muhammad Ali: 6–8, 59, 106–107, 126, 135, 187
Jirga (tribal or village council): 230
Joint Action Committee: 299(n12) (also see Women's movement)
Jomtein Conference for Education For All (EFA): 181
Jordanian: 196
Junejo, Muhammad Khan: 189

K

Kafir (nonbeliever): 7
Kakul Academy: 202
Kalabagh dam: 280–281
Kalabagh, Nawab of: See Nawab of Kalabagh
Kant, Immanuel: 23
Karachi (provincial capital of Sindh): 4, 17(n6), 109, 112, 116, 127, 131–133, 139, 161, 171, 174–176, 182–183, 196–198, 204, 249, 280, 291
Karamat, Jehangir: 134, 138, 139
Kargil (disputed area in Kashmir): 139–141, 170, 177
Kashaf Foundation: 272–273
Kashmir: 117, 140–141, 174, 177, 182, 186–187, 202, 208–209; Azad Kashmir: 195, 199; Indian Kashmir: 79
Katcha (area in Sindh): 200
Khan, Amir Muhammad: 127
Khan, Ayub: 8–9, 112–113, 127–129, 135–136, 143–144, 148, 163–164, 189, 191, 246(n8)
Khan, Ghaffar: 107
Khan, Ghulam Ishaq: 138, 146
Khan, Liaqat Ali: 8, 135, 187
Khan, Tikka: 137
Khan, Yahya: 136–138, 143–144, 189
Khar, Ghulam Mustafa: 137
Khatoon, Akram: 250
Khilafat Movement: 80
Khora (village in NWFP): 295
Khushab (city in Punjab): 88(n4), 199

Khoshki: 212(n11)
Khyber Agency: 230
Kissan Conference: 289
Kizilbash, Hamid: 11, 17(n9)
Kohat (district in NWFP): 193, 199
Kohistan (district in NWFP): 289
Kot Addu Power Station: 195
Kumar, Krishna: 23–24
Kurli (village in NWFP): 294–295
Kurram Rural Support Organization: 300(n26)

L

Lahore University of Engineering and Technology (UET): 211(n3)
Labour Unions: 113, 281 (also see Trade Unions)
Lahore: 69, 80, 88(n4), 96, 101, 137–139, 161, 176, 196–199, 212(n13), 230, 252, 259, 272, 280; Walled City of Lahore: 69, 72, 84, 88(n5), 96
Larkana (city in Sindh): 230
Leghari, Farooq Ahmad Khan: 134–135, 146, 166(n6)
Literacy: 78, 86, 170, 172, 180; adult literacy: 4, 78; female literacy: 4, 75, 77, 86; illiteracy: 170, 180, 257
Locke, John: 23
Lok Rehas: 299(n1)
Lok Tamasha: 299(n1)
London Business School: 161
London: 187

M

Madrasas (religious schools): 179, 276
Malakand (area of NWFP): 289, 299(n14), 300(n26)
Malnutrition: 225; underweight children: 4
Mamdot, Iftikhar: 107
Manchester (city in U.K.): 104
Manzai (tribe): 230
Mardan (city in NWFP): 71

Mardan (district in NWFP): 199
Marx, Karl: 23; Marxian formulations: 24, Marxian theorists: 18
Maslow, A.H.: 52
Maudoodi, Maulana: 207
Mazdoor Kissan Party: 299(n2)
Mehdi, Saeed: 131
Menon, Carlos: 153
Mianwali (district in Punjab): 127, 199, 270
Micro-lending/ micro-finance/ micro-credit: 15, 240, 248–250, 266, 271–273; delivery systems: 15, 248, 249; micro enterprise: 249; micro-entrepreneurs: 252, 257, 259, 261, 273; micro-lending institutes and facilities: 15, 248–250, 255, 257, 263, 270–272
Middle Eastern states: 124–125, 129, 165(n3), 170–174, 203, 209
Military: 75, 85, 97, 99, 101, 104, 106, 108, 117, 125, 127, 130–131, 134–148, 153–155, 169, 175, 177, 186–211; military elite: 33, 132, 136, 140–141, 144, 153, 188–190, 204, 206, 209–210; officials: 111, 136–137, 143, 186, 191–210, 213(n23) (also see Army)
Military government: ix, 9, 11, 15, 32, 112, 116, 123, 149, 164, 183,188, 189, 191, 192, 201, 204, 207, 211(n1), 276, 277; coup d'etats: 124, 130, 135; coup of 1958: 8, 135–136, 188, 205; coup of 1977: 137; coup of 1999: 125, 136; indirect: 189; martial law: ix, 143, 189, 204, 286; military ruler: 191, 277–278;
Ministry for Social Welfare: 281
Ministry of Defense: 194; Defense Production Division: 194, 195
Ministry of Women's Development (MOWD): 77, 252
Mirza, Iskander: 188
Mithankot (village in Punjab): 230

Modernization: 26, 34–35, 99, 105, 119, 127, 148, 150, 157; modern institutions: 144, 159; modern society: 28; modern state: 24, 28; modern world: 24, 92, 136; modernist worldview: 290
Moscow: 135
Movement for the Restoration of Democracy (MRD): 276–277, 299(n2)
Mughal: 96, 100–101, 108; court: 97; economy: 96–99; empire: 96–101; period: 98
Muhajir Qaumi Movement (MQM): 17(n6), 116, 175, 201
Muhajir(s) (migrants): 10, 17(n6), 183, 199, 200
Muhammad, Ghulam: 188, 193
Multan (city in Punjab): 69, 96
Multan (district in Punjab): 270
Mumtaz, Khawar: 77
Murree (hill station in Punjab): 78
Musharraf, Pervez: ix, 89(n15), 131–133, 139–147, 166(n5)
Muslim Family Law Ordinance: 80, 234, 246(n8)
Muslim League: 6, 7, 12, 85, 106–107, 147–148, 187, 277, 279–281, 285; Malik Qasim Group: 299(n2); Muslim Student's Federation (MSF): 280
Muslim(s): 17(n8), 81, 95, 100, 105–109, 124, 126, 130, 151; civil society in Muslim areas: 16(n3); Muslims of British India: 126; Muslim world: 81; non-Muslim(s): 105, 108–109; society in North Africa: 17(n8)
Muzzafargarh (town in Punjab): 270

N

National Conservation Strategy (NCS): 288
National Democratic Party: 299(n2)

National Plan of Action (NPA): 67, 77, 289

National Report for the Fourth World Conference on Women (NATREP): 81

National Security Council: 185(n1)

National University of Science and Technology (NUST): 212(n17)

Navy: 198–200, 205; Bahria organizations: 198; Naval War College: 138–139; Navy Chief: 205

Nawab of Kalabagh: 127–129, 149, 159

Nehru, Jawaharlal: 156

New York Times (newspaper): 134, 165(n4)

New York: 137

Newsline (magazine): 281

Non-Governmental Organization(s) (NGOs): viii, 5, 15, 19, 67, 78, 183, 217 220, 233, 235, 237–243, 249, 252, 259–261, 263, 265–272, 275–276, 281–298, 300(n18, 21); Advocacy Development Network: 287; coalitions: 287, 300(n18, 21, 26); Forestry Working Group: 293, 300(n26); Joint Action Committee: 291, 296, 299(n12); non-government action: 25; non-government actors: 283; NGO Bill: 287–288, 294

NGO Dialogue: 287, 300(n18)

Noor, Zainab: 225

North West Frontier Province (NWFP): 7, 9, 107, 126–127, 160, 199, 261, 280–281, 289, 293–294

Northern Areas (region of Pakistan): 195, 199, 249, 283

Nukerji: 212(n11)

O

Orangi Pilot Project (OPP): 249, 273

P

Pakhtun(s)/ Pashtun(s)/ Pathan(s): 176, 182, 199; movement: 8

Pakistan Commission on the Status of Women: 246(n6)

Pakistan Democratic Alliance (PDA): 299(n3)

Pakistan Democratic Party: 299(n2)

Pakistan Environmental Action Plan: 288

Pakistan Institute of Development Economics (PIDE): 183, 253

Pakistan Institute of Labour Education and Research (PILER): 298(n1)

Pakistan International Airlines (PIA): 131, 133 139, 153

Pakistan NGO Forum: 300(n21)

Pakistan Penal Code (PPC): 82; Section 11: 289

Pakistan People's Party (PPP): 113, 115, 128, 129–130, 138, 277, 299(n2)

Pakistan: vii–viii, 3–16, 16(n2), 17(n7), 20, 31–38, 49–63, 65–86, 93–120, 123–164, 165(n1, 2), 166(n7), 167–185, 186–209, 217, 220–221, 225, 228, 235–238, 241–242, 252, 275–279, 282–284, 292, 295–297; East Pakistan (now Bangladesh): 8–10, 17(n7), 109, 112, 124, 128, 136–137, 165(n1), 166(n7), 200; government: 76–77, 111, 123, 131–164, 168–183, 186–194, 205, 207, 209-210, 225-226, 233–234, 242, 248–257, 260–261, 264–273; one unit plan: 8; Pakistani: 3, 6, 50, 57–58, 60–61, 79, 111, 140, 148, 152–153, 165(n3), 170, 176, 181, 250, 253–255, 264–265, 277–278; peace coalition: 280; peace movement: 280, society: vii, ix, 5–6, 11–14, 20–22, 31–34, 37, 39, 40, 50, 66, 95, 125, 176–178, 186–187, 190–193, 204, 207, 210, 221–222,

250, 253–255, 264–265, 273, 275–276, 277–278; struggle for: 7, 12; studies: 79; West Pakistan (now Pakistan): 8–10, 124, 127–128, 136; women: 65, 67, 80, 229, 250, 253–257, 264, 270

Pano Aqil (town in Sindh): 201

Participatory Rural Appraisal (PRA): 293

Pataro (town in Sindh): 200

Payan (village in NWFP): 295

People's Representation Act: 234

Peshawar (provincial capital of NWFP): 88(n4), 196–197, 212(n13), 213(n23), 291

Peshawar University: 211(n3)

Pirs (religious leaders): 7, 12, 57–58

Pishin (city in Baluchistan): 88(n4)

Planning Commission: 282

Poland: 137; Polish: 137

Polanyi, Karl: 27

Political Parties Act: 234

Population Planning: 66; census: 151, 154; growth rate: 170, 171; explosion: 180

Poverty Alleviation Strategy: 282; task force: 284–285; Working Group on Poverty Alleviation: 285

Power: viii–ix, 5–16, 35–36, 49–52, 56–63; 65–69, 65–70, 74, 80–86, 93–99, 106–109, 113–114, 120, 123, 125, 127–128, 130, 133–138, 145–150, 159, 161, 169–171, 177–185, 187–191, 203–205, 210, 217, 220–228, 237, 241, 248, 252, 255, 258, 260, 264, 272, 277–286, 291, 298; attaining power: 5, 8; centers of power: 62; coercive power: 26, 103; contenders for power: 13, 65, 220, 243; distribution of power: 8, 11, 15, 35; economic power: 35, 102, 128, 146; foundations of power: viii, 12, 65; gendered power relations: 65–66, 70, 74–75, 80, 86, 191, 224, 240–241, 250, 278, 290; instruments of power: 5; political power: 32, 35,

40, 67, 80, 95, 104, 107, 119, 130, 134, 144–145, 186, 298; politics of power: 9, 123, 205; power crisis: 14, 15; power groups: 12; power of capital: 27; power relations: 6, 11, 14, 49–51, 58–61, 65–66, 70, 75, 80, 82, 86, 240–241, 250, 278, 290; power renegotiation: 12, 14–16, 66, 86; power structures: 9, 12, 33, 34, 190, 223, 241, 264, 294; powerful: viii, 7, 10, 29, 52–57, 83, 85, 113, 127, 149, 153–154, 190, 227, 278, 282; powerless: 35, 52–54, 62, 66, 72, 80, 224, 243, 285, 292, 294, 297; purchasing power: 4; social power: 5, 14, 22, 27, 49, 50, 58, 60, 67, 102, 146, 217, 220; traditional centers of power: 3, 49–51, 272

Presidential Orders: 146

Public Interest Organizations (PIOs): 291

Punjab NGO Coordination Council: 300(n21)

Punjab University: 211(n3)

Punjab: 4, 7, 100–109, 113, 127, 131, 147, 150–151, 160, 176, 193–194, 199, 224, 229–230, 235, 248–251, 258, 261–267, 269–271, 281; Punjab Alienation of Lands Act of 1901: 103; Punjab National Unionist Party: 106, 107; Punjab police: 73; Punjabi(s): 10, 107, 109, 183, 199

Purdah (seclusion): 69; *chador aur char diwari* (remaining veiled and secluded in the four walls of the home): 85

Q

Qaumi Mahaz-e-Azadi: 299(n2)

Qisas (retribution): 82

Quaid-e-Azam University (QAU): 193

Quaid-e-Azam: *See Muhammad Ali Jinnah*

Quetta (provincial capital of Baluchistan): 88(n4), 197

Qur'an: 7, 75; Qur'anic verses: 70
Qureshi, Moin: 3, 169

R

Rahimuddin, Air Marshal: 137
Raiwind (town in Punjab): 207
Rajanpur: 270
Rawalpindi: 88(n4), 132, 138, 193, 196–199, 212(n11), 267
Rehman, Saifur: 131
Resolution Trust Corporation: 155
Risalpur (town in NWFP): 198
RISE: 291
Rotating Savings and Credit Associations (ROSCAS): 253–254, 265
Rousseau, Jean Jacques: 16 (n1), 23
Rural Support Programme: 242, 285; National: 266–267; Northern Areas: 284; Punjab: 286; Rural Support Organization: 284–286
Russia: *See Soviet Union*

S

Safire, William: 133
Saigol, Robina: 223, 227
Sakrand (town in Sindh): 200
Salariat (state functionaries): 6, 8, 16(n5)
Sangla Hill: 212(n11)
Sanitation: 4, 278
Sargodha: 88(n4), 199
Sarhad NGOs Ittehad: 300(n21)
Saudi Arabia: 198 *(also see Arab States and Middle Eastern States)*
Shah, Sajjad Ali: 134
Shaheed, Fareeda: 77, 228
Shaheen: Aero Traders: 197; Air Cargo Service: 197; Air International: 197; Airport Service: 197, Foundation: 197; Knitwear: 197; Pay TV: 197; Systems: 197
Shaikh (kinship group): 109, 112
Shakargarh (town in Punjab): 265

Shanghai: 161
Sharif, Mian Nawaz: 3, 4, 78, 85, 88(n2), 117, 130–150, 154–155, 277, 279–281, 284, 289
Sharif, Mian Shahbaz: 131, 149
Shehri: 291
Shirkat Gah: 235, 237, 291; Women, Law and Status Programme: 235
Siachen Glacier: 140
Sialkot (city in Punjab): 88(n4), 265
Sierra Leone: 4, 16(n2)
Sikh(s): 100, 101, 105, 124
Simla: 140
Simorgh: 237
Sindh: 4,7, 102, 107, 109, 126, 132, 150–151, 160, 193, 199–200, 229–230, 251, 261, 280–281; Sindhi(s): 183, 194, 199–200
Sindh NGO Federation: 300(n21)
Singapore: 163
Sinha: 50
Sirhoey, Iftikhar: 138
Smith, Adam: 23
Social Action Program: 78
Social Darwinism: 37
Social Summit: 181
Society for the Advancement of Higher Education (SAHE): 298(n1)
South Africa: 142
South Asia: 98–102, 106, 160, 163, 168, 218, 223, 249, 263, 272, 280
South Korea: 163
Soviet Union: collapse of Soviet system 94; 174; troops: 208, 283; withdrawal from Afghanistan: 171
Sri Lanka: 131, 163
State: 6, 8–11, 15, 18, 20–23, 26–28, 30, 32–33, 35–40, 65–67, 79–83, 85, 94–95, 98–99, 101, 103–104, 110–120, 124, 126, 128–129, 133, 140, 151, 153, 159–162, 164, 168, 175–177, 186–188, 191, 202, 207, 217, 220–223, 225, 227–228, 230–239, 241–243, 275–278, 281–288, 290–298; state owned media: 34, 276

Structural Adjustment: 30, 169, 172
SUNGI Development Foundation: 291, 300(n26)
Sustainable Development Policy Institute (SDPI): 183, 246(n1), 300(n26)

T

Tableeghi Jamaat: 207
Taliban: 168, 179, 234
Tando Muhammad Khan: 212(n11)
Tarar, M. Rafiq: 134, 179, 279
Taunsa Barrage: 193
Taxila (historical site in Punjab): 196
Tehrik-i-Istiqlal: 299(n2)
The Globe and Mail (newspaper): 160
The Times of London (newspaper): 142
Third World: 22, 24, 27–31, 35; economies: 30
Tiwana, Khizr Hayat: 107
Trade Unions: 221, 281 (*also see Labour Unions*)
Tripathi, R.C.: 50

U

United Kingdom: 142 (*also see Britain*)
United Nations (UN): 182–183; peacekeeping: 203; Security Council: 137; UNDP: 76, 266; UNICEF: 266
UNICEF (United Nations Children's Fund): 266
UNDP (United Nations Development Program): 76, 266; Human Development Report (HDR): 16(n2), 89(n8, 9, 10)
United States of America/USA/America: viii, 9, 11–12, 21, 148, 156, 168, 187, 196, 201–202, 206, 208–209, 213(n28); Agency for International Development (US-AID): 286; Central Intelligence

Agency (CIA): 168, 213(n28); Drug Enforcement Agency (DEA): 213(n28); State Department: 169
Urdu: 59, 199, 201, 257
USSR: *See Soviet Union*

V

Violence: 53, 70, 99, 139, 174, 176, 185, 226, 229, 235, 291; abduction: 73; battery: 71, 228; communal violence: 186; custodial rape: 235; domestic violence: 70–74, 225, 243; gender-based violence: 72–73; marital rape: 72, 82, 84, 226–227, 243; mental abuse: 72; murder: 73, 89(n15); violence against women: 72–73, 84, 225–226, 229–232, 235, 238, 297

W

Waheed, Saima: 226
Wali (guardian): 82
War: 104, 124, 201–202; civil war: 124, 128, 136–137; Indo-Pak war of 1965: 9, 128, 186–187, 202, 206; Indo-Pak war of 1971: 137, 202, 206; Korean War: 111; war bands: 100; war veterans: 104, 195; World War II: 107, 201
War Against Rape (WAR): 298(n1)
Waseem, Mohammad: 36, 44(n41)
Washington, D.C.: 135, 141, 143, 168–170
Water and Power Development Authority (WAPDA): 139, 153, 281, 292
Watta sutta (reciprocal exchange marriage): 71
Wazirabad (city in Punjab): 69, 71
Westernization: 32–35, 79; non-western: 19, 32–34; west: 19, 81, 97, 100, 139, 143, 223; western: 31–34, 55, 58–59, 133, 142–143, 160, 279
White, R.W.: 52

Women: 65–86, 223–225; conflicting images of: 65; financial empowerment of: 15, 248–274; rights: 65, 67, 77, 80, 218, 220, 223, 225–228, 230, 233, 235, 238–243, 246(n6, 8), 283, 291

Women's Action Forum (WAF): 77, 231, 234, 237–239, 242, 298(n1) *(also see Women's movement)*

Women's movement: 15, 79, 88(n2), 217–222, 225–228, 230–243; Joint Action Committee: 299(n12); Women's Action Forum (WAF): 77, 231, 234, 237–239, 242, 298(n1)

World Bank: 117, 168–170, 249, 261, 265, 271, 292; World Development Report (WDR): 89(n9)

Y

Yaqub, Sahibzada M.: 133, 139

Z

Zia ul-Haq: ix, 10–12, 35, 39, 61–62, 72, 76, 85, 114–116, 130, 134, 137–138, 143–145, 148, 166(n10), 189, 191, 194–195, 201, 203–204, 206–209, 242, 246(n6), 276–277, 282, 289, 299(n1)

Ziauddin, Khwaja: 132, 139

Zina (extramarital sex): *See Hudood laws*